ARCHAEOLOGY OF
SALT

Sidestone Press

ARCHAEOLOGY OF

SALT

APPROACHING AN INVISIBLE PAST

EDITED BY

ROBIN BRIGAND AND OLIVIER WELLER

Published by Sidestone Press, Leiden
www.sidestone.com

ISBN 978-90-8890-303-8
    PDF e-book: ISBN 978-90-8890-304-5

Lay-out & cover design: Sidestone Press
Photograph cover: Salt layers in the Tàrgu Ocna salt mine
(county Bacău, Romania) Olivier Weller 2009

CNCS

Contents

Foreword

Common salt (sodium chloride) is an invisible object for archaeological research, but the ancient texts, the history, the ethnography and our everyday life confirm that both Man and Animal can not live without it. Salt is a primordial reference for humanity. This "fifth element" is universal in a double sense, diachronically and diatopically. How can archaeology and related disciplines or sciences approximate this soluble good, this "white gold", this invisible past? Giving visibility to more or less ancient activities such as rock salt extraction or concentration and crystallisation of natural brine is still a difficult task. It requires crossed perspectives, on different levels: systematic archaeological survey and excavation around the salt sources to identify exploitation techniques, chronological and production dynamics; paleoenvironmental analysis (*e.g.* pollen, charcoal and remains of soil combustion) to evaluate the relations and the impact of salt production on the environment; spatial analysis to correlate archaeological and salt resource data bases; ethnographic investigations to build different ethnoarchaeological models and enlarge the referential of techniques...

Within a brief enumeration, the salt related archaeological research theme are intriguingly various: explorations (hunting for salt), exploitation techniques, exploitation and used tools, transport and storage containers, human and animal feeding, conservation, manufacture related uses, barter, commerce, human and animal mobility, salt resources control, conflicts, strategic value, professions related to salt exploitation and uses, *etc*. All these themes already make a study object for an impressive amount of interdisciplinary archaeological approaches. This amount is continuously increasing, as the study of a universal element that only has indirect archaeological visibility requires a holistic approach.

Some forty years after the *Report on the salt weekend held at the University of Essex* (De Brisay and Evans 1975), this book brings out the most recent results in salt archaeology and displays the variety of approaches that are required to understand the whole complexity of this many-faceted object. The two international sessions which took place during the *7ᵗʰ World Archaeological Congress* (Dead Sea, Jordan, January 2013) and the *19ᵗʰ European Association of Archaeologist* (Pilsen, Czech Republic, September 2013) proved the need for a global review of recent orientations on the universal topic that salt is. This work follows on from previous European conferences about salt Archaeology, organised in 1998 and 2001 (Weller 2002), 2003 (Fíguls and Weller 2007), 2004 (Monah *et al.* 2007), 2006 (Weller *et al.* 2008), 2008 (Alexianu *et al.* 2011), 2010 (Nikolov and Bacvarov 2012) and 2012 (Alexianu *et al.* 2015).

If Europe is the host to some important archaeological research projects on the role of salt in the prehistory or the history as in Romania, Bulgaria, Germany, Spain, Great Britain or France, important research is also going on in Asia, South America and Africa. These new approaches, either historical, archaeological or ethnographical, prove that research on salt is becoming a topic in itself within humanities on a global scale. The twelve papers of this book cover a broad surface, both on a chronological level (from prehistory to nowadays), on a geographical level (South America, Japan and Europe) and on a thematic one (production and transport techniques, spatial analyses, traditional uses, environmental interactions, *etc.*).

This book is structured around four themes.

The first theme is ethnography and salt exploitation. Following research in West Africa (Niger), China (Sichuan area) and Oceania (West New Guinea), Pierre Gouletquer and Olivier Weller shape an overview of various technical processes of salt production. The diversity of production systems, all strictly adapted to the local climate and possibilities, their complexity and their level of technicality are linked to the social and economical aspects of this resource for human societies. Marianne Cardale Schrimpff's research in Colombia compares archaeological findings with the descriptions given in numerous historical documents, thus improving the understanding of pre-Columbian production techniques. Finally, Marius Alexianu and his team reflect on supply choices and strategies around the Romanian Carpathians, depending on the nature and the availability of the resource.

Part two focuses on salt production techniques. Olivier Weller's paper is a synoptic synthesis of the salt exploitation during the Neolithic in Europe. The various types of salt resources, the diversity of archaeological evidence as well as of exploitation forms are discussed. Following a different perspective, Maria Cristina Grossi and her team of archaeologists review the recent searches on the location of a former lagoon west to Rome, where sea salt production evidence was found for the Roman time. On the broader scale of Poland, Józef Bednarczyk and his colleagues review pre-medieval salt exploitation. Their focus on a region that had hardly been studied up to now (the Polish plain) is a heuristic study of a production site from the first centuries of our era.

Papers of the third part of this book address the issue of interactions between the first agro-pastoral societies and salt, either from the sea-salt in Japan or from salt spring in Rumania. Takamune Kawashima studies the origin and the development of salt production in Japan and questions its social and economical challenges during the last three millennia of the current era. A fundamental issue is addressed in the papers of Gheorghe and Cornelia-Magda Lazarovici on the one hand, Robin Brigand and Olivier Weller on the other hand, in the region of the Rumanian Carpathians: the structuring role of attraction played by salt resources on Neolithic habitat and trade networks. Using cartographical tools and geographical information systems, the authors were able to improve the understanding of various processes, including both circulation and controls of goods with a high social value.

The fourth and last part of the book is homogeneously focused on one chronological era – the Roman time – in a historical point of view. Thomas Saile studied the rhythms of salt production in Central Europe alongside the expansion of the Roman Empire north of the Alps. His point meets Ulrich Stochinger's approach: focusing on the Rhenodanubian regions, he confirms the existence of noticeable changes and moves of production systems along the extension of the Empire. He questions the salt demand as well as the trade routes and the economical importance of this mineral resource during the imperial period. Finally, Isabella Tsigarida's paper explains how the increasing salt demand during the expansion of the Empire in Great-Britain could be met by the authorities. Using archaeological data, she contributes to document the methods and infrastructures linked to salt exploitation.

The structure of this book as well as the variety of approaches and grounds which it displays remind that a better understanding of social, economical and territorial challenges surrounding salt can only be reached by gathering our knowledge and experiences in the peculiar domain of salt archaeology.

R.B. & O.W.

Acknowledgements

The quality of this publication is due to the financial support of the University Panthéon-Sorbonne in Paris (Projet de politique scientifique 2014-2015, *Les sources salées de Moldavie*, O. Weller), the Commission for Foreign Excavations (French Ministry of Foreign Affairs, *Exploitations pré- et protohistoriques du sel en Roumanie orientale*, O. Weller), the National Centre of Scientific Research (CNRS, UMR 8215 *Trajectoires*) and the Romanian National Authority for Scientific Research (CNCS-UEFISCDI project number PN-II-ID-PCE-2011-3-0825, 219/5.10.2011, *The ethno-archaeology of the salt springs and salt mountains from the extra-Carpathian areas of Romania*, ethnosalro.uaic.ro).

The editors thank Ştefan Caliniuc, Arielle Gévaudan-Dené and Anatole Lucet for translating some of the articles and for the language improvement of the English versions of some contributions to the present volume.

References

Alexianu, M., Curcă, R.-G. and Cotiugă, V. eds. 2015 (in press). *Salt Effect*. Proceedings of the 2nd Arheoinvest Symposium, april 2012, Al. I. Cuza University (Iaşi, Romania). BAR International Series. Oxford: Archaeopress.

Alexianu, M., Weller, O. and Curcă, R.-G. eds. 2011. *Archaeology and Anthropology of salt. A diachronic approach*. Proceedings of the International Colloquium, oct. 2008, Al. I. Cuza University (Iaşi, Romania). BAR International Series 2198. Oxford: Archaeopress.

De Brisay, K.M. and Evans, K.A. eds. 1975. *Salt. The study of an ancient industry*. Report on the Salt Weekend held at the University of Essex, 20-22 september 1974. Colchester: Colchester Archaeological Group.

Fíguls, A. and Weller, O. eds. 2007. *Trobada International d'Arqueologia envers l'explotació de la sal a la Prehistória i Protohistória*. Acts of the 1ˢᵗ International Archaeology meeting about Prehistoric and Protohistoric salt exploitation, Cardona, dec. 2003. Cardona: IREC.

Monah, D., Dumitroaia, G., Weller, O. and Chapman, J. eds. 2007. *L'exploitation du sel à travers le temps*. Actes du colloque international, Piatra Neamt, Roumanie, oct. 2004. Bibliotheca Memoria Antiquitatis, XVIII. Piatra Neamt: ed. C. Matasa.

Nikolov, V. and Bacvarov, K. eds. 2012. *Salt and Gold: The Role of Salt in Prehistoric Europe*. Acts of international colloquium Humboldt-Kolleg, Provadia, Bulgaria, oct. 2010. Provadia-Veliko Tarnovo : Faber.

Weller O. ed. 2002. *Archéologie du sel. Techniques et sociétés dans la Pré et Protohistoire européenne*. Actes du colloque international, XIVᵉ congrès UISPP, Liège (Belgique), sept. 2001 et de la table ronde du Comité des Salines de France, Paris, mai 1998. Internationale Archäologie, ASTK 3. Rahden : Verlag Marie Leidorf GmbH.

Weller, O., Dufraisse, A. and Pétrequin, P. eds. 2008. *Sel, eau et forêt. D'hier à aujourd'hui*. Actes du colloque international de la Saline Royale d'Arc-et-Senans, octobre 2006. Cahiers de la MSH Ledoux 12 (coll. Homme et environnement 1). Besançon: Presses Universitaires de Franche-Comté.

Part One

Ethnoarchaeological overview

Techniques of salt making: from China (Yangtze River) to their world context

Pierre GOULETQUER* and Olivier WELLER**

* CNRS, Centre de Recherche Bretonne et Celtique, F-29200 Brest, France (retired)
** CNRS, UMR 8215 *Trajectoires*, Université Paris 1 Panthéon-Sorbonne, Maison de l'Archéologie et de l'Ethnologie, 21 allée de l'Université, F-92023 Nanterre cedex, France

Abstract. Completed with some new observations and experimentations, this paper is the abstract of the lecture gave in several places by the authors during their journey in China (2001-2002). Irrespective of the different techniques to get salt itself (salt marshes, boiling brine of different origin, burning salted plants or clays, *etc.*), since the Neolithic times, the producers invented methods to make standard blocks able to resist manipulation during travelling and, especially, the humidity of the atmosphere. Here and there in the world one can observe the natural phenomena of "glassy salt" at the surface of salt heaps of the salt marshes, in the salt pots of the kitchens, in the desert sebkhas, or on the ribs of brine-boiling pots. In specific conditions of heat and humidity, the thin layer of water surrounding each salt grain dissolves the salt, and this brine, getting colder, transforms itself into an uncrystallized, amorphous salt. Different processes strictly adapted to the nature of the brines, to the climate and to the local possibilities can be used to product such salt blocks. The so-called "briquetages" of Europe, West Africa, Asia and Mesoamerica illustrate one of these processes, but there are others methods using fire or not.

Keywords. Traditional techniques, China, West Africa, New Guinea, ethnoarchaeology.

Résumé. Complété par quelques observations nouvelles et expérimentations, cet article est le résumé de la conférence que les auteurs ont donné à plusieurs endroits lors de leur voyage en Chine (2001-2002). Indépendamment des techniques de production du sel proprement dit (marais salants, bouillage de saumures d'origines diverses, brûlage de plantes ou d'argile, *etc.*), depuis le Néolithique, les producteurs ont inventé des méthodes pour fabriquer des blocs capables de résister aux manipulations et au transport et, plus spécialement, à l'humidité ambiante. Un peu partout dans le monde on peut observer le phénomène naturel de « glaçage » du sel à la surface des mulons de sel des marais salants, dans les pots de sel de nos cuisines, dans les sebkhas des déserts ou sur les rebords des marmites de bouillage des saumures. Dans certaines conditions d'humidité et de température, la fine pellicule d'eau qui entoure chaque grain de sel dissout la surface de celui-ci ; quand la température baisse, cette saumure se transforme en un sel amorphe, non cristallisé. Différents procédés strictement adaptés au climat et aux possibilités locales peuvent être utilisés pour fabriquer de tels blocs. Les briquetages d'Europe, d'Afrique de l'Ouest, d'Asie et de Méso-Amérique illustrent l'une de ces techniques, mais il existe d'autres méthodes utilisant ou non le feu.

Mots-clés. Techniques traditionnelles, Chine, Afrique de l'Ouest, Nouvelle Guinée, ethnoarchéologie.

Living near the sea side or some salt springs, everyone can get salt water, and boil vegetables, meat or anything in it. During the summer season, it is even possible to find salt crystallizations in small natural ponds on the rocky coasts, and add it to food. One can hear such evidences everywhere in the world, and we heard it about the ancient salt wells of Tujing and Weixingqia (Sichuan province, China).

The history and archaeology of the ancient world show that from time to time the salted areas were required to give salt to other regions. In that case, those domestic uses of local salt resources weren't sufficient. Concerned people had to invent adapted technologies to answer external and important needs since Neolithic times (Gouletquer *et al.* 1994; Weller 2002; Harding 2013; Cassen and Weller 2013).

The reasons for those demands can be varied. It can be the consequence of a new type of economic development, for instance the development of cattle-breeding, new ways of preserving meat or fish, some industry using salt, *etc.* New production sites can emerged to replace ancient ones, if those had been abandoned for a reason or another, or if the trade routes were no longer secure. It can be for political reasons, for instance when concerned provinces decide to become independent, and to develop their own economy, cutting out the trade with their former suppliers.

When this happens, each producing region must invent two things:
- First, it must develop ways of taking salt out of their natural raw materials. Usually, the techniques are strictly adapted to the natural and social possibilities of the concerned area. The production must require as few as possible artefacts, materials and people coming from outside.
- Second, it must invent packaging adapted to the transportation possibilities. The packaging itself usually being an identifying sign of the producers: far from the production sites, one can recognize the origin of the salt.

Raw materials

The ethnological evidences show that people don't try necessarily to get sodium chloride, but a "generic salt", the composition of which can be very different in terms of its origin.

Generic salt can be extracted from four types of raw materials:
- rock salt;
- saline waters (sea water and lakes, salt springs);
- saline soils (sand, earth, clays);
- saline or non-saline plants.

Rock salt is composed of the natural evaporating seas, from which the volatile components (iodine, for instance) and a great part of impurities (clay, magnesium salts, *etc.*) have disappeared. Conversely, new impurities can enter the salt mass such as iron oxides. The extraction techniques for rock salt can be the same as for other rocks: open-air quarries or underground mining. The extracted salt is then cut into blocks having the desired shape and dimensions for trade. But it can also be washed, transformed into brine, and treated as brine is. The problem is exactly the same, when wells are drilled into the rock salt layers, water poured in, the brine soaked up, and evaporated.

Getting concentrated brine

Concentrating a natural brine

Usually, natural saline waters are not concentrated enough to be directly transformed into salt through evaporation. This needs a series of operations (called "gradation"), which consists in increasing their concentration. This can be obtained by natural evaporation (salt marshes, for instance), by washing salty raw materials with the brine itself[1] (earth, seaweeds, salt plants), but rarely by artificial evaporation, which would need a great expense of energy.

Washing salty raw materials with fresh water

The technique which consists in washing salted earth with the lightly concentrated brine is very close to the techniques using fresh water. The result is definitely the same, a concentrated brine, but the fresh water helps to wash away some undesired chemical components from the finite product. Of course, even when fresh water is used to get brine, the composition of this and of the obtained salt will depend of the composition of the original product.

We know at least one case in which the extraction of salt from salted mud was different. In some areas of the French Atlantic coast (Vendée and Charente), the sea side is very clayey. The salt could not be directly washed out. During the Late Iron Age, the salty surface layer was scraped; the thin fragments of clay thus obtained were burnt, then washed to get brine (Rouzeau 2002).

---

1   The soils which have been wetted with brine contain more salt than the brine itself.

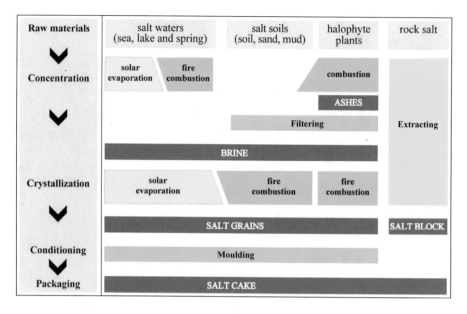

Figure 1. General principles of salt production (drawing O. Weller).

Burning plants and washing the ashes

Of course, saline plants can be directly consumed, but when it is necessary to get salt, they usually are burnt, their ashes collected and washed, usually with fresh water. The range of plants suitable for this process is very large. It goes from plants which contain sodium chloride, to plants which have not (but which are soaked or irrigated with saline water). Of course, the resulting brine is more or less rich in sodium chloride, and always contains a lot of potassium salts.

This quick view over the different saline raw materials and ways to get salt out of them shows that brine-making is one of the main keys in salt-making techniques (fig. 1). For obtaining a concentrated enough brine, two operations must take place: evaporating the brine to get the salt crystals, and preparing the salt for trade.

Getting crystallized salt

Three ways can be used to obtain crystallized salt: burning salted plants and collect the salt grains from the ashes and charcoals (as in New Guinea), natural evaporation (as it can be seen in salt marshes in numerous regions of the world), or boiling the brine (as it used to be done in the Zigong and Chengdu areas of China or in West Africa).

Burning salty materials: the evidence of New Guinea

In New Guinea there are different ways to get salt but the natural support used is always some vegetal raw material (Weller 2007). In Papua (western part of New Guinea, Indonesia), the Western Dani will conduct expeditions and live in temporary habitations built near the springs, where they would work to product

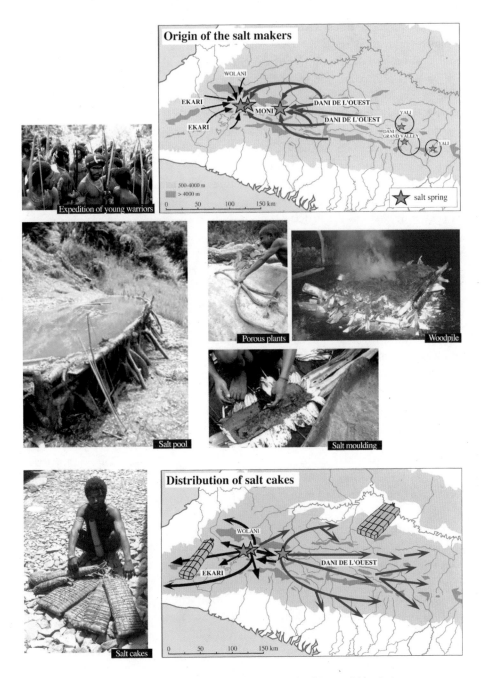

Figure 2. Salt exploitation and circulation in the Highlands of Papua (New Guinea, Indonesia): The Western Dani expedition (photos O. Weller, drawing P. Pétrequin and O. Weller).

large and hard salt cakes (Weller *et al.* 1996; Pétrequin and Pétrequin 2006). After an agreement with the land's owners (the Moni), who will furnish the necessary food against shells, fineries, pigs or stone axes, men will look in the forest for the necessary raw material: young stems of porous edible plants (*Elatostema macrophylla Brogn.* from *Urticaceae* family) and trunks of peculiar trees which produce scant ashes and large charcoals after burning. After cleaning the spring pool, and reinforce the dam to prevent the inflow of fresh water from the nearby river, plants are soaked for more than a day and a night. While the plants are soaking in salty water, men go and collect vegetal material (leaves, bark and rattan) to pack the salt, and clean the flat terrace in front of the houses, in order to install the woodpile where salted plants will be burnt (fig. 2).

Plants are taken out of the pool, and put together near the woodpile during the following night, after the night rains. The slow and controlled combustion of the plants lasts for seven hours. The flames are blown-out with brine. In the early morning, during long hours, from amongst the ashes and charcoals, men will carefully sort out the little salt concretions in the shape of the hollows of the plants. Collected in a great wooden plate, these concretions are piled and riddled with a portage net, and the charcoal rejected down the terrace.

The salt and ashes powder is placed on long pandanus leaves in a rectangular frame limited with thin little boards held vertical by little pegs. Mixed with brine, the paste is compressed and packed down in the mould before the leaves are folded. The salt cake will be carefully dripped and dried during more than a week above the fire place, until it becomes a hard and compact "stone salt", resistant to dampness and long-distance transport.

The obtained salt is a light-grey product, rich in sodium chloride and having very few impurities. In order to get a salt of great quality, as white as possible, with no charcoal, the Western Dani give a great importance to the sorting stage. They also give attention to the shape of the salt cake and basketwork packaging.

The fittings of the salt spring, some light structures, the terrace, and the combustion leftover are the main evidences of the production. Threw down the terrace, with the passing of the years, the combustion leftover above the salt spring forms coaly heaps of several meters high. These are eroded by the torrential floods of the stream, which wash and deposit the charcoal downstream.

From this predictive ethnoarchaeological model from New Guinea, the archaeological study in eastern France, given the total absence of crudely-fired clay artefacts (*briquetage*), was based on deep drillings to explore the marshy depressions close to the salt springs, date any charcoal deposits, and reconstitute the forest cover based of the pollen and the anthracologic diagrams (Pétrequin *et al.* 2001). We have thus been able to demonstrate a genuine exploitation of salt springs as far back as the 5th millennium BC, which only intensified during the Middle Bronze Age, and culminated with the Gallic salt production. We then reach the limits of the predictive model (Pétrequin and Weller 2008). At the technical level first of all, the salt was probably not produced by soaking, as in New Guinea, but by pouring the brine on bonfires. Furthermore the production of salt using this method fluctuated substantially after the Neolithic. Finally, we need to ask ourselves why certain areas of salt production led at specific points in time to particular accumulations of wealth, whilst other salt springs were ignored, notwithstanding their high concentration levels of salt.

Figure 3. Salt evaporation ponds in Teguidda-n'Tessum (Niger) (photo P. Gouletquer).

Natural evaporation: an example in Africa, Teguidda-n'Tessum (Niger)

In Teguidda-n'Tessum (Niger), the salty water springs from the sandstone in the bottom of a kind of pond near which the village has been built (Bernus 1972). The village well itself is salty. During the rainy season, the saline water level rises up to the level of the surrounding grounds, which soak themselves with salt. Once a year, the Tuareg nomads from across the country come here and meet for "the salted treatment", in which camels and sheep can eat salty pastures (Gouletquer and Kleinmann 1976).

During the dry season, the water evaporates leaving the earth salty. People use to mix this earth with saline water in great basins made of clay, let it settle, then take the clear brine and pour it in storage basins, where the evaporation begins under the effect of the wind and sun. When the quantity of brine is sufficient, and when the right concentration is achieved, the brine is poured into small basins where evaporation is conducing to crystallization. The wet salt is scraped of the bottom of those small basins, and stored in barrels. Later, it will be shaped and dried (fig. 3).

Boiling brine: an example from Africa, Dallol Fogha (Niger)

In Dallol Fogha (Niger), the natron brine is obtained from salty pools, boiled in metallic vessels until turning into a kind of pasty salt. This is stored still wet, before being pressed, ball-shaped in the hands, and let to dry on a mat in the sunshine. When dried, the salt-cake looks like a brioche on which the pattern of the mat is impressed.

Amorphic salt

More or less present in our old publications since 1970 (see P. Gouletquer' bibliography in Gouletquer *et al.* 1994), the idea of "amorphic salt" got strength during this mission, through two ways. First when evoking the salt quarries of the Sahara for our Chinese colleagues; second, when visiting the saltworks of the Zigong area.

Salt in Saharan sebkhas

In the sebkhas of the Sahara desert, salt exploitation is done through open-air trenches that permit to reach and choose the best salt layers and to cut them in standardised slabs that will be carried, sold and potentially divided on the markets, sometimes some hundred kilometres far. By their nature, these salt layers have all the qualities necessary for trade, especially purity and hardness. During their formation, they gradually eliminated the greatest part of their impurities (clays, secondary salts, water, *etc.*), and made themselves hard and sometimes translucent levels, in which the very last impurities made thin layers.

In the rubbish of the exploitations, one can see abandoned salt fragments, which have been exposed to dampness and sun drying (which can reach 60° C or more). The purification process goes on these samples, and salt becomes glass-like transparent.

Salt in the Zigong area

A similar phenomenon takes place in the Zigong area of China. We have been very interested by the end of salt making process in the Shen Hai Well Museum, and especially by a process which seems to accelerate the purification.

First, the boiling brine is "washed" (it is the term used) by adjunction of soy-bean milk (about 20%). It seems that the intended effect is to accelerate the flocculation of impurities and, perhaps, to break the crystallization. Taken with a shovel from the boiling basin, salt is deposited in cylindrical and flexible bottom-less baskets (formerly bamboo, nowadays rubber), packaged, and finally washed again with soy-bean milk. These two operations probably contribute to get hard blocks of salt, consistent enough to be unmoulded and handled (fig. 4). The process lasts for some minutes.

During brine boiling, it happens that brine spills over and deposits itself as salt out of the basins rims. When workers take the salt off, brine and salt trickle from the shovel. From time to time this deposit is more or less packed with the shovel. This salt becomes transparent. In the abandoned Aihe Xian Salt Factory, one can see transparent salt around the boiling vessels. It looks like the naturally purified salt of the Saharan sebkhas.

Figure 4. Salt making in the Shen Hai Well Museum (Zigong, China) (photos O. Weller).

"Glassy salt" and traditional salt cakes

One could call this "glassy salt". It seems amorphic, and resists well to dampness, the hygrometric effect being limited to the surface of the block instead of affecting each crystal. Thus this salt has a structure very similar to that of rock salt, as a result of a technical process. This "glassy salt", shaped like conical sugar-cakes, is of course the ideal structure for salt to be traded. That does not mean that such a perfection had ever been obtained, but it is quite certain that the processes to make normalized salt cakes tended towards such a structure and quality.

Figure 5. Mould in rolled palm-tree barks in Bilma (Niger) and salt cones on the Agadez market. One can recognize the three strips forming the mould, the larger being flared at the opening and the seam's mark (photos J.-L. Manaud and P. Gouletquer 1974).

In Zigong the process is stopped beforehand, because the handling and transport of salt takes place in the factory itself, where the blocks are immediately crumbled with a shovel, and the salt packed in plastic bags. Somebody told us that in Yunnan Province the blocks are very hard, and "one must use a hammer to break them".

Figure 6. Salt cakes modelling in Teguidda-n'Tessum (Niger) (photo P. Gouletquer).

All the conditioning of salt in hard blocks could be resumed in this process which consists in favouring the migration of the impurities out of the blocks, in order to strengthen the internal coherence. Properly speaking, it is not a baking process, because this could only reach to crystallization, which is not the intended goal. The process diverts the crystallisation. In some cases, the adjunction of some products can help the process: soy-bean milk in Zigong, cow dung and probably something else in Manga region of Niger (Gouletquer and Kleinmann 1984).

This process does not need high temperatures: about 60°–80° C which is the temperature reached in the sebkhas, and probably outside the boiling basins of Zigong, in the two cases in damp atmosphere. The slower the process, the purer the salt, and the more developed the anamorphic its structure will be. One can experiment the process at the surrounding temperature in Europe by pouring small quantities of water into a pot full of crystallised salt, and turning it as often as possible during some days. During the day hours, the dissolution of salt is higher than during the night. When the right dissolution is obtained, the un-dissolved salt turns into a glassy salt. The same process takes place near the salty marshes on the Atlantic coast, when the heaps of salt remain with no protection during winter time. A hard crust of glassy salt forms at the surface of the heap.

At higher temperatures, the crystallization goes on, which is not the aim. At lower temperatures, the process can develop itself so that the coherence between the grains of salt does exist and is sufficient to make the block hard enough to be handled. This solidification process seems independent of the container size. That's what happens in the Bilma and Tegidda-n'Tessum saltworks (Niger). In the first case, the pasty salt taken out of the salty pools is moulded in a thick bark stitched of palm-tree – often considered by mistake as a hollowed trunk – rolled in the shape of a cone (the process looks like the one from Zigong) (fig. 5). Unmoulded, as children do with sand on the beach, the salt hardens, and the blocks can be transported on camels or nowadays by lorries across the desert, to the Agadez market, some 500 kilometres far. There, it is broken with an axe before being sold in little quantities to its final customers.

In Teguidda-n'Tessum, the salt-cakes are made during two times. First, a "sole" of salt, about half a centimetre thick is deposited on the sand, and let to dry. When this slab is dry and hard, the worker takes wet salt and moulds a 2 or 3 cm thick level, giving the definite shape of the salt-cake, which will be dried in the sunshine and hardened during the night by coldness (fig. 6). This process is the same as in the Dallol Fogha for natron cakes before packing and drying over a domestic fire (fig. 7).

Lastly, on the Atlantic coast, from Guinea to Brittany, in the salt marshes, during the wet season, salt is let uncovered outdoor. Rain washes the impurities from the surface of the heaps, and the sun dries and hardens it, in a kind of process which looks like the beginning of "fractioned crystallization". After a short time, the heap is covered by a hard crust.

As far as we know, the rare attempts of archaeologists to reconstruct the briquetage ware focused only on making salt. This is easy, but it is not the intended goal. The experimentation efforts must be done in the direction of getting this "glassy salt" which best resists to the effects of dampness and transport accidents. As a matter of fact, we can compare it to a kind of "salt ingot".

From ethnological generalities to archaeological remains

In conclusion, we can draw several remarks from those ethnological evidences:

1. Apart from some cases in which the quality of rock salt is very good, the first objective of salt makers is to get a concentrated brine, whatever the initial material will be. Usually, this is done by techniques which enrich the brine concentration. In Sichuan, during the last 1000 years, the innovation consisted in more and more deep drilling, in order to get directly concentrated brine.
2. Whatever the initial product (saline water, saline earth, saline plants, ashes, *etc.*) or the technique used to get crystallized salt (burning, natural or artificial evaporation) are, the final product will be a "salt cake", a "salt artefact".
3. Whatever the technique to harden it (natural or artificial drying), this salt cake must be hard enough to be stored, traded, exchanged, and so on, as a unit. By its composition, its aspect, its shape, and, eventually the designs decorating its surface or the quality of its packaging, this unit points out the producing group, far from the production site.
4. Whatever its precise chemical composition and the techniques, this salt artefact can be used as a pre-monetary wealth, able to be used as an ordinary food for men or cattle, used for trade and barter, offer as a gift or hoarded. That is why one can call it an "ingot".

All that means that, regarding the result (generic salt artefact), there is no great difference between the techniques which are used to obtain it. The technological differences are strictly dependent on the nature of the initial raw material and to the local possibilities to assume the three main operations of the process (collecting raw material, getting concentrated brine, crystallisation and hardening salt ingots).

On the contrary, an archaeologist looking at a general board of the different techniques will see great differences between the techniques using fire or not.

Figure 7. Natron cakes packing in Dallol Fogha (Niger) (photo P. Gouletquer).

The experience of salt archaeology shows that evident remains occur when fire is used during the salt making process. Techniques using clay vessels and clay supports to boil brine or to dry salt, offer structures which had been called "briquetages" since the 18th century. These have captured the attention of archaeologists during the last 120 years in the areas where firing was necessary to get salt or salt cakes. Their typology and their geographical and chronological situation are rather well known, but the researches about the processes taking place before firing are dramatically lacking. In the best cases, people can only describe basins which are probably brine storage or concentrating structures.

One can understand how difficult it will be to look for the other types of remains, such as those we have shortly described in Teguidda-n'Tessum, or even to recognize classical salt marshes when those will have been abandoned during several hundred years or more.

Our knowledge on pre- or protohistoric salt making is still very poor and limited, regarding its economic, social and political importance.

Acknowledgements and context

Completed with some new observations and experimentations, this paper is the abstract of different lectures gave in several places by the authors during their journey in China from December 2001 to January 2002.

Thanks to Pr. Lothar von Falkenhausen (UCLA) and Pr. Hua Sun (Beijing University) who invite us to join their Project in Sichuan, in order to get an idea of their research, and to compare the salt making archaeological remains along the

Yangtze River (Three Gorges Dam archaeological rescue) with other archaeological and ethnographical evidences.

During one month, we visited sites, storage rooms and museums in Chongqing (Zhongba, Ganjing, Zhongxian, Tujing, *etc.*), Chengdu and Zigong areas[2]. We had long discussions with our colleagues excavating salt making sites in Sichuan Province and Chongqing Municipality, and we gave lectures about the use of ethnographical evidences in salt archaeology at the Chengdu Provincial Museum, at the Zigong Salt Museum, and in the Chongqing Museum. The present paper sums up these lectures and try to answer the public's questions.

References

Bernus, E. and Bernus, S. 1972. *Du sel et des dattes : introduction à l'étude de la communauté d'In Gall et de Tegidda-n-tesemt.* Etudes Nigériennes 31. Niamey: CNRSH.

Cassen, S. and Weller, O. 2013. Idées et faits relatifs à la production des sels marins et terrestres en Europe, du VIe au IIIe millénaire. In: Soares, J. ed. *Prehistory of Wetlands. Landscapes of salt.* Setúbal Arqueológica 14. Setúbal: Museum of Archaeology and Ethnography of the District of Setúbal (MAEDS), 255-304.

Gouletquer, P. and Kleinmann, D. 1976. Structure sociale et commerce du sel dans l'économie touarègue. *Revue de l'Occident musulman et de la Méditerranée* 21, 131-139.

Gouletquer, P. and Kleinmann, D. 1984. Les salines du Manga. *Techniques & Culture* 3, 1-42.

Gouletquer, P., Kleinmann, D. and Weller, O. 1994. Sels et techniques. In: Daire, M.-Y. ed. *Le sel gaulois.* Dossiers de Centre de Recherche Archéologique d'Alet, Suppl. Q, 123-161.

Harding, A., 2013. *Salt in Prehistoric Europe.* Leiden: Sidestone Press.

Pétrequin, A.-M. and Pétrequin, P., in coll. with Weller, O. 2006. *Objets de pouvoir en Nouvelle-Guinée.* Catalogue de la donation Pétrequin au Musée des Antiquités Nationales, Saint-Germain-en-Laye. Paris: Réunion des Musées Nationaux.

Pétrequin, P. and Weller, O. 2008. L'exploitation préhistorique des sources salées dans le Jura français. Application et critiques d'un modèle prédictif. In: Weller, O., Dufraisse, A. and Pétrequin, P. eds. *Sel, eau et forêt. D'hier à aujourd'hui.* Cahiers de la MSHE 12. Besançon: Presses Universitaires de Franche-Comté, 255-279.

---

2   We must acknowledge all the persons who made this journey possible, and who presented us with the great opportunity to discover China and some of its archaeological problems. Pr. Hua Sun and Pr. Lothar von Falkenhausen for their kind invitation to participate to the Project, and for their receptiveness all along the days we spent together. Pr. Li Feng, Pr. Sun Zhibin, Pr. Wang, Yi Huang, Jian Huang, Huang Xiaodong, Pr. Li Shuicheng, who gave us time and attention, and who agreed on our visit and comment on sites and collections. We friendly add our own ideas and hypothesis to the discussion about salt making techniques in China, with no more ambition than to enrich the debate about salt making archaeology in general. All the colleagues and the staffs of Institutes, Museums, and Laboratories we met made this journey a success. The welcome we were given was greatly more than an ordinary hospitality. Of course, we can't forget Pochan Chen, full of attention translator and friend, always available, ready to listen the less of our demands. Thanks again to all.

Pétrequin, P., Weller, O., Gauthier, E., Dufraisse, A. and Piningre J.-F. 2001. Salt springs exploitations without pottery during Prehistory. From new Guinea to the French Jura. In: Pétrequin, P. and Beyries, S. eds. *Ethno-archaeology and its transfert*. BAR International Series 983. Oxford: Archaeopress, 37-65.

Rouzeau, N. 2002. Sauneries et briquetages. Essai sur la productivité des établissements salicoles gaulois du Centre-Ouest atlantique d'après l'étude du gisement de Nalliers (vendée). In: Weller, O. ed. Archéologie du sel: techniques et sociétés dans la Pré et Protohistoire européenne. Internationale Archäologie, ASTK 3. Rahden: VML GmbH, 99-124.

Weller, O. 2002. Aux origines de la production du sel en Europe. Vestiges ; fonctions et enjeux archéologiques. In: Weller, O. ed. *Archéologie du sel: techniques et sociétés dans la Pré et Protohistoire européenne*. Internationale Archäologie, ASTK 3. Rahden: VML GmbH, 163-175.

Weller, O. 2007. Exemples ethnographiques d'organisation du travail : les différentes exploitations de sel en Nouvelle-Guinée. *Techniques & Culture* 46-47, 51-61.

Weller, O., Pétrequin, P., Pétrequin, A.-M. and Couturaud, A. 1996. Du sel pour les échanges sociaux. L'exploitation des sources salées en Irian Jaya (Nouvelle-Guinée, Indonésie). *Journal de la Société des Océanistes* 102, 1, 3-30.

Pre-Columbian salt production in Colombia – searching for the evidence

Marianne CARDALE SCHRIMPFF

Pro Calima Foundation for Archaeological Research,
Calle 92, No. 11A – 56, Ap. 701, Bogotá, Colombia

Abstract. The study of the pre-Columbian salt industry in Colombia suffers from the same problems of invisibility as in most other part of the world. Although the country has two coastlines, one on the Pacific and one on the Caribbean, with a number of maritime salterns that were worked during antiquity, it is only in the mountainous regions of the country that the evidence for past salt works becomes visible. Since weather conditions did not favour evaporation by sun and wind alone, the brine was boiled in earthenware vessels until a cake of solidified salt was obtained. The vessels were then broken to extract the salt, as a result of which the salt exploitation can be identified by the enormous accumulations of potsherds that result from this process. In some cases, at least, these sherds have special characteristics that are easily recognizable. A number of salt exploitation areas are described, with particular emphasis on those from Zipaquirá, Nemocón and Tausa, in the mountains of Cundinamarca and Boyacá. These salterns were exploited from at least as early as the third century BC, during the Herrera period, and later by the Muisca Indians. Descriptions in a number of historical documents give some idea of the methods used. The evidence is examined for features that enable salt works to be identified as such, on exploitation techniques, on the tools used and on the salt trade. In this case a detailed study of the salterns provides important information on the ancient peoples that worked them.

Keywords. Colombia, salt-making pottery, salt production, ethnohistory.

Résumé. L'étude de l'exploitation du sel précolombien en Colombie souffre des mêmes problèmes d'invisibilité que dans les autres parties du monde. Bien que le pays ait deux côtes, l'une sur l'océan Pacifique et l'autre sur la mer Caraïbe et que de nombreuses salines maritimes étaient pratiquées dès l'antiquité, ce n'est que dans les régions montagneuses du pays que l'exploitation précolombienne du sel a été mise en évidence. Comme les conditions d'évaporation naturelle par le soleil ou simplement le vent n'étaient pas favorables, la saumure était chauffée jusqu'à ébullition dans de grands récipients en terre cuite jusqu'à l'obtention d'un pain de sel. Le récipient devait être ensuite rompu pour extraire le sel, ce qui a provoqué d'importantes accumulations de tessons de céramique qui témoignent de cette exploitation précolombienne. Au moins dans certains cas, ces tessons de céramique possèdent des caractéristiques particulières qui permettent de les reconnaître facilement. Certaines exploitations de sel ont été décrites de manière plus détaillée comme celles de Zipaquirá, Nemocón et Tausa qui se trouvent dans les montagnes des départements de Cundinamarca et Boyaca. Ces exploitations ont fonctionné au moins à partir du IIIe siècle av. J.-C, pendant la période Herrera, et plus tard assurées par les indiens Muisca. Les descriptions fournies par de nombreux documents historiques nous apportent quelques idées sur les méthodes utilisées. Des caractéristiques particulières ont permis de mettre en évidence et d'identifier certaines activités comme les techniques d'exploitation, les instruments utilisés ainsi que le commerce du sel. Une étude détaillée de ces exploitations de sel permet d'enrichir remarquablement nos connaissances sur les peuples qui les ont conduites.

Mots-clés. Colombie, céramique, production, ethnohistoire.

There have been relatively few studies of pre-Columbian salt production in Colombia precisely because, in most cases the evidence is so hard to find. Since Colombia has two coasts, one on the Caribbean and one on the Pacific, evaporation of sea water has undoubtedly been an important source since early times (fig. 1). However, although there may be useful information on these activities still to be found in early historical documents, they have probably left little or no physical evidence. This is underlined by the situation at the important coastal salterns at Manaure, in the Guajira peninsula (fig. 2). When the eminent archaeologist Junius Bird visited it in the early 1970s, they were still being exploited by the Wayuu (known in the earlier literature as Guajiro) Indians using methods that had probably changed little since pre-Colombian times. The brine was left to concentrate in shallow inlets of the sea where, in the hot and arid climate, it soon formed salt crystals which could be shovelled into heaps to drain and then packed into sacks for transport. Unlike coastal salterns in other parts of the world such as the Essex coast (de Brisay 1975, 5), any ad hoc arrangement in the conditions of year-long sun and wind in the Guajira peninsula would have been useful. Probably these activities would have left almost no physical evidence further that the occasional broken shovel, a tool which in pre-Columbian days would almost certainly have been made of perishable wood.

The first Spaniards to explore Colombia found that abundant sea salt of excellent quality was available. This salt was traded inland for a certain distance (some 300 kilometres), but, as Jimenez de Quesada and his soldiers discovered on their journey up the river Magdalena, the further they got from the coast, the scarcer and more expensive this commodity became (such as attested by an anonymous 16th century writer published in Friede 1960, 259). Indeed, salt was one of the reasons for the success of their expedition since, pressing forward, they began to find salt available once more. But this time instead of granular sea salt it

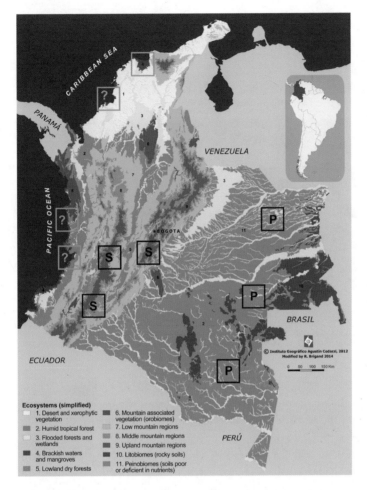

Figure 1. Ecosystem map of Colombia (after IGAC 2012 modified and simplified) with the locations of different sources of salt shown schematically. Blue squares mark the approximate positions of some coastal salterns, the letter S the mountain salterns and the letter P the regions with no natural sources of sodium chloride where salt was obtained from the ash of certain plants.

was in the form of large blocks, in the words of the Spaniards "shaped like a sugar loaf" and each weighing about 50 pounds (Fernandez de Oviedo 1959, XXVI, chap. 19). Intrigued by this and by the reports that the Indians who produced the salt "wore clothes" (a sign, for the Spaniards, of a superior race), Jimenez de Quesada decided to leave the hot and steamy jungles of the Magdalena valley and make his way up through the mountains in search of the salterns. Thus was discovered the territory of the Muisca Indians and the highlands of what are now the departments of Boyacá and Cundinamarca where the capital of Colombia was to be founded.

Figure 2. The salt works at Manaure, Guajira, exploited by the Wayuu Indians. Photograph: Junius Bird (1970).

Saline springs are found in a number of places in Andean Colombia. These vary considerably in the quantity of brine produced and in the degree of salinity. The latter depends on the time of year, rising with the dry season and decreasing with the rains. Some of these are only sufficient for local needs and, in some cases, the brine was used directly without processing. Until relatively recently it was still possible to see people collecting brine in an earthenware pot or leather bag and taking it home to use in liquid form, adding the brine directly to the cooking vessel – an activity that would not have left physical evidences. In other places such as Azufral, on the flanks of the Puracé volcano in the mountainous border between the territory of the Paez and the Guambiano Indians, a salt spring in an area of thermal springs has been used by the Indians of both groups for generations. The brine forms a salty crust on the surrounding rocks and can be scraped off and transported in sacks. Probably the only evidence of this activity would be the paths leading to the spring through an otherwise uninhabited and precipitous landscape (personal communication, Alberto Flor y Dominga Tumiña, 2014).

Unlike the situation in many other parts of the world, salt in Colombia never seems to have been mined in pre-Columbian times so we have none of the concentrated evidence from sites such as Hallstatt. Even during the Colonial and early Republican periods, salt was usually exploited in the form of brine, although an exception to this is described by the French traveller, Edouard André (1884, 580-584) who, in the second half of the 19th century, visited the Salinas de Upín where an outcrop of very pure salt was being worked.

The archaeological visibility is very different at salterns where the salty water was sufficiently abundant and concentrated to supply long-distant trade and so justified the process of evaporating this brine. In the more arid regions of the world or where there is a long dry season, this can be achieved by building salt pans such as those of the Salineras de Maras, near Cuzco, a system which should be reasonably visible in the archaeological record. However the salt exploitation sites in the Colombian Andes all appear to be in areas of high rain fall where there is insufficient evaporation for the success of this system and a process was evolved whereby the brine was boiled in earthenware pots until it evaporated and formed a solid cake which could be transported easily.

Springs with these characteristics are found in various places in the Colombian Andes, particularly in the Tierradentro region in the south, in the middle region of the river Cauca valley, in what are now the departments of the Quindío, Risaralda, the northern part of the Valle del Cauca, and Antioquia. Many of them are mentioned in chronicles of the early colonial period and some of these, such as Consota, near Pereira (Tistl 2004; Acevedo and Martinez 2004; Pino 2004), have been exploited until relatively recently. A number of these springs bubble up inside the river bed, making their use a challenge while the course of the river often changes during floods: the spring may therefore be destroyed or lost. Archaeological studies of human activities at these springs include that of Groot (1974) in Tierradentro, at La Insula (*parcialidad* of San Andrés de Pisimbalá), Bruhns (1976) at the Salado de los Quingos (Valle del Cauca), and Consota (Tiestl 2004; Acevedo and Martinez 2004; Pino 2004). Unfortunately none of these salterns were still in use at the time of the excavations so it was not possible to make an ethnoarchaeological study of the methods and tools used like the valuable documentation compiled by Eduardo Williams (2003) for western Mexico, aspects of which can provide useful clues for the detection of salt works and techniques.

The early history of these Colombian salterns is another aspect which so far, remains invisible. It is probable that they were discovered, initially, by animals as salt licks. Human hunters would undoubtedly have been hot on their trail. However for the exploitation to become "visible", testified to by the sherds from the pottery vessels used in the evaporation process, the population needed to be competent potters. Although pottery vessels were being made in northern Colombia from as early as the fourth millennium BC (Oyuela and Bonzoni 2014, 8; Reichel-Dolmatoff 1965) the history of the development of ceramics in more southerly regions is still far from clear. For Consota there is a date of 550 ± 50 BC (Beta 190727) associated with "the first significant density of sherds from the large pottery vessels used for boiling the brine" with a later one of AD 120 for a subsequent level (Cano 2004, 81). So far the first of these two dates is the earliest associated with salt exploitation anywhere in the country. Occasionally sherds of domestic pottery are found in association with those of the evaporation vessels and fragments of Incised Brownware are reported from the earliest levels (Carmen Elisa Henao, personal communication 2013). This pottery style is associated with gold of the Classic Quimbaya style, made and used by a rich and sophisticated society that occupied an extensive territory of the central and western Cordilleras (from about

Figure 3. Carrying the moyas to the furnace at a salt works in Nemocón. 1970.

4.5° to 7° N) and whose wealth, it has been suggested, came partly from working the salt and from the salt trade (Neila Castillo, personal communication 2014).

The geology of the salt deposits of the eastern Cordillera or mountain range has been studied fairly extensively (summarised in Cardale Schrimpff 1981, 45-6, 242). They are believed to have formed in shallow inlets of the sea where the brine evaporated and, as a result of the orogenesis of what is now the eastern Cordillera they are now preserved as horizons of salt bounded by layers of sedimentary rocks. These salt deposits may be hundreds of metres thick (Zipaquirá) and in the case of the main salterns of Nemocón, Tausa, and particularly, Zipaquirá, the salt springs are on the slopes of a hillside, the result of rain water draining through the top soil and a thick layer of *rute*[1] until it reaches the underlying block of salt.

These salterns tend to be more permanent and easier to exploit than the springs within the river. In this area the method of solidifying salt by boiling brine continued in use until about fifty years ago and the method employed recently has been studied by Groot (2008, Appendix) and by Cardale Schrimpff (1981). Very large pottery vessels, nearly two metres tall and made by the slab technique were mounted on brick columns in a furnace. The vessels were filled with brine and hot brine was added while the liquid evaporated, until a solid cake of salt had formed. The process was not very different from that described by the baron von Humboldt (1952) when he visited Zipaquirá at the beginning of the 19th century and lamented the waste of time and materials since the pots had to be broken to extract the salt (figs. 3-4).

---

1   Rute is an almost impermeable layer of soft black clay, the residue left when the salt is dissolved through contact with water. It is composed of impurities in the salt and includes mudstone, pyrites, calcite and other materials.

Figure 4. Evaporating brine at the same salt works in the early 1970s. On the left the very large pots known as moyas have been mounted in the furnace and are ready to receive the brine. To the right, granular salt is draining in baskets over metal evaporation pans.

The method appears to be a development of the one used by the Muisca Indians and their forebears but on a larger scale. Partly because of their greatly increased need for salt, the Spaniards took over the running of the salterns in 1599 and the *visita* of the *Oidor* Luis Henríquez a year later, the first official visit to the salterns after this appropriation, sheds some light on the traditional methods (Cardale Schrimpff 1981, 27-32). Until the Spanish administrator had huts built specially for the evaporation process, this was carried out by the women in their own homes (the men were responsible for providing the firewood). As far as can be deduced from the document, no specialised structures were involved and the vessels used for boiling were still fairly small with sufficient capacity to produce two cakes of salt of up to two arrobas each (a total of up to 100 lbs of salt in each pot). The process took two days and three nights and required constant attention. Not only was it essential to maintain the fire at the right temperature but the vessels needed frequent topping-up with hot brine to replace the water as it evaporated. As the salt solidified it formed a hard crust on the walls of the pots. It is probable that a similar crust also formed on the surface. This was the case at the salterns observed in the early 1970s when the crust had to be moistened with hot brine, poured over it every half hour, to avoid it becoming too hard and so causing the pot to break. The Spanish administrator employed a number of women, working in shifts and it is not hard to imagine that, previously, and during the dry season when the brine was more concentrated, several families would have got together for the process, each one, perhaps, putting a distinguishing mark on their particular pots. It was customary for the women to place small pot of varying sizes known

Figure 5. The salt hill at Nemocon, 1991. A cut made by a bulldozer reveals an accumulation many metres thick of fragments of the pots that had been used for evaporating brine at different periods.

as *catalenicas* in the spaces between the larger vessels. Ana Maria Groot (2008), using contemporary documents, compiled a detailed history of the three salterns (Zipaquirá, Nemocón and Tausa) for the period 1537-1640, covering technical, economic and social aspects.

The springs at both Zipaquirá and Nemocón appear to have been exploited on a considerable scale since the Herrera period and the earliest reliable date associated with salt production is 150 ± 60 BC (GrN 8452, uncalibrated, Cardale Schrimpff 1981, 57) and for Nemocón, 260 ± 65 BC (GrN 6544, uncalibrated, Cardale Schrimpff 1975, 84). A number of later dates are associated with different stages in the development of the process (Cardale Schrimpff 1983). These dates were all obtained during the 1970s and early 1980s and unfortunately, with the notable exception of the work of Ana Maria Groot, little work has since been carried out at these important sites. It seems perfectly plausible that careful field work could reveal evidence of earlier exploitation and, at the same time, would contribute valuable evidence for the development of the Herrera culture (fig. 5).

The pottery used in the process at these sites is highly characteristic since the inner face has been carefully smoothed, almost polished, to prevent the brine entering the pores where it would solidify and crack the pot. Furthermore the

Figure 6. Sherds characteristics of the pottery used for evaporating brine during the Herrera period at Zipaquirá and Nemocón. The inner wall (right) has been very carefully smoothed, almost polished to provide a sufficiently compact surface to prevent the brine seeping into the pores in the clay where it would solidify and crack the vessel. The outer wall, in contrast, is rough and the junctions of the coils are still visible.

solidified salt adheres less firmly to a smooth surface, making it easier to extract at the end of the process. Possibly the vessels were first "cured" in some way before filling them with brine; at Nemocón in the 1970s Groot (2008, 152) documented the use of a solution of a mixture of salt and lime applied two or three times to the heated pots. Only once this mixture had dried were the vessels filled with brine. Treatments of this sort might possibly be detected by a careful chemical analysis of the inner surface of the potsherds. The outer surface of the pre-Columbian vessels were left rough, in contrast, with the junctions of the coils still visible. The sherds have often broken along the junctions and these weak points would have been an advantage when the time came to break the pots and extract the salt (Cardale Schrimpff 1981, 111). Another diagnostic feature associated with boiling brine is the occasional occurrence of patches of glaze. This salt glaze can occur when brine spills onto the surface of the pottery vessels at temperatures in excess of 800° and is fairly common at salterns in the Old World. At Nemocón and Zipaquirá it is rare but becomes more frequent with time, indicating the use of higher temperatures in the later periods (Cardale Schrimpff 1981, 112; de Paepe and Ghijsels 1981, 259-262) (fig. 6).

Used tools associated with the salt boiling process have seldom been detected, although Bruhns (1976, 95-96) mentions some interesting examples of forms rarely or never found on local habitation sites. "Large stone knives chipped from river boulders of local basalt" were found by hundreds and although very roughly made, follow a definite pattern in size and shape. There was also a large number of rough basalt flakes which Bruhns (1976, 98) suggests may have been used in preparing the firewood used for boiling the brine while the large quantities of stone split by fire would have been the remains of the hearths. No specialised tools are mentioned for the salterns in Tierradentro or Consota, nor were any found at the Herrera period sites in Zipaquirá and Nemocón. At these two sites stone tools of any kind were relatively rare and limited to such domestic items as axes, grinding stones and rough chert flakes. At this period lumps of prepared clay and fragments of accidentally fired coils indicate that pottery was being made on site and some of the pebbles found may have been used for smoothing the surface of the vessels (Cardale Schrimpff 1981, 136-141).

Documents from the beginning of the Colonial Period indicate the importance of the salt trade both locally, through a system of markets, and over long distances beyond the limits of Muisca lands. The importance and territorial range of barter in salt through the markets during the early years of this period has been extensively studied by Langebaek (1987) and, more recently, by Groot (2008, 120-123). For information on long-distance trade, the literature relies mainly on the available early Spanish accounts (summarised in Cardale Schrimpff 1981, 15-17; Groot 2008, 117-126). These are in agreement that this salt was of enormous importance economically and was traded far into the eastern plains (the *llanos orientales*)[2], to the area of present day Neiva to the south as well as the considerable distances to the north that we have already mentioned. Groot (2008: 117-132) documents considerable trade in salt during the early colonial period with populations to the west of the river Magdalena. However, a commentary by Aguado ([1582] Book VII, Chap. 3) suggests that it had been very scarce in the region formerly, probably because many Indian groups in the region were at war with their neighbours during the centuries immediately preceding the arrival of the Spaniards.

Again traces of this very important activity are very hard to find in the archaeological record. Most of the items the salt was exchanged for were perishable products of warmer climates: cotton, fruits and vegetables and items such as feathers and pelts. One of the few non-perishable items was gold, essential to the Muisca for their religious offerings. The fact that, according to the documents evidence, most of this gold came from the Neiva area should, at least, be verifiable from trace elements, although this may be complicated by the large quantities of copper added by the Muisca to most items. The recent and extremely interesting study by Uribe on the significance of colour in Muisca metal work includes detailed analyses of numerous pieces but leaves the sources of the metals used as a subject for further study (Uribe 2012, 63).

Although the salt trade with the tribes of the llanos was undoubtedly important, there are hints that the Muisca Indians were not the only ones to provide salt for this region and here archaeology can supplement the historical information. During a visit to the Salina de Upin in the 1970s, I was able to explore briefly a buried soil with considerable quantities of sherds characteristic of the Guayupe Indians who, presumably, had also exploited this saltern.

---

2   Groot (2008, 118-119) summarizes information on the salt trade with the llanos in a document of 1560, a *Visita anónima*, which suggests that it was bartered over a distance of up to 800 kilometers "adonde se cree que llegaba por trueque hasta doscientas leguas tierra adentro". Those unable to acquire this product had to make do with a substitute obtained from the ash of certain plants.

An item of trade not mentioned by the Spanish chroniclers is stone. An iron-using society would be unlikely to take an interest in the sources of stone tools. However the geology of most of Muisca territory is composed mainly of sedimentary rocks and the most abundant material is chert, usually of poor quality and unsuitable for making some essential items such as axes. A fragment of an axe excavated at the Herrera period saltern at Zipaquirá was identified as andesite, a volcanic rock which could hardly have been obtained locally and would almost certainly have been brought from the mountains of the central Cordillera, a small hint of what may well have been another important material traded for salt, probably already in the finished form of axes. This suggestion appears to contradict the apparent scarcity of salt in this region mentioned above. However for trade prosperity peace was as important then as it is now and the archaeological evidence suggests that the Herrera society flourished during a period of relative peace in Southern Colombia during which long-distance trade was able to prosper. The fact that so little suitable stone is available locally makes the study of axes and the identification of the rock types used a promising field for detecting pre-Columbian trade in the area.

One tantalising hint is that sometimes the salt appears to have been transported as a complete cake and still in the vessels in which the brine was evaporated. Occasionally, small numbers of the highly characteristic potsherds have been found in archaeological excavations at sites in other parts of the neighbouring highlands[3]. For practical reasons it would seem logical to suppose that this would have been more common in the earlier periods when the pots were still fairly small with the addition, perhaps, of the salt boiled in the little *catalnicas*.

Local trade in materials needed for the consolidation was also important, particularly in the later periods as production increased. As already mentioned, in the early levels at Nemocón and Zipaquirá there is evidence of the pottery being made locally while at la Insula, the Tierradentro site, the saltern was adjacent to a source of good clay (Groot 1974, 49) and chunks of the prepared material were also found among the fragments of the pots that had been used for boiling the brine (Groot 1974, 63). However by the early Colonial period most, if not all, the vessels were brought from the neighbouring pueblos of Cogua and Gachancipá (Cardale Schrimpff 1981, Chap. II). In the case of Cogua, at least, it is clear that this practise had earlier roots. An indication of when the practice began should be possible to obtain archaeologically from the analysis of the clay of the sherds in different periods at the salterns. By the Colonial period, enormous quantities of wood were needed to fuel the furnaces. This is hard to document for earlier periods where there are no written records but areas where the local vegetation is severely impoverished, such as the neighbouring valley of Checua, may owe their condition to the over-exploitation of the woods for the salt industry.

---

3   The sites include CHN-IV-2 and 3a in the *vereda* Chinec, *municipio* of Tenjo (Bernal 1992, 69), the Valle de Samacá (Boada 1998, 92) as well as Cachipay and Apulo (Pena 1991, 13). At the Cachipay site they were associated with pottery of the Herrera period. Additional sites of the Herrera period are mentioned in Cardale Schrimpff (1987, 118).

Salt is such an important commodity that in many parts of the world it has been a source of great wealth or a valuable "card" in regional politics. Eduardo Williams considers that the need to provide its subjects with an adequate salt supply was one of the reasons behind the expansion of the Tarascan Empire in western Mexico (Williams 2003, 207 and Chap. III). However, there does not seem to be any evidence, either archaeological or documentary, that wealth or power were important factors in the case of the eastern Cordillera salterns. No outstandingly rich graves have been found near the salterns and documents of the early colonial period do not mention the chiefs in whose territories the saltern are found as being either particularly rich or particularly powerful. In this respect it is interesting to take into account the attitude of traditional gold miners, still working the alluvial deposits in the rivers of parts of Antioquia (Castillo 2007, 283). Rather than considering it as a source of accumulated wealth, they extract from the river only small quantities, no more than the miner requires for his needs. Taking more than necessary, accumulating it or using it for communicating the owners social status are options which, for them make little sense; furthermore misuse of this wealth may lead to the diminishing of the supply. Although rivalry and battles between different Muisca chiefdoms are documented – and were exploited – by the first Spaniards to reach the area, they do not appear to have been related to dominance of the salt springs.

While salt is, indeed, an invisible object in the archaeological record, its study can also throw light on other aspects of the society that was producing or using it. Prior to the excavations at Nemocón and Zipaquirá, there was almost no information on the Herrera period which bridges the gap, chronologically, between the end of the Pre-Ceramic period and the fully-developed Muisca society. Although tentative evidence for the existence of this period had been recovered by Broadbent (1970) and, previously, by Duque Gómez (1955, 100) and Hernández de Alba (1937, 14-15) these excavations have proved key to the construction of a chronology for the central area of the eastern Cordillera. Stratified sites are rare in the region and the deep stratigraphy at some points of the salt sites could undoubtedly prove an enormous help in refining these chronologies in the future. One of the problems with working at these sites is the sheer density of the material. This makes excavation extremely slow and the classification of such huge amounts of material can take a very long time indeed. At the Herrera period site of Zipaquirá V, an excavation measuring 3 × 3 m with a depth of 1.50 m produced almost a ton of cultural material, chiefly fragments of pottery. However, their careful study made it possible to follow an increase in salt production over time with change in the size and shape of the vessels used as well as technical advances in the way the pottery was made. At both Nemocón and Zipaquirá these changes were particularly marked towards the end of the 1st century BC. Previously the vessels used for evaporating the salt were small (some 25 cm in diameter at the rim) with an abundance of very shallow bowls in which the brine would have evaporated rapidly, but the cake of salt would have been correspondingly small. These vessels were replaced by deeper varieties of different forms and of a greatly increased capacity (Cardale Schrimpff 1981, figs. 49-50). At the same time the colour of the pottery reflected increases

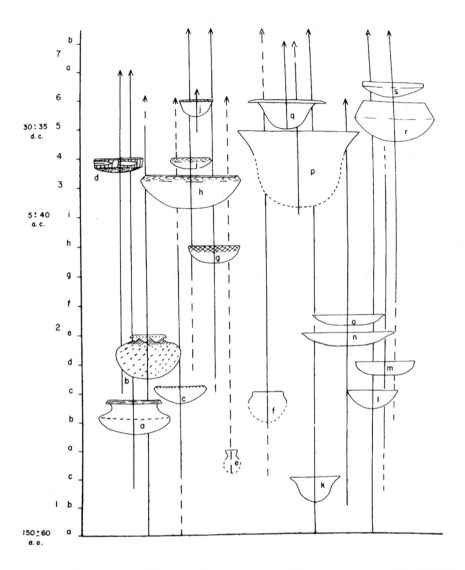

Figure 7. Changes in vessel shapes during the Herrera period between approximately 150 BC and the 1ˢᵗ century AD.

in temperature, changing from a brownish colour in the earlier levels to a brighter, more orangey tone once the vessels became fully oxidised. Clearly there was some mechanism which fired the increase in salt production at this time, a mechanism which we are currently unable to explain. Since the salt workers were living in the area where they boiled the brine, considerable amounts of domestic pottery were also recovered, and changes in the shape and decoration of these vessels could also be documented. These changes were approximately contemporary with those detected in the evaporation vessels and, as I have suggested elsewhere (1981, 63-65, 87), may have been due to technical rather than cultural preferences (fig. 7).

One further valuable bit of information that the salterns can offer is a tentative estimate of population density, based on the quantities of sherds remaining from the pottery vessels used in the evaporation process, and a calculation of the amount of salt that these vessels would have produced. Initially these calculations suggested that by the 1st century AD sufficient salt was being produced at the three salterns of Nemocón, Zipaquirá and Tausa for a population of some 30,000 people (Cardale Schrimpff 1981, 160). Knowledge of the Herrera culture was still in its infancy at the time, few archaeological sites of this period were known and a suggestion that the salt was supplying a population of this size was surprising. However subsequent research revealed even greater quantities of the sherds used in the process indicating that, in fact, the population would have been considerably larger (Cardale Schrimpff 1987, 118). It is worth bearing in mind that the traditional salt requirements of the populations in the area would have been very different to that of the Hispanicised society of the early colonial period. With their arrival the need for salt escalated and the production levels at the salterns was jacked up to levels that were difficult to sustain in terms of the quantities of pottery vessels and firewood required. Not only did the recent arrivals require salt for their own personal consumption, but the new society consumed large quantities in ways that were entirely different. These needs included salt for the large numbers of cattle that now roamed the country and salt for preserving meat and fish, replacing the traditional, indigenous method of preserving these items by smoking[4]. By the end of the 16th century large quantities of salt were also needed for the silver mines at Marquita (Groot 2008, 71), a metal that was not used by the indigenous population. A contemporary calculation of the quantities required annually was 25,000 *arrobas* which, at 25 lb per *arroba* would have come to something in the region of three hundred tons.

One final and almost totally invisible aspect of salt is in the realm of past indigenous belief systems. Nonetheless it is important to take into account their probable existence. Although much appreciated, and not only just as a necessity, it is also considered a very "powerful" and "dangerous" substance. Starting with the 16th century work of Fernandez de Oviedo (1959, XXVI, Chap. 28, 121) and continuing with an ample spectrum of ethnographic literature, we learn that salt and sexual intercourse were forbidden at certain time of the year or on particular occasions. Oviedo was told that this was "to avoid angering the sun". The literature reveals an extremely complex system of beliefs that varied from one indigenous group to another. For the U'wa Indians, for example, salt represents an extreme of mortality and death. It is never added to food but is eaten aside, as hot peppers (which share some of the connotations of salt) are eaten separately, outside in the porch. The combination of salt with other foods is seen to "kill" the essence of that

---

4   I have not come across any early historical references to Indians using salt to preserve meat and the absence of this custom was something which clearly surprised the Spaniards. In the anonymous description of their first expedition to the highlands of the central part of the Eastern Cordillera under Jimenez de Quesada, there is a description of a village or small town where the Spaniards came across a house "full of venison **that had been cured without salt**". (Anonymous 1960, 235). Author's translation and emphasis.

food (Osborn 2009, 126-127 and 186-187), a concept which may explain the fact that, as mentioned above, Colombian Indians did not traditionally preserve meat by salting. A rather widespread belief in the Andean regions of Colombia is that spirits, or *mohanes*, dwell in certain mountain lakes and will become extremely angry if salt is thrown into the water. In Boyacá, on one occasion, the infuriated *mohan* raised a violent storm (Graciela Salcedo Sua, personal communication 2002) while some years ago in Guambía the result was even more dramatic: a man who was carrying loads of salt on mules from the saltern on the limits of Guambiano/Paez territory threw a sacksful into a lake he passed on his route. By the following morning the lake had dried up and the man was found dead (Alberto Flor, personal communication 2010).

References

Acevedo, T.A. and Martinez B.S. 2004. La Sal y las Mercancías en la Provincia Quimbaya. Primeras noticias y crónica de los salados del río Consota. In: Lopez, C. and Cano, M. eds. *Cambios Ambientales en Perspectiva Histórica*. Pereira: Universidad Tecnológica de Pereira, Facultad de Ciencias Ambientales, Centro de Investigaciones y Extensión, vol. 1, 169-189.

Aguado, F.P. [1582] 1956-7. *Recopilación Historial*. Bogotá: Biblioteca de la Presidencia de Colombia, vol. 31-34.

André, E. 1884. *América Pintoresca. Descripción de Viajes al Nuevo Continente por los más modernos exploradores. Carlos Wiener, Doctor Crevaux, D. Charnay, etc, etc.* Barcelona: Montaner y Simón, Editores.

Anonymous 1960. Epitome de la Conquista del Nuevo Reino de Granada. In: Friede, J. *Descubrimiento del Nuevo Reino de Granada y Fundación de Bogotá, 1536-1539.* Bogotá: Banco de la Republica.

Bernal, R.F. 1992. *Prospección preliminar en el Municipio de Tenjo, Cundinamarca.* Unpublished manuscript. Tenjo: Casa de la Cultura.

Boada, Rivas, A.M. 1998. *Bases of Social Hierarchy in a Muisca Central Village o the Northeastern Highlands of Colombia.* Unpublished doctoral thesis for the University of Pittsburgh.

De Brisay, K. 1975. The red hills of Essex. In: de Brisay, K.W. and Evans, K.A. eds. *Salt. The Study of an ancient Industry.* Report on the Salt Weekend, held at the University of Essex, September 1974. Colchester: Colchester Archaeological Group, 5-10.

Broadbent, S. 1971. Reconocimiento arqueológico de la laguna de La Herrera. *Revista Colombiana de Antropología* XV (1970), 171-213.

Bruhns, K. 1976. La salina de los Quingos: nueva información sobre el intercambio prehispánico de sal. *Cespedesia* V/17-18, 88-100.

Castillo, N. 2007. Minería aurífera. Etnografía de las formas materiales y simbólicas en el noroeste andino de Colombia. In: Lleras Pérez, R. ed. *Metalurgia en la América Antigua.* Bogotá: Fundación de Investigaciones Arqueológicas Nacionales, Banco de la República - Instituto Francés de Estudios Andinos, 281-322.

Cano, M. 2004. Los Primeros Habitantes de las Cuencas Medias de los Ríos Otún y Consota. In: Lopez, C. and Cano, M. eds. *Cambios Ambientales en Perspectiva Histórica*. Pereira: Universidad Tecnológica de Pereira, Facultad de Ciencias Ambientales, Centro de Investigaciones y Extensión, vol. 1, 68-91.

Cardale Schrimpff, M. 1975. Prehistoric salt production in Colombia, South America: a brief survey. In: de Brisay, K.W. and Evans, K.A. eds. *Salt. The Study of an ancient Industry*. Report on the Salt Weekend, held at the University of Essex, September 1974. Colchester: Colchester Archaeological Group, 84.

Cardale Schrimpff, M. 1981. *Las Salinas de Zipaquirá: su explotación indígena*. Bogotá: Fundación de Investigaciones Arqueológicas Nacionales, Banco de la República.

Cardale Schrimpff, M. 1983. Ocupaciones humanas en el Altiplano Cundiboyacense. *Boletín Museo del Oro*. Año 4, septiembre-diciembre 1981. Bogotá: Banco de la República, 1-20.

Cardale Schrimpff 1987. En busca de los primeros agricultores del altiplano Cundiboyacense. *Revista del Departamento de Antropología*, Universidad Nacional de Colombia, Maguaré 5, 99-125.

De Paepe, P. and Ghijsels, J. 1981. Some Chemical and Petrographic Characteristics of glazed Pottery from Zipaquirá (Colombia). In: Cardale Schrimpff, M. ed. *Las Salinas de Zipaquirá: su explotación indígena*. Bogotá: Fundación de Investigaciones Arqueológicas Nacionales, Banco de la República, Appendix 4, 259-262.

Duque Gómez, L. 1955. *COLOMBIA. Monumentos Históricos y Arqueológicos*. Mexico: Instituto Panamericano de Geografía e Historia. México.

Fernández de Oviedo, G. 1959. *Historia General y Natural de las Indias, Islas y Tierra Firme del Mar Océano*. Madrid: Ed. Juan Pérez de Tudela Bueso. Biblioteca de Autores Españoles.

Groot, A.M. 1974. *Excavaciones arqueológicas en Tierradentro, Cauca: estudio sobre cerámica y su posible uso en la elaboración de sal*. Unpublished Thesis, Universidad de los Andes, Bogotá.

Groot, A.M. 2008. *Sal y poder en el altiplano de Bogotá, 1537-1640*. Bogotá: Facultad de Ciencias Humanas, Universidad Nacional de Colombia.

Hernández de Alba, G. 1937. Excavaciones arqueológicas del Templo al Sol de Goranchacha. *Revista de Indias* II/7, 10-18.

Osborn, A. 2009. *The Four Seasons of the U'wa. A Chibcha Ritual Ecology in the Colombian Andes*. Wantage: Sean King.

Oyuela-Caycedo, A. and Bonzoni, R.M. 2014. *San Jacinto 1. Ecología histórica, orígenes de la cerámica e inicios de la vida sedentaria en el Caribe colombiano*. Barranquilla: Universidad del Norte.

Pena León, G.A. 1991. *Exploraciones Arqueológicas en la Cuenca Media del río Bogotá*. Bogotá: Fundación de Investigaciones Arqueológicas Nacionales, Banco de la República.

Pino, J.I. 2004. Reconocimiento arqueológico en el Salado de Consota. In: Lopez, C. and Cano, M. eds. *Cambios Ambientales en Perspectiva Histórica*. Pereira: Universidad Tecnológica de Pereira, Facultad de Ciencias Ambientales, Centro de Investigaciones y Extensión, vol. 1, 237-258.

Reichel-Dolmatoff, G. 1965. *Excavaciones Arqueológicas en Puerto Hormiga*. Antropología 2. Bogotá: Publicaciones de la Universidad de Los Andes.

Tistl, M. 2004. Sal, Cobre y Oro en el Consotá. In: Lopez, C. and Cano, M. eds. *Cambios Ambientales en Perspectiva Histórica*. Pereira: Universidad Tecnológica de Pereira, Facultad de Ciencias Ambientales, Centro de Investigaciones y Extensión, vol. 1, 43-55.

Uribe Villegas, M.A. 2012. Contexto, significado y color en la selección de materiales en la orfebrería Muisca. Un estudio analítico e interpretativo de la composición química de artefactos. *Boletín de Arqueología* 23, 3-98.

von Humboldt, A. 1952. *Memoria Raciocinada de las Salinas de Zipaquirá*. Bogotá: Publicación del Banco de la República, Archivo de la Economía Nacional.

Williams, E. 2003. *La sal de la tierra. Etnoarqueología de la producción salinera en el occidente de México*. Michoacán: El colegio de Michoacán, Secretaria de Cultura del estado de Jalisco.

The salt from the Alghianu beck (Vrancea County, Romania): a multifaceted ethnoarchaeological approach

Marius ALEXIANU*, Felix Adrian TENCARIU*,
Andrei ASĂNDULESEI*,
Olivier WELLER**, Robin BRIGAND**,
Ion SANDU*, Gheorghe ROMANESCU*,
Roxana-Gabriela CURCĂ*, Ștefan CALINIUC*
and Mihaela ASĂNDULESEI*

* "Alexandru Ioan Cuza" University of Iași, Arheoinvest Interdisciplinary Platform, Carol I, no. 11, 700506 Iași, Romania
** UMR 8215 *Trajectoires*, Université Paris 1 Panthéon-Sorbonne, Maison de l'Archéologie et de l'Ethnologie, 21 allée de l'Université, F-92023 Nanterre cedex, France

Abstract. This study presents the first results of the ethnoarchaeological investigations in the microzone of the salt outcrops from Alghianu using original questionnaires, as part of a Romanian project (cf. ethnosalro.uaic.ro). Since animal (cattle, ovicaprid, swine, caballin) husbandry is the main occupation of the inhabitants of this microzone with a quasi-autarchic economy, this allowed us to study in detail the multiple aspects concerning the role played by rock-salt boulders particularly in animal feeding and human alimentation, as well as in food preservation. In this context, it became possible to elaborate spatial models of supplying of rock salt from Alghianu within local and pendulatory pastoralism.

Keywords. Romania, ethnoarchaeology, traditional economy, pastoralism.

Résumé. Cette étude présente les premiers résultats d'une étude ethnoarchéologique menée dans le département de Vrancea autour des affleurements de sel gemme d'Alghianu à partir des questionnaires établis pour le projet Ethnosalro. Dans le cadre d'une économie qui tend à l'autarcie, l'élevage est l'occupation principale des habitants de ce petit secteur. Cette caractéristique nous autorise à étudier dans le détail la place tenue par les blocs de sel gemme en premier lieu dans l'alimentation animale et humaine, mais aussi pour la conservation de certaines denrées. Dans le contexte d'un pastoralisme local et pendulaire, il devient alors possible d'élaborer des modèles spatiaux qui éclairent les modalités de l'approvisionnement en sel.

Mots-clés. Roumanie, ethnoarchéologie, économie traditionelle, pastoralisme.

With approximately 300 salt massifs and around 3000 salt springs (Romanescu 2014), with a remarkable density of archaeological sites, and, most noteworthy, with numerous resilient areas where traditional behaviours of salt supplying in the rural and sometimes even urban areas continue to this day, at an unexpected degree of intensity for a EU-member country, Romania (for the most part) meets the ideal conditions for undertaking ethnoarchaeological researches focused on investigating the role of salt in the evolution of prehistoric communities. This opportunity didn't pass unseized, so that a conjoint endeavour by Romanian and French specialists managed to win the first grant for ethnoarchaeological researches on the salt springs (Ethnosal 2007-2010) funded by the Romanian Government (Alexianu and Weller 2009). During the research carried out in the Carpathian piedmont and mountainous area from eastern Romania (Weller *et al.* 2010), particularly in the southern part of the study area, a series of traditional practices of salt exploitations were also encountered, which led to the necessity of a new research grant (EthnosalRo 2011-2015), extended to the entire area of Romania outside of the Carpathian range (Alexianu *et al.* 2012).

Methodological aspects

Immediately after the EthnosalRo project commenced, one of us (M.A.), on the basis of the experience acquired in developing questionnaires concerning the salt springs (produced through the collaboration between O.W., M.A. and L. Nuninger), elaborated new types of questionnaires (at the source, the sheepfolds and the consumer villages), this time concerning the salt cliffs/mountains (fig. 1).

The main themes addressed (with the afferent aspects presented selectively below) in the case of the questionnaire at the salt outcrop concern:

- The identification of the salt outcrops in the studied microzone, including micro-toponymic aspects;
- The harvesting of the salt (extraction periods and parameters, tools employed);
- Spatial analysis (the settlements and sheepfolds supplied, the time required for reaching the salt outcrop on foot or by various transportations means);
- Transportation (transportations means, packaging);
- Uses: human consumption (private, collective, commercial), animal feeding, preservation (cheese, meat and fat, vegetables), halotherapy, *etc.*;
- The ratio between the use of rock salt, natural brine from salt springs and artificial brine (obtained by dissolving rock salt into the water);
- The attraction exerted by the salt outcrop on wild animals, hunting;

Figure 1. Field images of the ethnoarchaeological campaigns conducted in the microzone of the Alghianu outcrop. Photos by F.A. Tencariu and (bottom-right) O. Weller.

- Frequency of salt supplying;
- Trade and barter;
- Behaviours/ethnoscience;
- Symbolism of salt.

The questionnaires for the consumer settlements and the sheepfolds contain other questions suitable for the respective situations. The questionnaires were not elaborated rigidly, but had a deliberate open character, as not once have we found that a less prohibitive approach to inquiries shed light on countless unknown, unforeseen and sometimes completely surprising aspects.

In Romania, the research on the primitive exploitation of the salt outcrops, from the ethnological or ethnoarchaeological standpoint, is very recent (Weller *et al.* 2010, 497-498; Ciobanu 2011; Brigand *et al.* 2015). Unlike previous works, the present study is based for the most part on the questionnaires newly conceived in 2012. The problematics around the outcrop from Alghianu (rock salt and natural brine) has been tackled during three investigations conducted in 2010, one in 2012, and eight in 2014 (table 1).

Geographical and geological context

The rock-salt outcrops on the right bank of the Alghianu beck are part of a salt massive located at the intersection of the 45°52'28"N lat. parallel and the 26°44'20"E long. meridian. The terrain is hilly, with an average elevation of 500 m, specific to sub-mountainous depressions. The investigated area is found within the Alghianu geological and landscape reserve, which occupies an area of 10 ha in the centre of the Vrancea Depression. The area is drained by the Zmeul beck (Alghianu beck). On the sixth terrace of the Putna River repause the Burdigalian-Aquitanian salt deposits, with a holokarst microrelief of the karren type.

The salt outcrops from Alghianu belong to the Poiana salt massif, itself surrounded by the Tulnici, Nistoreşti and Năruja massifs. The massif is a klippe with an area of 1 km² and a thickness of 1 km. The thickness of the overlying layer is 0-1 m. The concentration of NaCl is 70-90% and the reserve is estimated at 769 Mt.

Halotoponym

The studied outcrop has several variants of toponymic syntagmas: La sare la Pârâul Alghianului (lit. "at salt at the beck of the Alghianu"), La sare la Alghian/Alghean (lit. "at salt at (the) Alghian/Alghean"), La sare la Gura Algheanului (lit. "at salt at the mouth of the Alghean").

Description of the salt and the saline water. Uses

Most of the informers specify that the salt collected from the outcrop is suitable for feeding domestic animals (ovicaprids, cattle, horses), as it contains dirt. Nonetheless, some consider that this salt too is suitable for human consumption. The elderly use even nowadays the salt from Alghianu for preparing food, just as in the past when its use was ubiquitous. There are areas of the outcrop where the salt is of a higher purity, which makes it fully qualified for human consumption. In any case, the local users are aware of the fact that the salt boulders from the Târgu Ocna salt mine or from the outcrop from Valea Sării are the best for human consumption. When the salt spring from Alghianu ("down at the brine") is cleaned, the brine is of high quality and favoured by people for consumption.

Access, frequency of supplying from the outcrop

Supplying is currently done in the upper part of the outcrop, on the right side of the beck, since in 1986-1987 a small dam was built on Alghianu beck. Before the erection of this small dam, the access to the salt outcrops was done by travelling in wains (Rmn. căruţă) along the bed of the Alghianu.

The halite outcrop from Alghianu is most often visited during spring and fall. During summer, access is hindered by the fact travelling over unmowed lands is prohibited. Herders come in spring to collect salt for the mountain sheepfolds and in autumn to provision with salt for the use of animals (sheep, goats, cattle) during winter. Spring also witnesses supplying for the local cattle husbandry. According to denizen Gh. Stana, congestion occurs during fall and the Christmas Lent. Herdsman F. Aniţoiu stated, during an investigation in a sheepfold, that he collects salt whenever he needs it, as his sheepfold is located at 1-1.5 km from the source, and for this reason only quantities under 20-30 kg are collected.

Extraction

Unearthing the portion of the outcrop that will be exploited is done using a spade or pick and a shovel. For detaching the boulders from the outcrop, the following tools are used in this order: pickaxes, axes, iron wedges/chisels/bolts, levers, and hammers/sledgehammers. The most basic *chaîne opératoire* is the following: the axe is used to cut a small ditch into the salt, deep enough to accommodate a wedge; the latter is blown with a hammer until salt "chunks" (Rmn. *grunz*) of various weights (from 1.5 kg upwards) are detached (I. Dumitru). This technique is used when the portion of the outcrop has a flat surface. Where the "salt is tender", according to D. Vasile, for extracting the salt boulder, the method "in the wheel" is employed, which uses first the chisel and then the iron nails. Particularly the top part of the outcrop is exploited, as it cleaner, "more washed" (I. Ţoiu).

Settlements and sheepfolds supplied with salt from Alghianu

All the villages and sheepfolds (Rmn. *stână* pl. *stâni*; in effect, a provisional complex of enclosures and structures found in remote areas, with specific characteristics, see Nandris 1985 for a detailed discussion) around the Vrâncioaia commune fall into this group. Respondents mentioned localities part of the Vrâncioaia commune and outside of it: Bârseşti, Bodeşti, Hăulişca, Muncei, Năruja, Negrileşti, Nistoreşti, Păuleşti, Ploştina, Poiana, Prisaca, Spineşti, Tulnici, Valea Sării, and Vrâncioaia (fig. 2, top). Because no other outcrop in the area can be exploited, the attractivity of the outcrop from Alghianu increased accordingly. Thus, the respondend mentioned that only after the "mine" from Valea Sării was covered after heavy rains, did the inhabitants from Valea Sării, Prisaca and Năruja started to come to Alghianu. Respondents provided particular information for the sheepfolds within the boundaries of the Bârseşti, Negrileşti, Păuleşti and Spineşti localities. A respondend stated that, generally, all the settlements and sheepfolds within a 15 km radius around the Alghianu outcrop are supplied from here.

In order to understand more thoroughly the role of salt in animal husbandry, it is necessary to turn to the ethnological research into this issue. In the specialised literature, there have been acknowledged "four structural morphological and functional types of pastoralism: sedentary, local (agricultural), pendulating, and transhumant" (Dunăre 1972, 158). Currently, only the first three types can be found in the studied area.

Sedentary pastoralism consists of "raising cattle around the peasant homestead within the confines of the village... This domestic manner of husbandry did not involve gathering animals into herds, nor the daily movement for pasturing. However, for watering the cattle are droved outside, usually to a well or running water, if one is found nearby. The cattle are fed in above mentioned pens or around them, inside the farmyard" (Dunăre 1972, 173).

Local or agricultural pastoralism takes place "during the entire warm season inside the village domain, in the land boundaries of each village. For this type of pastoralism, the movement of herds doesn't go beyond the land boundaries. Similarly, no human collective (herdsmen) leaves during the respective time period the native village" (Dunăre 1972, 174). This type of pastoralism has three subtypes: local (agricultural) pastoralism without shed and sheepfold; local (agricultural) pastoralism with shed and race, but without a sheepfold; local (agricultural pastoralism) with shed, race and sheepfold (Dunăre 1972, 175).

Pendulating pastoralism presents two forms, namely the simple-pendulating pastoralism and the double-pendulating pastoralism. The *simple-pendulating pastoralism* is "characterised by the fact that the sheep flocks, often also the pig as well as the cattle and horse herds, move *each summer* between the village and the mountain for pasturing, always wintering in home village of the owners. In this case, the pastoral calendar is rather simple: the herds spend the *spring* on the fields of the respective village, pass the *summer* in the mountains, the *fall* on the stubble fields, and the *winter* in the village, through the care of each village" (Dunăre 1972, 190). The *double-pendulating pastoralism* differs foremost in that "wintering takes place in the area of the forest or sub-forest meadows, that is in between the village and the summer pastures" (Dunăre 1972, 192).

The calendar of the sheep pastoralism in the area is the following: from December to the 10th-15th of April, the sheep are kept home. From the middle/late April until after Saint Demetrius Day (26th of October), the animals are turned to the sheepfolds. Between the end of October and the first snow, people graze them by their own (C.S. Lepădatu).

Transportation

The transportation of the salt extracted from Alghianu consists of the stage in which goods are transported from the outcrop to the wain, and the stage in which they are transported using a wain or a horse to the final destination (settlement or sheepfold).

Usually, roles are assigned by turns: "one digs, the other picks up, carry up the hill, taking turns". In the first stage, the rock-salt boulders weighing 5-10 kg or more are packed into hemp or raffia sacks and carried on the back up to the wain. The distance from where the wain is left and the outcrop is *c.* 60 m. If the horses are strong, one can drag the sacks with salt or the salt chunks on a tree branch (Rmn. târn; a large, flat tree branch, regularly used to carry hay, or in this case the salt boulders) to the top of the hill (fig. 1, bottom left). The larger chunks are put as such into the hutch of the wain, while the smaller ones and the broken salt are placed into sacks.

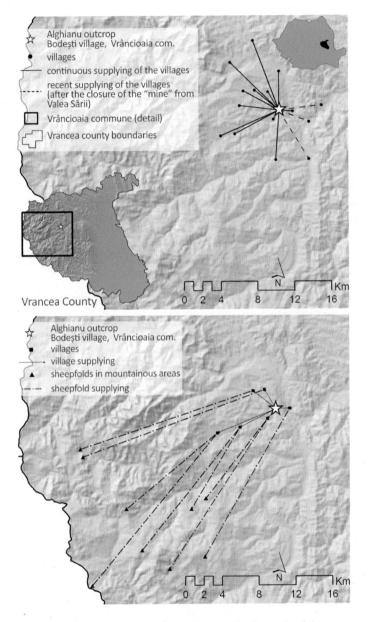

Figure 2. *Supplying with salt boulders strictly for the needs of the inhabitants and the animals from private homesteads (top), and of the villages as well as sheepfolds from isolated areas (bottom).*

The transport of the salt to the consumer settlement is usually done with the wain. Conversely, transport from the consumer settlement to the consumer sheepfold is done either with the horse, either with the wain, according to the difficulty of reaching the sheepfold. In some case, for example when the sheepfold has around 500 animals and the salt has been depleted, the sheepfold is supplied two or three times more directly from the source (fig. 4, interrupted line), with the salt transported in sacks placed on the horses' saddles so that the weights "even out" (D.Vasile).

Long-distance trade and barter

I. Dumitru (55 y.o.) from Poiana, Vrâncioaia commune, stated that in the past (towards the middle of the 20th century), locals exchanged salt from Alghianu with maize, though he was unable to provide names of settlements. P. Tufănoiu recalled how in the past the impoverished denizens from Bodeşti carried salt to the great markets in Focşani (c. 60 km away) and Odobeşti using wains, 200-300 kg with each transport, in exchange for money and especially for wheat or maize. C. S. Lepădatu expounded how his godfather Roşca extracted salt for the villagers of Bârseşti in exchange for a bushel of maize, and in exchange for wood for the mountain forest rangers who used the salt as fodder for wild animals. I. Danţiş mentioned that his son Fane Danţiş, transported salt to sheepfolds, to Negrileşti and Bârseşti, where the salt was needed but the location of the outcrop was not known.

Collecting, quantities used

The salt is not collected by standard quantities, but according to the necessities of the homestead or the number of animals. The variety of answers which we report are illustrative in this sense: thus, I. Ochean carries with the wain 50-100 kg at once, a quantity of salt extracted by two men in one-two hours; F. Aniţoiu habitually transports a wain fully load with 500-600 kg of salt, the maximum weight the animals can pull after an extraction work of half a day. C. S. Lepădatu loads the wain with approximately 200 kg of salt extracted by two-three men who put an effort for at least three hours. Gh. Stana specified that the extraction of 7-8 chunks (approx. 100 kg) takes around half a day, and the entire activity, from the moment he departs his home until he returns, takes a day. For F. Murgu, a toil of half a day produces c. 200 kg. V. Chetreanu mentions that he sometimes extracted between 100 kg and 200 kg, and between 300 kg and 400 kg on other occasions; this took from half to an entire day of work. An informant at a very advanced age, D. Vasile, recalled how he left early in the morning (around 4, 5 or 6 a.m.) from the village of Poiana with the wain drawn by two horses, accompanied by a companion, travelling for half an hour to the Alghianu outcrop, where the extraction took them two hours, if they had good tools, since at that place "the salt is tender, that is, it's not too hard and can break well". T. Caba specifies that the salt was not allotted (divided) to the two workers evenly, even though both put the same amount of work into extracting it, but according to the number of animals each possessed.

Storage

In the village homesteads, part of the salt boulders are put directly into the cattle's rack, part is kept away from moisture in a dry place inside the shed. D. Vasile develops on this: "I purposely had at the shed a bole, a trunk with branches in the ground, and you put (salt chunks) inside and the cows come to it to lick salt". Other informants mention storage in a dry place in the shack. In sheepfolds, the salt boulders were partially put in the pen for the sheep (directly on the ground or fixed on a piece of a branch with three offshoots), and partially somewhere in the sheepfold protected from the rain. A respondent mentions the storage in the sheepfold in a dry place inside an improvised light shack.

Pounding for pig fodder

The salt boulders were once pounded with a stone (hone, Rmn. *cute*), and a specific quantity of salt was added to the pig's fodder (swill). This method is now dated, and nowadays the salt is pounded with a rock or with the axe's blade. For use in swill, the salt was pounded directly at the outcrop, but also home. Some denizens put into the swill brine collected from the Alghianu spring.

Pounding for human consumption

The salt chunks were washed carefully, pounded/grinded with a smasher (Rmn. *chilug*) inside a wooden mortar (Rmn. *piuă*, var. *chiuă*), passed through a strainer, washed again and then it was ready for use. Others passed it through a sieve, cleared with water. Another method for crushing the salt was to place it inside a rag, pound it and then passed through a sieve (the kind used for sieving flour); the finest salt was used for salads, maize porridge (Rmn. *mămăligă*) and eggs. The crushed salt was also used as such, without any further processing, as a responded amusingly recalled: "it was also used dirty like this, and I haven't died (from it)!". The same point is implied by the statement of another villager (I. Dumitru): "When you come (home) from scything, you don't have any pretence", or in other words, "if the salt is not white, that is not a problem".

Uses of natural brine

The brine extracted from the Alghianu salt spring is used for preparing pickles and preserving meat and cheese. It is also used directly in human alimentation, as done for instance by F.C. Dănilă, as the brine is clear, himself cleaning the spring. Low-quality fodder is sprinkled with saline water in order to stimulate the appetite of the animals.

Uses of artificial brine

The brine obtained by dissolving salt into water has two main uses: preservation and therapeutics. Salt is dissolved in the water until the obtained brine is sufficiently concentrated to hold a raw egg on its surface. Meat absorbs as much salt as it needs, so any amount of salt can be put to produce the brine. The brine obtained by dissolving rock salt is used for pickling in barrels. For cabbage, the salt chunk with was placed directly into the wooden barrel, even if it had inclusions of dirt. For therapeutic use, artificial brine is obtained by dissolving salt in hot water. Combined with various herbs, the brine is used for feet baths. Another use of artificial brine is also adjuvant to the pigs' fodder.

Human halotherapy

M. Aniţoiu mentions in general terms that hot water with salt dissolved in it and combined with various herbs is used for feet baths. A more detailed description of the procedure is provided by P. Tufănoiu: "the salt is dissolved, put into hot water, and the feet are bathed for rheumatism or the flu". For backaches, salt is grounded, heated in a tray on the stove, put into gauze cloth and placed on the painful spot for half an hour (P. Tufănoiu). Others heat the salt boulder, cover it with cloth, and place it over the aching area (F. C. Dănilă). Salt inhaling is also attested: "salt boulders are placed in boiling-hot water and inhalings are done". Likewise, salt is placed on wounds. For stomach aches, D. Vasile grandmother drinks a small cup brandy mixed with a spoon of fire ash (Rmn. *spârlă*) and with "a little, but little salt".

Animal halotherapy

The vermifugal quality of salt is well known among husbanders. For instance, to the question why is salt given to animals, T. Caba mentioned among others that salt is given to calves so that they do not become infested with roundworms.

Quantities of salt necessary for various animals

The answers to this question have specific characters, according to the perception of each responder. Accordingly, some considerations on the equivalent in kilograms of the salt chunks should be taken with caution.

I. Ochean estimates that 10-15 kg/year of salt is required for a cow, and 20-30 kg/year for 15 sheep. F. Aniţoiu estimates that 100 goats need 1000 kg/year, and a cow 20-30 kg/year. For P. Tufănoiu, three cows need approximately 60 kg/year. C. S. Lepădatu states that at the sheepfold 50 sheep need four large chunks, or *c.* 100 kg for a winter, and a cow needs around 30 kg/year. Both F. Danţiş and his father I. Danţiş consider that a cow requires approximately 30 kg of salt each year. The same individuals, herders in a sheepfold, state that a wain of 200 kg of salt is needed for the summer for approximately 300 sheep. The winter is passed only with their sheep, around 70, which consume more salt than during the summer, also *c.* 200 kg. For F. Murgu, a wain with 200 kg of salt is enough for more than a year of consumption by four cows and ten sheep. Apparently in opposite view with the respondents above, V. Chetreanu states that a chunk of 5 kg is enough for a cow during the winter.

Sometimes the estimations rely on the number of necessary salt chunks, and no information on the weight is provided. Thus, T. Caba states that in the sheepfolds, from spring till fall, 300-400 sheep need 20 salt boulders, and that for the winter, during which the sheep are kept home at their owners, 50 sheep require three or four salt boulders.

What type of salt chunks do animals prefer

All the informants mentioned that animals prefer to lick the darker salt. F. Aniţoiu (herder) thinks this is due to the presence of supplemental elements than in white salt. P. Tufănoiu considers that the salt for animals should be grainier and softer than the hard white one, which could break the teeth of the animals which desire (that is, which haven't licked for a long time) salt and sometimes bite from the boulder. The same informer states that when the animal has not licked salt for a long time, the salt boulder is not left inside the animal's rack for more than half an hour, because it is bad if the animal over-consumes salt. For C.S. Lepădatu, sheep prefer to lick the darker salt, which is less the "steely" (that is, hard) than the bought white one, and melts better in the mouth. He is also of the opinion that the darker salt is more adding (that is, nourishing) for animal as well as human food than the commercial one. Herder I. Danţiş likewise considers that the salt bought from the Tulnici market is harder, and not so good, since animals chew it with their teeth. Gh. Stana too considers that the salt from Alghianu is better than the commercial one, "even like this with dirt, it's not like the guts will turn black". Currently, only the impoverished and destitute use it, to avoid buying commercial salt. The majority of people avoid it however, since it is dirty.

Salt for fodder

"Some people sprinkled (salt) on the greener hay so it doesn't spoil, the animals it better too", state I. Ochean and P. Tufănoiu. Even if the animals lick the salt, the fodder is sprinkled with brine and salt, particularly "when the fodder is a little green of even spoiled" (F. Aniţoiu). Brine is also sprinkled on the maize combs for preserving them (P. Tufănoiu).

Crystallised salt in human food and preservation

Crystallised salt is used for salting various foods and preparing various dishes (maize porridge, sour soups, *etc.*). For preserving cheese for instance, 50 g of fine salt are put to 10 kg of cheese, which is then kneaded, placed into firkins, covered with a fir cap and fastened with fir twigs, "so not even a fly can enter" (D. Vasile).

Animal attraction

F. Aniţoiu stated that the area around the Alghianu outcrop attracts boars and roe deer. D. Vasile stated that even nowadays roe and red deer come to Alghianu for salt, and that "in the past there were also magpies, falcons, ravens, (they) pecked salt, but now they disappeared, there are not so many birds".

Social chain

F. Aniţoiu stated that he also travelled alone for collecting small quantities, but it is not recommended because the activity is dangerous. Generally, the people going to the outcrop belong to a family. For example, I. Ţoiu went goes with his son, sometimes with his brother and with his wife (M. Ţoiu) who waits at the wain.

P. Tufănoiu stated that a wain has at least two persons, and that two or three wains go at the same time to the outcrop. I. Dumitru stated that the outcrop is visited by a wain with three of four persons, but that has also witnessed groups of two or three families from the village travelling in wains to Alghianu. Women seldom go to the outcrop, as they are unable to dig out and carry up the hill the heavy boulders. F.C. Dănilă stated that herders "sometimes come with people from the village to help them".

The most destitute extract salt by request, which they then sell or trade for food products. The salt requirements of some individuals can also be met through donations: "the one who takes out more salt also give it to his friends, if they ask".

Superstitions

For the first time during the investigations conducted until the summer of 2014, there have been recorded superstitious beliefs concerning salt, particularly that used for animals. Thus, I. Danţiş claimed that "if (somebody) steals salt from the animals, you (will) have troubles, they fall sick, the wild animals (will) eat them. If somebody wants to do you harm, they take a piece of salt from the animal, out of revenge or envy". In other words, F. Murgu believes that "if (somebody) takes the salt from the animal it causes harm". In the same vein, Gh. Stana considers that stealing salt from animals is a bad omen — it happened to him that "salt was stolen from the sheep and until he realised, four of his most beautiful lambs died". Also for the first time ever, we have recorded interdictions concerning the borrowing of salt during certain days of the week. For example, C.S. Lepădatu, I. and F. Danţiş are aware that "some people believe it is not good to give salt from the house on a Wednesday or Friday, (because) you will have trouble, (your) lamb, cow will die". According to a very common superstition, "when the milk boils over, salt is put (on the stove), so that the tit of the cow or sheep will not break, (so that) milk (source) doesn't dry" (P. Tufănoiu). Elder D. Vasile clarifies: "well it is not allowed (to let the milk spill over the stove) because the animal tit sores, the tit breaks, you must be careful that (the milk) doesn't boil over, and to sprinkle a little salt and say 'away from my cow the sore (Rmn. *spuză*)".

Interdictions

The salt started by an animal is not given to another animal of the homestead. When the animal has not licked salt for a long time, the salt boulder is not left inside the animal's rack for more than half an hour, because the animal licks to much salt. When a cow is gestating, for a period of two or three months at the beginning of the gestation period, it should not lick salt, nor after delivery should salt be left all the time in the rack.

Symbolism

The investigations carried out in the Alghianu area confirm a series of known symbolical uses of salt. Thus, C.S. Lepădatu stated that "during bathing it is put salt, wheat, maize and others so that the baby will be wealthy". M. Aniţoiu recalls that salt was once put into the tub of the newborn. D. Vasile stated that "when the mother-in-law bathes the baby, a little salt, flowers, rice are put into the water, so that the baby will strengthen, be hard". Furthermore, during the wedding when the gifts were collected, salt was involved in this ritual. For example, F. Murgu says that "in weddings, (during) the toast, bread and salt are placed on a plate". Gh. Stana goes into further detail: "(during) the wedding bread and salt, (and) rice on a plate when the gifts are collected".

Salt in weather forecasting

During New Year's Eve night, an onion is cut into twelve layers corresponding to the twelve months of the year, and the same quantity of salt is sprinkled into each. If the salt moistens in certain layers, it means that the respective months will be rainy, and if the salt stays dry, it means that the respective months will be dry too.

Behaviours/Ethnoscience

The first knowledge concerning the location of the outcrop are received as early as three of four years of age, occasioned by the children accompanying their fathers to the place of exploitation.

There exists a genuine set of precepts concerning the satisfaction of the salt requirements of domestic animals. Thus, cattle, ovicaprids and caballines are given exclusively salt boulders for licking, and are not allowed to water from the salt springs because herders found that ingurgitating salt water in larger quantities, particularly during the extremely hot periods of the summer, induces disorders (firstly the abrupt increase of the blood pressure) that can even lead to death. The scientific explanation is that in the case of licking the ingurgitation of salt in done gradually, and the existence of sensors of the sympathetic nervous system warns the brain of the quantity of salt necessary for the organism has been reached. In the case of the saline water, this self-regulating mechanism is overridden, and salt is consumed well above the limits from which the ingestion of salt becomes toxic. With respect to the pigs' fodder, the quantity of salt is controlled by the husbander by adding limited quantities of either raw salt, either brine from salt springs.

In what concerns the role of salt for cattle fodder, the husbanders know that it stimulates the animal's appetite and strength. At the same time, even though the quantity produced remains unchanged, the milk has superior organoleptic qualities when the cow is fed with salt.

Results and conclusions

The elaboration of the questionnaires as all-encompassing as possible, the numerous and sometimes surprising information obtained from ethnological investigations, the complexity of the phenomena and processes revealed by the systematic approach of certain specific parameters have fully demonstrated the saliency of this multifaceted ethnoarchaeological approach.

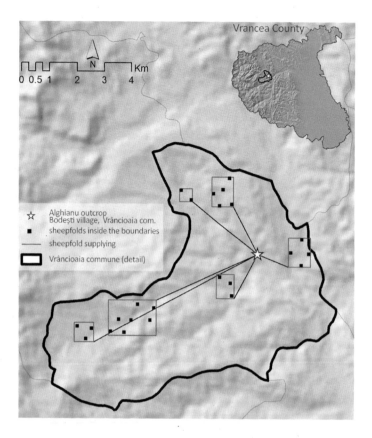

Figure 3. Supplying with salt boulders for the needs of the inhabitants and the animals from private homesteads and sheepfolds located within the boundaries of the settlements.

The investigations of this salt outcrop as part of the EthnosalRo project has allowed us to elaborate a complex epistemic grid, the validity of which shall be tested for other salt outcrops from the Carpathian piedmont areas of Romania.

With respect to the exploitation of salt from Alghianu, it should obviously be ascribed to a phase preceding the actual mining exploitation, respectively the quarrying of rock salt (Harding 2013, 34, 61). Even if it constitutes quarrying, this type of exploitation of the rock salt during prehistoric times required, as evinced from our investigations, particularly hard tools (at least axes, chisels and hammers fashioned from stone or metal). From another point of view, this type of exploitation of rock salt involves a number of activities (extracting, transporting and crushing the salt) much more labour-intensive than those of the exploitation of the salt springs.

The existence in the area of the Alghianu outcrop of rural communities with quasi-autarchic economies centred on animal husbandry (cattle, ovicaprids, swine) allowed us to highlight the role held by salt in animal feeding. In this context, it was possible to develop new models of salt supplying of the settlements and sheepfolds from this area witnessing intensive animal husbandry:

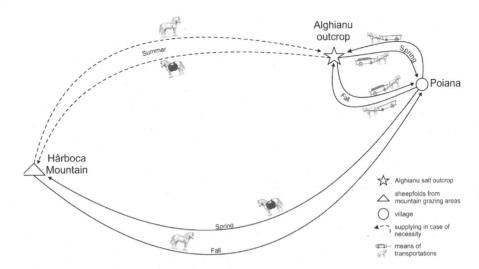

Figure 4. Schema of direct supplying with salt boulders of the Poiana village; from here, a portion of the salt is transported to the sheepfold using a horse (continuous line). When the sheepfold's initial salt reserves are depleted, direct supplying from the outcrop occurs (interrupted line).

(1) Supplying with salt boulders strictly for the needs of the inhabitants and the animals from private homesteads (for human and animal consumption, for preserving foods and fodder) (fig. 2, top);

(2) Supplying with salt boulders of the settlements in the sense of point 1, to which is added the supplying of sheepfolds located within the boundaries of the settlements (fig. 3);

(3) Supplying with salt boulders of the settlements in the sense of point 1, to which is added the supplying of isolated sheepfolds located in mountainous areas (fig. 2, bottom and fig. 4, the continuous line);

(4) Direct supplying with salt boulders of the sheepfolds located in mountainous areas (when they have exhausted the initial salt reserves), as well as of the sheepfolds found near the salt outcrop (fig. 4, the interrupted line).

Notwithstanding the results of the twelve investigations carried out in the area of the Alghianu outcrop, in the user settlements and sheepfolds, further ethnological investigation must be carried out here for the following two reasons: (a) the necessity to elucidate a series of unforeseen aspects (*e.g.* the typology of the sheepfolds from the area, the changing supply relationships between the settlements and the sheepfolds); and (b) the necessity to fully comprehend a series of predicted aspects of an unforeseen complexity. In other words, the research carried out so far concerning this outcrop have yet to meet the exigencies of a saturated model (Alexianu 2013).

No	Year	Name of informant	Age/Sex	Residence
1.	2010	Ion ȚOIU	53/M	Poiana, Vrâncioaia, Vrancea county
2.	2010	Milica ȚOIU	48/F	Poiana, Vrâncioaia, Vrancea county
3.	2010	Ion DUMITRU	55/M	Poiana, Vrâncioaia, Vrancea county
4.	2010	Titi CABA	48/M	Poiana, Vrâncioaia, Vrancea county
5.	2012	Dumitru VASILE	85/M	Poiana, Vrâncioaia, Vrancea county
6.	2014	Ion OCHEAN	82/M	Vrâncioaia, Vrâncioaia, Vrancea county
7.	2014	Fănică ANIȚOIU	54/M	Sheepfold on the Scapătului Hill, Bodești, *etc.*
8.	2014	Magdalena ANIȚOIU	79/F	Sheepfold on the Scapătului Hill, Bodești, *etc.*
9.	2014	Pavel TUFĂNOIU	67/M	Bodești, Vrâncioaia, Vrancea county
10.	2014	Constantin S. LEPĂDATU	72/M	Bodești, Vrâncioaia, Vrancea county
11.	2014	Fane DANȚIȘ	36/M	Sheepfold on the Crucii Hill, Bodești, *etc.*
12.	2014	Ion DANȚIȘ	66/M	Sheepfold on the Crucii Hill, Bodești, *etc.*
13.	2014	Gheorghiță STANA	73/M	Muncei, Vrâncioaia, Vrancea county
14.	2014	Fănică MURGU	54/M	Spinești, Vrâncioaia, Vrancea county
15.	2014	Fănică Costică DĂNILĂ	80/M	Bodești, Vrâncioaia, Vrancea county
16.	2014	Vasile CHETREANU	76/M	Bodești, Vrâncioaia, Vrancea county

Table 1. List of the responders to the ethnologic inquiries during the three series of investigations (2010, 2012 and 2014).

The most comprehensive conclusion is that the survival in a number of micro-areas from Romania of these genuine behaviours/practices of surface exploitation of the salt outcrops constitutes a quite exceptional opportunity, an inescapable point of reference for understanding the workings of similar processes from prehistory. Unique in Europe, these resilient behaviours, threatened to the point of extinction by the inherent globalisation, must be studied intensively and urgently in order to record as much as possible of this precious intangible heritage.

Acknowledgement

This work was supported by a grant of the Romanian National Authority for Scientific Research, CNCS–UEFISCDI, project number PN-II-ID-PCE-2011-3-0825, 219/5.10.2011, The ethno-archaeology of the salt springs and salt mountains from the extra-Carpathian areas of Romania – ethnosalro.uaic.ro.

References

Alexianu, M. 2013. The saturated model: a first application in world and Romanian ethnoarchaeology. In: Marciniak, A and Yalman, N. eds. *Contesting ethnoarchaeologies.* New York: Springer, 211-225.

Alexianu, M. and Weller, O. 2009. The Ethnosal project. Ethnoarchaeological investigation at the Moldavian salt springs. *Antiquity* 83/321, September 2009.

Alexianu, M., Weller, O. and Brigand, R. 2012. EthnosalRo: an ethnoarchaeological project on Romanian salt. *The European Archaeologist* 38, 17-22.

Brigand, R., Weller, O. and Alexianu, M. 2015 (in press). A new technique for salt block preparation at Coza (Tulnici, Vrancea County, Romania). In: Alexianu, M., Curcă, R.-G. and Cotiugă, V. eds. *Salt Effect*. Proceedings of the 2nd Arheoinvest Symposium, april 2012, Al. I. Cuza University (Iaşi, Romania). BAR International Series. Oxford: Archaeopress.

Ciobanu, D. 2011. Traditional Methods of Salt Mining in Buzău County, Romania in the 21 Century. In: Alexianu, M., Weller O. and Curcă, R.-G. eds. *Archaeology and Anthropology of Salt: A Diachronic Approach*. Proceedings of the International Colloquium, 1-5 October 2008 Al. I. Cuza University (Iaşi, Romania). BAR International Series 2198. Oxford: Archaeopress, 35-36.

Dunăre, N. 1972. Forme de viaţă pastorală. In: Dunăre, N. ed. Ţara Bârsei. Bucharest: Ed. Academiei, 257-241.

Harding, A. 2013. *Salt in Prehistoric Europe*. Leiden: Sidestone Press.

Nandris, J. G. 1985. The Stina and the Katun: Foundations of a Research Design in European Highland Zone Ethnoarchaeology. *World Archaeology* 17(2), 256-268.

Romanescu, Gh., Alexianu, M. and Asăndulesei, A. 2014. The distribution of salt massifs and the exploitation of ancient and current reserves of mineralized waters within the Siret hydrographical basin (Romania). Case study for the eastern area of the Eastern Carpathians. In: *Hydrology & Water Resources*. Conference Proceedings of the 14th Geoconference on Water Resources, Forests, Marine and Ocean Ecosystems. International Multidisciplinary Scientific Conferences, 17-26 June 2014, Bulgaria. Sofia: STEF92, 731-746.

Weller, O., Brigand, R. and Alexianu, M. 2010. Recherches systématiques autour des sources salées de Moldavie. Bilan des prospections 2008-2010. *Memoria Antiquitatis* 25/26, 437-504.

Part Two

Archaeological evidences and applications

First salt making in Europe: a global overview from Neolithic times

Olivier WELLER

CNRS, UMR 8215 *Trajectoires*, Université Paris 1 Panthéon-Sorbonne, Maison de l'Archéologie et de l'Ethnologie, 21 allée de l'Université, F-92023 Nanterre cedex, France

Abstract. This paper deals with the origin of salt production and discusses different approaches ranging from technology, ethnoarchaeology and paleoenvironmental studies to chemical analyses. Starting from the current research on the Neolithic exploitation of salt in Europe, we examine the types and nature of the salt resources (sea water, salt springs, soil or rock), the diversity of archaeological evidence as forms of salt working. We also scrutinize the types of production for these early forms of salt exploitation, with or without the use of crudely-fired clay vessels (*briquetage*). Finally, we contextualize the socio-economic dimensions and highlight both the diversity of salt products, as well as their characteristics, which go well beyond dietary roles.

Keywords. Salt production, Neolithic, Europe, methodology, archaeological evidence.

Résumé. Cet article traite de l'origine de la production de sel et aborde différentes approches allant de la technologie, l'ethnoarchéologie, les études paléoenvironnementales aux analyses chimiques. A partir des recherches actuelles sur l'exploitation néolithique du sel en Europe, nous examinons les types et la nature des ressources en sel (eau de mer, source salée, sol ou sel gemme), la diversité des indices archéologiques comme les formes d'exploitation. Nous examinons également les types de production pour ces premières formes d'exploitation du sel, avec ou sans utilisation de terre cuite (*briquetage*). Pour finir, nous cherchons à mieux définir les dimensions socio-économiques de ces productions ainsi la diversité des sels produits qui dépassent de loin le seul rôle alimentaire.

Mots clés. Production de sel, Néolithique, Europe, méthodologie, indices archéologiques.

If today salt is an ordinary good, a practically inexhaustible substance, both alimentary and industrial, this hasn't been the case in countless pre-industrial societies. It is at least since the Neolithic that European agropastoral societies have sought to extract it from its natural sources, or more precisely since the 6th millennium BC. Nowadays we likely associate the exploitation of salt with coastal salt marshes. Yet a great share of the production still comes from artificial heating of brine or simply from the extraction of rock salt. If regular table salt, or sodium chloride, seems an inexhaustible natural commodity, neither its geographic distribution, nor its physical forms are uniform. Salt is found in either solid (rocks, outcrops, earths, sands, plants) or liquid form (sea or spring waters, bodily fluids). Furthermore, it is present in highly variable concentrations, ranging from a few grams for blood or urine, to almost 200 g/l for certain salt springs or enclosed seas, attaining an average of 30 g/l for oceanic waters. It crystallizes at concentrations of around 330 grams per litre of water.

Faced with this disparity in concentration and distribution, humanity resorted to a wide assortment of extraction techniques. Nonetheless, apart from the exploitation of rock salt, salt extraction most often consists, in some cases after the lixiviation of a salty solid, of processing a liquid by subjecting it to a natural (solar salt) or artificial (ignigenous salt) evaporation process, until crystallisation is achieved (see Gouletquer and Weller, in this volume, fig. 1). The grained salt obtained can be then used as such or packaged as hard blocks of standardised shapes and weights. In this form, it can be preserved or readily transported and then traded over long distances.

The diversity of methods observed across the world seem intimately linked to the environmental contexts and the type of saliferous resources exploited; it also mirrors the quality of the sought product (type of salts, salted ashes, grained salt, or salt blocks), and to the specificities of the demand and of the social context (Gouletquer et al. 1994).

The issue of origins

If archaeologists and scholars have examined the ancient mines or the abundant debris of fired clay (briquetage) from after the Iron Age up to the 18th century, research on the origins of salt exploitation, harking to the Early Neolithic, has not yet even commenced. At a first glance, one can easily understand why, in the absence of the very object of research, the issue of salt exploitation remained poorly addressed for the prehistoric period. However, if nothing has remained of the product, the archaeological realities around salt exploitation have been ascertained in the field with the help of various types of evidences, which inform us non-vicariously of the techniques employed (catchments, pottery or charcoal accumulations), or more indirectly of their impact on the environment, the territorial organisation, or the circulation of goods.

Besides the discussion on the archaeological remains themselves, it is the general question of the function of salt which emerges. Indeed, how can we explain the appearance of this new exploitation of the natural environment? What were the reasons for which the simple occasional collecting from a furrowed rock or from the edge of a salt spring were not sufficient anymore to these early Neolithic salt-producing communities, which now set themselves to separate the salt from its natural support (water, rocks, soils or plants) and, as such, to produce a hard, transportable and shaped salt? While many researchers have turned to biology and psychology to answer this question, others have looked for answers in ethnographic investigations. Indeed, does the biological hypotheses, according to which salt was an essential nutritional element within the new Neolithic alimentary diet, suffices to explain its exploitation?

In order to confront the hypotheses of the nutritionists with the archaeological realities, and to characterise the production of salt and its socio-economic implications, it is necessary to develop a pluridisciplinary approach and to multiply the ethnographic, historical, environmental, archaeometric, and experimental observations. It was therefore necessary to make use of several methods that, conjoined, can shed light on the archaeological realities. By illustrating our set goal with various case studies from across Europe, we seek to tackle the issue of salt exploitation from the methodological standpoint of different approaches that may be incurred, and of the elements that so far seem diagnostic. Also, we will see how the study of known or newly brought to light vestiges and of relative archaeological contexts can allow a reconsideration of the diversity of functions performed by salt, in which alimentation is not necessary the cornerstone.

Archaeological evidences

Whether or not one adheres to the biological argument, prehistorians have only recently considered other possible functions of salt in these early agricultural societies. Yet we know that the scarcity of exploitable natural resources meant that at specific times in history salt played an important economic and social role, prior to being bestowed with the multiple day-to-day applications we are now fully aware of (preservative, adjuvant for the dairy industry, tanning agent, metallurgy of precious metals, dye-fixing, medication…). Moreover, it has long been held that – just like with the production techniques of the Iron Age – salt exploitation was dependent just on the identification of vestiges or fired-clay structures collectively known as briquetage. Today, the variety of forms of exploitation recognised by both ethnography and archaeology (Alexianu *et al.* eds. 2011; Cassen *et al.* 2008; Cassen and Weller 2013; Fíguls and Weller 2007; Harding 2013; Hocquet *et al.* 2001; Monah *et al.* 2007; Nikolov and Bacvarov 2012; Pétrequin *et al.* 2001; Weller 2002; Weller *et al.* 2008) allows us to return to the issue of the function of certain material remains, and to advance new hypotheses on the place of this irreplaceable substance also in the domestic, technical and socio-economic spheres.

The directly-observable material remains of prehistoric salt production can sometimes be found in the form of wooden catchments or fittings, but most often it consists of accumulations of fired clay (or briquetage) comprising debris from ancient heating installations and fragments of salt pans, accumulations of charcoal and ashes, unearthed structures, or, in the case of rock salt exploitation, of stone

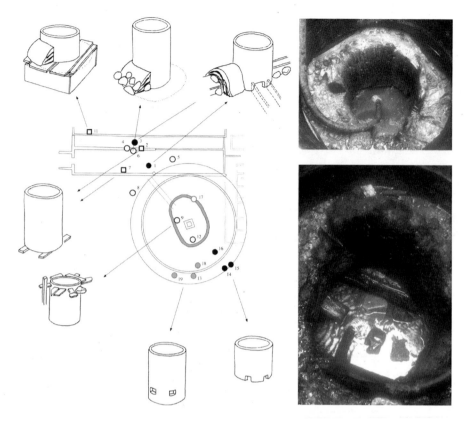

Figure 1. Neolithic wooden wells from Fontaines Salées, Saint-Père-sous-Vézelay, Yonne, France (drawing P. Pétrequin and photos O. Weller).

tools. We should note that no such remains are known at present for salt marshes, and that such inventions should be placed to the Roman period (not the Middle Ages), as shown by the excavations from Vigo in Portugal (Castro Carrera 2008).

Spring catchment and fittings

The construction of catchment systems and retention basins around the salt springs is difficult to ascertain in cases of heavy erosion or rapid sedimentation. However, French examples such as the spring from Moriez in the Alps, where researchers unearthed the frame of an ancient wattle dated to around 5600 BC (Morin *et al.* 2008), or that from Grozon in the Jura, where the salt workers erected a true horseshoe-shaped bulwark for protecting the spring (Pétrequin *et al.* 2001), suggest that the search for such structures should continue.

In the past, many wooden structures were observed during works of rehabilitation or for capturing the salt springs, but their dating is often problematic (missing elements, brief remarks at the moment of discovery…). The most eloquent are the 19 oak trunks from Fontaines Salées in Saint-Père-sous-Vézelay (Yonne, France) (fig. 1), formerly attributed to the onset of the Iron Age and nowadays re-examined and dated dendrochronologically to the 23rd century BC, that is to say contemporary with the Bell Beaker culture (Bernard *et al.* 2008).

Figure 2. Evidences of salt exploitation in Central and Eastern Europe between the 5ᵗʰ and 4ᵗʰ millenniums BC: 1- accumulation of firewood places from the Early Neolithic at Lunca-Poiana Slatinei (Romania); 2- Succession of archaeological layers extremely rich in pottery from the Precucuteni and Cucuteni cultures at Ţolici-Hălăbutoaia (Romania); 3, 4- Briquetage from the Cucuteni culture (Lunca and Ţolici, Romania); 5- Briquetage from the Vinča culture (Tuzla, Bosnia-Herzegovina); 6- Briquetage with an element of a stove, corroded ceramic and model from Barycz VII (Poland) (photos and drawings O. Weller except drawings 5- Benac 1978 and 6- Jodłowski 1977).

Fired-clay vessels (or Briquetage)

The exploitation of salt during the Neolithic and Chalcolithic seems to have been in some cases particularly dynamic, on account of the considerable quantities of fragments of ceramic moulds accumulated around certain salt springs, sometimes associated with combustion structures or residues (Weller 2002a). This is the case with salt springs from Little Poland, Bosnia-Herzegovina, Romanian Moldavia

Figure 3. Chalcolithic salt moulds accumulation in Solnitsata, Provadija, Bulgaria (photos O. Weller).

(fig. 2, 2-6), or, more recently, Bulgaria (fig. 3), all exploited using fired-clay moulds, during the middle of the 5th millennium BC (Weller 2012). Around 3000 BC, on the Atlantic coast, it is the enclosures around the Poitevin Marsh in France which produce a very large quantity of briquetage (Ard and Weller 2012), while in Germany the salt springs from Halle furnish the first fired-clay moulds.

This specific ceramic ware, in all instances abundant and clearly distinct from the domestic pottery, displays the same general characteristics: clay of local provenance, numerous inclusions sometimes taking a quite large share of the paste, abundant tempering (sand, plant matter, grog, *etc.*), open shape, crude fashioning from a clay lump or from coils, finger or plant imprints, traces of wickerwork on the bottom; the edges and the outer walls are not finished but the interior is neatly smoothed. Fragmentation is nonetheless significant, due to their deliberate breaking for extracting the salt cakes. Across different producing sites, the vessels' bottoms, sometimes complete, constitute in some cases the majority of the ceramic harvest; the edges adhere to the salt cakes and can serve to trace the distribution paths.

These salt moulds thus serve both as moulds and crystallizers. If for some their function still remains at the level of hypothesis (Cassen *et al.* 2012), we were able to confirm it, for others, through a series of chemical analyses based on the assay of the element chlorine (Weller 2002a; Weller and Ard, forthcoming). Basically, the levels of chlorine in the salt moulds are 2 to 20 times higher than in domestic contexts. These values are greater still, as the meteoric waters infiltration is lower.

The use of ceramic moulds of practically identical shapes and volumes by each cultural group attests to the commitment to produce and package the salt according to a predefined shape, compact and easy to transport. The production is not aimed at simply producing salt, but salt cakes of a standardised quality, size and weight. The salt cake thus becomes a social object, an identity marker of the producers. In this form, it will circulate conveniently, be divided without losing its use value, and be stored for many years.

It is Central and Eastern Europe which in the early-middle Chalcolithic, specifically the middle of the 5th millennium BC, develops the crystallisation and moulding of salt in vessels of fired clay (Weller 2012). The appearance of these chemical techniques alongside the first copper objects, similarly casted, betray a new conception of the properties of matter, of making visible and manipulable a substance that is initially invisible. Nonetheless, with the exception of a fragment of a furnace discovered in Little Poland, there are no known genuine combustion structures from this era, and Western Europe had to wait the Bronze Age to first produce such structures, and then the Iron Age for saltworks in the true meaning of the word.

The charcoal accumulations

It was for a long time thought that in the absence of fired clay (ceramics, supports, accessories and fragments of furnaces or kilns), we could not demonstrate the exploitation of salt. However, there are other techniques of salt production, which do not necessitate the use of fired clay or kilns. The ethnographic studies conducted in New Guinea (Pétrequin *et al.* 2001; see Gouletquer and Weller in this volume) and their archaeological work in eastern France (Franche-Comté) revealed methods of exploitation that do not require the use of fired clay or furnaces, but other techniques involving the use of vegetal matter as raw material and produce considerable quantities of charcoal and ashes (Pétrequin and Weller 2008). Finding ancient accumulations of charcoal around the salt springs or littoral marshes thus becomes a new challenge for the research on ancient forms of salt production.

To have an image, if not for the production of salt, at least for the approximate volume of charcoal and waste on the river, the case of Salins-les-Bains (Jura) is exemplary: the charcoal from the production of salt during the 18th century is visible in the alluvial deposits to a distance of up to 10 km downstream from the saltworks; with respect to the charcoal produced during the Neolithic dated to around 3000 BC, it is still present in large quantities in the clogged meanders 7 km downstream of the salt exploitation area.

Over thousands of years, it is therefore a massive quantity of fuel that has been consumed in order to produce salt. For instance, the longitudinal section of the Grozon basin (Jura) across 400 m has revealed carbonaceous layers over 7 m thick, dated to between the early 4th millennium BC and the Roman period (fig. 4). The end of the exploitation during the Gallo-Roman era is marked by the entrenchment of the Romans around the salt springs (or the coastal marshes, respectively) presumably to put a halt to the Gallic exploitation and to sell their own Mediterranean salt.

As for the paleoenvironmental approaches, the palynologic and anthracologic analyses represent the most promising research directions. By studying the sedimentary sequences spread across the depressions near or immediately downstream of the salt exploitation points, it is possible to trace the management of the fuel and the history of deforesting (Dufraisse and Gauthier 2002). It is particularly possible to differentiate the deforesting for agricultural purposes (where the pollen of certain crops are well represented) and deforestation associated

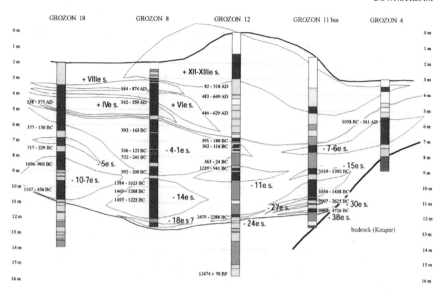

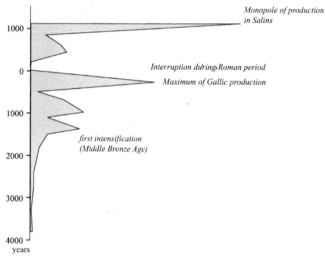

Figure 4. Salt exploitation in Grozon (Jura, France): Longitudinal stratigraphic cut of the Grozon basin (400 m) based on drill cores and dated by radiocarbon. The depression was created after the underlying salt-rock was dissolved (top). Schematic chronological evolution of the charcoal sediments volume related to salt exploitation (bottom) (drawings P. Pétrequin).

only with the exploitation of salt, in the case of the spring located at that moment outside of the permanent settlement and cultivated land. But the accuracy of the pollen diagrams is directly affected by the quality of the preserved pollen and the recording of the chronological sequences; this means that the marshes and depressions with wet environments should be the prime targets of core boring and sample collecting.

With respect to the exploitation techniques, in light of our own ethnographic study in the Indonesian New Guinea (see Gouletquer and Weller in this volume), following a re-examination of the ancient sources (foremost Pliny, Tacitus and Varro) and a series of life-size experiments (Pétrequin and Weller 2008), the extraction of salt without recipients is today better known for the Middle Neolithic of eastern France, and similarly proved for the Early Neolithic of Romania (fig. 2, 1) (Weller and Dumitroaia 2005; Weller *et al.* 2008). They involve the direct spill of the saline water over an incandescent pyre covered by a vegetal blanket meant to slow down the falling water. The saline water gets concentrated along the running path, just like in the techniques used in the gradual-evaporation salt factories of 16th-19th century Germany and eastern France; in contact with the incandescent embers, the salt crystallizes instantly. The small salt crystals are subsequently recovered from the ash and cinders, and packaged in a form that still eludes us.

The exploitation structures and buildings

Always built in the immediate proximity and view of the salt springs, according to the ethnographic data, the buildings and structures for exploitation are still largely unknown. Examples include the saltworks from Little Poland (pits, ditches and foundation post holes from the site of Barycz VII), the pits from Provadija in Bulgaria (Nikolov ed. 2008), or the Neolithic pits from Sandun (Loire-Atlantique, France), justly interpreted (Cassen *et al.* 2008) as pits for filtering salty sand and collecting brine, just like the pre-Hispanic vestiges from Mexico (fig. 5) (Liot 2000), or the Gallic sites from northern France (Edeine 1970). In the case of Sandun, it is therefore the real functions of the site considered so far as marsh-edge settlement that must be reconsidered. S. Cassen also invites us to readdress the functions of the different structures unearthed in several sites presumed to be settlements from France and Italy, or the so-called *Cultura de los silos de Baja Andalucía* for which he proposes to be reinterpreted as places for producing salt foremost by washing very fine sand. Intriguing hypotheses which must be tested in the field.

The first Neolithic mining tools

The only salt mountain in Western Europe is found in Cardona in Catalonia, at about 80 km northwest of Barcelona. This varicoloured *Muntanya de Sal* reaches more than 140 m in height. Despite the abundant research on the Neolithic burials of the region in the early 20th century and the discovery of numerous stone tools around this landform, the hypothesis of a Neolithic exploitation of this remarkable outcrop was hastily abandoned after the 1930s. After that moment, this region from the foothills of the Pyrenees remained outside of the large research endeavours and archaeological campaign concentrated along the Catalan shoreline.

However, starting from a series of chance findings gathered since the start of the last century by prospectors, farmers or workers from this salt mine, we were able to study several hundred stone tools represented by hammers, reused axes, pestles, and bushhammers (Weller 2002b; Fíguls *et al.* 2013). Their technological analysis showed that the Neolithic workers were using mining tools (usually stone axes

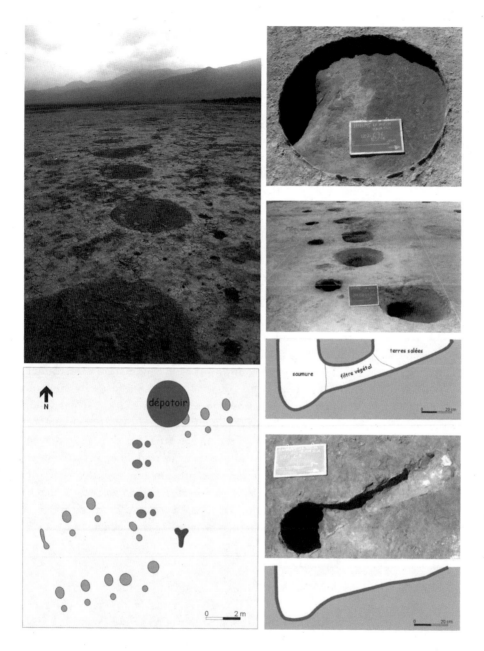

Figure 5. Pits for leaching salty soils, with watertight facing, simple, double or multiple from the Pre-Hispanic salt production centre on the edge of the Sayula basin (Jalisco, Mexico) (photos O. Weller-left and C. Liot-right, drawings C. Liot).

reused) associated with the exploitation of rock salt in the form of an open quarry. The salt blocks extracted from the outcrop were transported to the surrounding settlements in order to be transformed using mortars, and probably regularised, into blocks of salt of standard shapes and weights.

The socio-economic implications

Discerning the economic and social aftermath of the production and trade of salt consists firstly in the identification, in the vicinity of the salt springs, of the specific concentrations of settlements, and therefore of a population (Brigand and Weller 2013; *id.* in this volume), or of valuables in the form of deposits (Harding 2013), of imported goods or of spectacular graves. But this is where interpretation is most difficult, particularly since the ethnographic model of chieftain/leader societies specific to the highlands of the Indonesian New Guinea is only one among many other examples of ways in which a society can be structured. Here there are no buried treasures, no graves of momentarily prominent individuals, simply because the forms of power are transmitted equally through exchange and redistribution of wealth. Other ethnoarchaeological models should be tested before attempting to characterise social behaviours founded on social inequality, for instance like those which around the middle of the 5th millennium BC engendered the monumental tombs from the Gulf of Morbihan (France), a particularly suitable area for the exploitation of salt (Gouletquer and Weller 2002; Cassen *et al.* 2012).

On the question of the type of organisation and a conceivable specialisation of the crystallised salt production by the Neolithic groups from northern Catalonia (Weller and Fíguls 2013), the great portion of tools reused and fashioned from fractured polished axes, their distribution in an area of more than 20 km around the salt deposit, their low degree of technical development, and foremost the plausible absence of any major fortified control settlement, all suggest an open exploitation, not one reserved for a single small group of local specialists. However, the relative richness of the graves of this group in goods imported from the coast (variscite pearls from Gavà, the largest ever known, bracelets and pearls from shells, blond flint imported from Haute-Provence) suggests an elevated position of salt within a wider regional exchange network.

We may also mention the tight spatial correlation observed in Germany between the salt springs and the distribution of greenstone long alpine axes, which demonstrate that salt could have played a key role in the acquisition of these wealth and ceremonial objects (Weller 2002a). The age of the exploitation of these highly saline springs remains nonetheless to be established, only fired-clay remains used since the late Neolithic have been subject of studies.

In any case, throughout Western Europe during the 5th millennium BC, certain saliferous resources, be they inner-continental or coastal, appear to act as hubs capable of "drawing" into their networks these large polished alpine axes with attached social value, while in Carpathian-Balkan Europe, the first copper and gold objects likely integrated such networks. It is thus necessary to turn decisively towards a political geography of salt.

Depending on the nature of the salt exploitation and the modes of occupation of territories rich in saliferous resources, this production was occasional, regular or heavily invested, and also modulated by the different uses and functions of the product. These different organisations responded to the different uses of the salt, varying according to the social context, and salt most definitely did not have the same value irrespective of the time and place. The circulation paths, the exchange networks, and the social context are from this point of view the determining factors.

If the prevailing hypotheses on the function of salt during the Neolithic are primarily biological ones, in line with the ubiquitous adage "Salt is essential to humans", the substance further acquired other uses, more recently established: preserving foods, dairy making, fixing dyes, hide processing, *etc.* However, the existence of idiosyncratic configurations of spatial organisation around the saliferous resources opens the door for other hypotheses besides the strictly utilitarian or functionalist explanations so far sanctioned by prehistorians. The diversity of functions played by salt in contemporary traditional societies shows that its status cannot be reduced to that of a simple household and nutritional chemical substance, especially because during the 5th millennium BC it was the focus of a massive technical and economic investment, as evidenced by its forging into cakes in Central and South-eastern Europe.

The appearance of the first Neolithic moulds means that salt, in the form of salt cakes, became a standardised item, dividable, transportable and storable, or, briefly said, a socialised good, an identity marker, capable of enabling long-distance exchange networks. Besides its role in human and animal alimentation, salt could have played, in certain contexts, the role of exchange good as a form of durable storage of a substance that is unique in terms of its qualities, of the areas suitable for its exploitation, and of its technical and economic charge.

We also notice that this intensification of exploitations of moulded salt in Central and South-eastern Europe coincides with periods of expansion of major groups such as the Lengyel (Poland), Vinča (former Yugoslavia), Cucuteni (Romania), or Hamangia (Bulgaria) cultures. The salt cakes could have been one of the means by which the social tensions generated by these population movements were defused. However, they were not necessarily used by all the expanding groups during this period of intensification of social relations, and were not routinely involved in all the processes of social regulation. It was just one possible form of storing wealth, one of the ways of taking part in the exchange.

As for the present, we are moving towards a European-wide geography of techniques of salt production (fig. 6), in which the technical investments, the economic and social status of this activity, but also the accompanying mental and social representations, can be pinpointed. It remains to define more precisely the forms of exploitation used in certain areas particularly suitable for extraction, for which only indirect evidence are available, but where the socio-economic contexts suggest a remarkable production (the lagoon areas of Morbihan, the highly saline springs from Halle/Salle and Bad Nauheim in Germany, the salt springs and saline lagoons from inner Spain…).

This study on an eminently soluble object is just the beginning, and future research should prioritise not only to search for undiscovered traces of exploitation (salt moulds, ceramics for boiling, filtration or storing structures, wooden catchment fittings, accumulations of ashes and charcoal, extraction implements and tools…), but should also seek to characterise the social behaviours of the groups that manipulated this substance and the historical processes that were engendered by them.

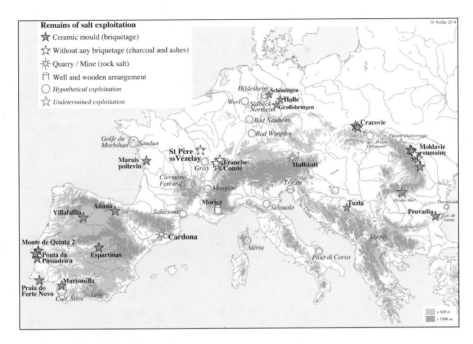

Figure 6. An European assessment for the Neolithic and Chalcolithic periods (6000-2300 BC): the various archaeological evidences for salt production (drawing O. Weller).

References

Alexianu, M., Weller, O. and Curcă, R.-G. eds. 2011. *Archaeology and Anthropology of salt. A diachronic approach*. Proceedings of the International Colloquium, 1-5 October 2008, Al.I. Cuza University (Iaşi, Romania). BAR, International Series 2198. Oxford: Archaeopress.

Ard, V. and Weller, O. 2012. Les vases de « type Champ-Durand » : témoins d'une exploitation du sel au Néolithique récent dans le Marais poitevin. In: Joussaume, R. ed. *L'enceinte néolithique de Champ-Durand à Nieul-sur-l'Autise (Vendée)*. Chauvigny: Association des publications chauvinoises, 309-333.

Benac, A. 1978. Neke karakteristike neoliskih naselja u Bosni i Hercegovini. *Materijali* 14, 15-27.

Bernard, V., Pétrequin, P. and Weller, O. 2008. Captages en bois à la fin du Néolithique: les Fontaines Salées à Saint-Père-sous-Vézelay. In: Weller, O., Dufraisse, A. and Pétrequin, P. eds. *Sel, eau et forêt. D'hier à aujourd'hui*. Cahiers de la MSH Ledoux 12 (coll. Homme et environnement 1). Besançon: Presses Universitaires de Franche-Comté, 299-333.

Brigand, R. and Weller, O. 2013. Neolithic and Chalcolithic settlement pattern in central Moldavia (Romania). *Documenta Praehistorica* 40, 195-207.

Cassen, S., de Labriffe, P.-A. and Menanteau, L. 2008. Washing and heating on the Neolithic shores of Western Europe. An archaeological hypothesis on the production of sea salt. In: Weller, O., Dufraisse, A. and Pétrequin, P. eds. *Sel, eau et forêt. D'hier à aujourd'hui*. Cahiers de la MSH Ledoux 12 (coll. Homme et environnement 1). Besançon: Presses Universitaires de Franche-Comté, 175-204.

Cassen, S., Viguier, E., Weller, O., Chaigneau, C., Hamon, G., de Labriffe, P.-A. and Martin, C. 2012. Neolithic flat-based pots from the Carnac Mounds in the light of Cycladic 'frying pans'. *Documenta Praehistorica* 39, 309-324.

Cassen, S. and Weller, O. 2013. Idées et faits relatifs à la production des sels marins et terrestres en Europe, du VIe au IIIe millénaire. In: Soares, J. ed. *Prehistory of Wetlands. Landscapes of salt.* Setúbal Arqueológica 14. Setúbal: Museum of Archaeology and Ethnography of the District of Setúbal (MAEDS), 255-304.

Castro Carrera, J.C., 2008. La saline romaine de 'O Areal', Vigo (Galice): architecture d'une installation industrielle de production de sel marin. In: Weller, O., Dufraisse, A. and Pétrequin, P. eds. *Sel, eau et forêt. D'hier à aujourd'hui.* Cahiers de la MSH Ledoux 12 (coll. Homme et environnement 1). Besançon: Presses Universitaires de Franche-Comté, 381-399.

Dufraisse, A. and Gauthier, E. 2002. Exploitation des sources salées en Franche-Comté: impact sur l'espace forestier du Néolithique à la période médiévale. In: Weller, O. ed. *Archéologie du sel. Techniques et sociétés.* Internationale Archäologie, ASTK 3. Rahden: VML GmbH, 243-257.

Edeine, B. 1970. La technique de fabrication du sel marin dans les sauneries protohistoriques. *Annales de Bretagne* LXXVII, 95-133.

Fíguls, A. and Weller, O. eds. 2007. *Trobada International d'Arqueologia envers l'explotació de la sal a la Prehistória i Protohistória.* Acts of the 1st International Archaeology meeting about Prehistoric and Protohistoric salt exploitation, Cardona, 6-8 dec. 2003. Cardona: IREC.

Fíguls, A., Weller, O., Grandia, F., Bonache, J., González, J. and Lanaspa, R. 2013. La primera explotación minera de la sal gema: la Vall Salina de Cardona (Cataluña, España). *Chungara. Revista de Antropología Chilena* 45, 1, 177-195.

Gouletquer, P., Kleinmann, D. and Weller, O. 1994. Sels et techniques. In: Daire, M.-Y. ed. *Le sel gaulois.* Dossiers de Centre de Recherche Archéologique d'Alet Q, 123-161.

Gouletquer, P. et Weller, O. 2002. Y a-t-il eu des salines au Néolithique en Bretagne ? In: Péron, F. ed. *Patrimoine Maritime sur les façades maritimes de l'Union Européenne.* Actes du colloque international CNRS-UBO-IEUM, Brest, 2000. Rennes: Presses Universitaires de Rennes, 449-453.

Harding, A. 2013. *Salt in Prehistoric Europe.* Leiden: Sidestone Press.

Hocquet, J.-C., Malpica Cuello, A. and Weller, O. 2001. *Hommes et paysages du sel.* Paris: Actes Sud.

Jodłowski, A. 1977. Die Salzgewinnung auf polnischem Boden in vorgeschichtlicher Zeit und im frühen Mittelalter. *Jahreschrift für mitteldeutsche Vorgeschichte* 61, 85-103.

Liot, C. 2000. *Les salines préhispaniques du bassin de Sayula (Occident du Mexique). Milieu et Techniques.* BAR International Series 849, Monographs in American Archaeology 6. Oxford: Archaeopress.

Monah, D., Dumitroaia, G., Weller, O. and Chapman, J. eds. 2007. *L'exploitation du sel à travers le temps.* Actes du colloque international, Piatra Neamt, Roumanie, oct. 2004. Bibliotheca Memoria Antiquitatis XVIII. Piatra Neamt: C. Matasa.

Morin, D., Lavier, C., Guiomar, M. and Fontugne, M. 2008. Aux origines de l'extraction du sel en Europe (VIe millénaire av. J-C). La source salée de Moriez, Alpes de Haute Provence. In: Weller, O., Dufraisse, A. and Pétrequin, P. eds. *Sel, eau et forêt. D'hier à aujourd'hui*. Cahiers de la MSH Ledoux 12 (coll. Homme et environnement 1). Besançon: Presses Universitaires de Franche-Comté, 281-297.

Nikolov, V. ed. 2008. *Праисторически солодобивен център Провадия-Солницата. Разкопки 2005-2007 г.* Sofia.

Nikolov, V. and Bacvarov, K. eds. 2012. *Salt and Gold: The Role of Salt in Prehistoric Europe*. Acts of international colloquium Humboldt-Kolleg, Provadia, Bulgaria, oct. 2010. Provadia-Veliko Tarnovo : Faber.

Pétrequin, P., Weller, O., Gauthier, E. and Dufraisse, A. 2001. Salt springs exploitations without pottery during Prehistory. From New Guinea to the French Jura. In: Beyries, S. and Pétrequin, P. eds. *Ethno-Archaeology and its Transfers*. BAR, International Series 983. Oxford: Archaeopress, 37-65.

Pétrequin, P. and Weller, O. 2008. L'exploitation préhistorique des sources salées dans le Jura français. Application et critiques d'un modèle prédictif. In: Weller, O., Dufraisse, A. and Pétrequin, P. eds. *Sel, eau et forêt. D'hier à aujourd'hui*. Cahiers de la MSH Ledoux 12 (coll. Homme et environnement 1). Besançon: Presses Universitaires de Franche-Comté, 255-279.

Weller, O. ed. 2002. *Archéologie du sel. Techniques et sociétés dans la Pré et Protohistoire européenne*. Internationale Archäologie, ASTK 3. Rahden: VML GmbH.

Weller, O. 2002a. Aux origines de l'exploitation du sel en Europe. Vestiges, fonctions et enjeux archéologiques. In: Weller, O. ed. *Archéologie du sel. Techniques et sociétés*. Internationale Archäologie, ASTK 3. Rahden: VML GmbH, 163-175.

Weller, O. 2002b. The earliest rock salt exploitation in Europe. A salt moutain in Spanish Neolithic, *Antiquity* 76, 1, 317-18. Available at: http://www.antiquity.ac.uk/ProjGall/Pre2003/Weller/weller.html

Weller, O. 2012. La production chalcolithique du sel à Provadia-Solnitsata: de la technologie céramique aux implications socio-économiques. In: Nikolov, V. and Bacvarov, K. eds. *Salt and Gold: The Role of Salt in Prehistoric Europe*. Provadia-Veliko Tarnovo: Faber, 67-87.

Weller, O. and Ard, V. forthcoming. Prehistoric salt production: technological approach in ceramic studies. *European Journal of Archaeology*.

Weller, O., Dufraisse, A. and Pétrequin, P. eds. 2008. *Sel, eau et forêt. D'hier à aujourd'hui*. Cahiers de la MSH Ledoux 12 (coll. Homme et environnement 1). Besançon: Presses Universitaires de Franche-Comté.

Weller, O. and Dumitroaia, G. 2005. The earliest salt production in the world: an early Neolithic exploitation in *Poiana Slatinei*-Lunca, Romania. *Antiquity* 79, 306. Available at: http://www.antiquity.ac.uk/ProjGall/weller/index.html.

Weller, O., Dumitroaia, Gh., Sordoillet, D., Dufraisse, A., Gauthier, E. and Munteanu, R. 2008. Première exploitation de sel en Europe : Techniques et gestion de l'exploitation de la source salée de Poiana Slatinei à Lunca (Neamt, Roumanie). In: Weller, O., Dufraisse, A. and Pétrequin, P. eds. *Sel, eau et forêt. D'hier à aujourd'hui.* Cahiers de la MSH Ledoux 12 (coll. Homme et environnement 1). Besançon: Presses Universitaires de Franche-Comté, 205-230.

Weller, O. and Fíguls, A. 2013. Die erste Steinsalzgewinnung Europas und der Tauschhandel als wirtschaftlicher Dynamisierer der Mittleren Jungsteinzeit in Katalonien. Das Vall Salina von Cardona (Katalonien, Spanien). *Archäologisches Korrespondenzblatt* 43, 2, 159-173.

Weller, O., Pétrequin, P., Pétrequin, A.-M. and Couturaud, A. 1996. Du sel pour les échanges sociaux. L'exploitation des sources salées en Irian Jaya (Nouvelle-Guinée, Indonésie). *Journal de la Société des Océanistes* 102, 1, 3-30.

A complex relationship between human and natural landscape: a multidisciplinary approach to the study of the roman saltworks in "Le Vignole-Interporto" (Maccarese, Fiumicino-Roma)

Maria Cristina GROSSI*, Sandra SIVILLI*,

Antonia ARNOLDUS-HUYZENDVELD**,

Alessandra FACCIOLO*, Maria Lucrezia RINALDI*,

Daria RUGGERI* and Cinzia MORELLI***

*archaeologists, independent researchers
**geo-archaeologist Digiter s.r.l., Via della Fortezza 58, 00040 Rocca di Papa, Roma, Italy
***Soprintendenza Speciale per il Colosseo, il Museo Nazionale Romano e l'Area Archeologica di Roma, Viale dei Romagnoli 717, 00119 Ostia Antica, Roma, Italy

Abstract. In this paper we will present the results of a series of archaeological excavations directed by the *Soprintendenza Speciale per i Beni Archeologici di Roma - sede di Ostia* over the years 2001-2008, in an extended part of the ex-lagoon of Maccarese (170 hectares). This area has been inserted in the wider environmental context of the coastal belt of Rome, which especially in the last decade has been subject to a considerable number of studies.

For three thousand years, from the recent prehistoric period to the modern ages, the lagoon waters and borders represented major human resources, determining the dynamics of occupation and resource exploitation in the area. Our commitment so far has been to improve our understanding of the area and to explore how landscape modification can be interpreted.

With a special focus on the Roman Age, the excavations carried out in the ancient lagoon have brought to light a large hydraulic structure, dating back to the first half of the 1st century AD. This site, which for the moment doesn't seem to compare to any installation in the areas pertaining to the ancient Roman world, was intended to isolate a large bay from the main body of the Maccarese lagoon and to control the water flow, in particular for activities related to salt extraction. The structures discovered seem to have a chronological connection with the harbours of *Claudius* and *Traianus* and with the *Via Portuensis*.

Keywords. Roman period, saltworks, channels, Italy, Maccarese Lake.

Résumé. Dans ce document on présentera les résultats de plusieurs excavations archéologiques dirigées par la *Soprintendenza Speciale per i Beni Archeologici di Roma - sede di Ostia* (dans les années 2001-2008) sur une zone étendue de l'ancienne lagune de Maccarese (170 hectares). Cette zone est insérée dans le contexte plus large de la ceinture côtière de Rome qui a été l'objet de plusieurs études pendant les dix dernières années.

Pendant trois mille ans, depuis la récente préhistoire jusqu'à l'époque moderne, les eaux de la lagune et ses rivages ont représenté la majorité des ressources humaines, déterminant la dynamique d'occupation et d'exploitation des ressources. Nous nous sommes engagés jusqu'à maintenant à élargir notre connaissance de la zone et à comprendre comment les changements du paysage peuvent être interprétés.

En se concentrant sur l'époque romaine, les excavations faites dans l'ancienne lagune ont mis à jour une grande structure hydraulique, datant de la première moitié du 1er siècle ap. J-C. Cette découverte, qui pour le moment ne semble pas pouvoir se comparer à d'autres établissements connus du monde romain, devait contrôler l'écoulement des eaux de la section de la lagune de Maccarese, tout particulièrement pour ce qui concerne les activités liées à l'extraction du sel. Les structures découvertes semblent avoir un lien chronologique avec les ports de *Claudius* et de *Traianus* ainsi qu'avec la *Via Portuensis*.

Mots-clés. Antiquité romaine, saline, canal, Italie, Lac de Maccarese.

Location-Paleoenvironment

The investigated area is located in the delta plain of the Tiber river, 25 km SW of Rome, delimited to the south by the Tiber, to the west by the Tyrrhenian coast, to the north by the Arrone river and to the east by a series of low Pleistocene hills. The coastal area of Rome is divided in an external delta plain formed by beach ridges of different Holocene depositional phases, and a flat inner plain characterized by wide depressions that were occupied originally by two ponds, of which the *Stagno di Maccarese* is the northern one (figs. 1 and 2).

In this area there have been considerable environmental landscape changes between about 20,000 and 3000 years ago. The beginning of this period coincided with the last glacial peak, when the sea level was extremely low and the Tiber valley was deeply incised. With the subsequent increase in temperature, the sea rose stepwise from *c.* -120 m until approximately the present level, and the lagoons and the Tiber valley began to fill in (Bellotti 2000; Bellotti *et al.* 2007). The sea level has been rising until approximately 6000 years ago, when a series of coastal barriers were laid in place, gradually isolating the lagoon from the sea (Bellotti

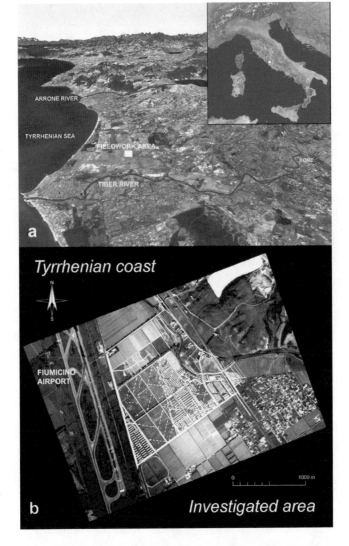

Figure 1a. Location of the area "Le Vignole - Interporto". Figure 1b. Explorative trenches realized between years 2003-2008.

et al. 2011). The peat sediments encountered at the base of the stratigraphy of the investigated area are dated to this period. Geomorphological investigations revealed that the beach ridges were broken up a number of times during the last thousands of years, determining connections between the sea and the Maccarese pond (Giraudi 2004). The river system has continued to slowly fill in the lagoon and the valley with clayey and silty sediments. At the time, the coastline was set back a few kilometres compared to the current one.

The Holocene paleo-vegetational record from the *Stagno di Maccarese* indicate a sequence of abrupt landscape changes, driven by local geomorphic coastal processes and by variations of the sea level (Di Rita *et al.* 2010; 2011). So, between *c.* 8300 and 5400 cal BP it was a freshwater basin, surrounded by a forested landscape, which changed until 5100 cal BP in an open marshy environment, probably due to a lowering of the water table. Between 5100 and 2900 cal BP there has been a remarkable expansion of riparian trees, possibly triggered by an increased water

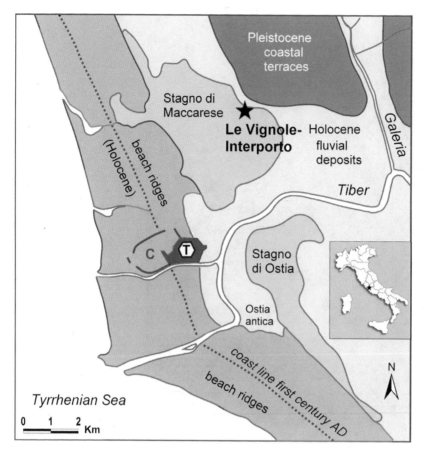

*Figure 2. Location of the area "Le Vignole-Interporto". C, harbour basin of Claudius;
T, harbour basin of Trajan.*

influx. Until 2000 cal BP an unstable marshy environment is registered, "formed by ponds, wetlands, sedge fens and salted soils" (Di Rita et al. 2010, 64).

An important environmental event that occurred, before or during the Etruscan period, with an almost stable sea level, is the transformation of the water of the Maccarese lagoon from fresh to salt/brackish, enough to allow the construction of saltworks. This change is recorded by Giraudi (2004, 485) to have occurred after 910-800 cal BC (calibrated ^{14}C data). Di Rita et al. (2010) report an increased salinity of the Maccarese basin around 2600 cal BP, based upon pollen and carpological data. The cause of this transformation should have been the (natural?) re-opening of the connection with the sea.

In Roman times, the sea level was slightly lower than nowadays, which must have influenced the water level of the lagoon. It was established at 0.80 m below present sea level in the 3rd-5th century AD (Goiran et al. 2009). The low tidal range of only 30-40 cm, common to all coastal plans along the Tyrrhenian Sea, should make it impractical, but not impossible, to use the high tide for letting the marine waters enter the salt basins.

Nowadays, the landscape, characterized by a flat morphology, is crossed by numerous channels and covered with cultivations, mostly cereals. Inland, the area is delimited by dissected Pleistocene coastal terraces while, towards the sea, the coastal dunes covered with *maquis* (a typical Mediterranean vegetation) can barely be perceived behind the extensive urban areas. What remains today of the lagoon of Maccarese is, actually, a flat artificial landscape resulting from the land reclamation started in 1883 by the newly established Italian state and carried out in the first decades of the 20th century (Biglieri 1896; Lugli and Filibeck 1935; Chiumenti and Bilancia 1979; Ministero Agricoltura and Foreste 1947; Parisi Presicce and Villetti 1998; Morelli *et al.* 2011b) by the owners of the large coastal estates. The reclamation works, besides cancelling the wide Maccarese Pond, have buried or destroyed the traces of pre-Roman and Roman settlements that had developed along its borders.

Methods

In range of works for the construction of a large industrial area (Interporto Roma-Fiumicino), the *Soprintendenza Speciale per i Beni Archeologici di Roma – sede di Ostia*, under the direction of Dr. Cinzia Morelli, undertook a preventive archaeological excavation, partly published (Castelli *et al.* 2008; Grossi *et al.* 2008; Morelli 2008; Arnoldus-Huyzendveld *et al.* 2009; Ruggeri *et al.* 2010).

Explorative trenches and selected excavation area were carried out (a large research team[1] excavated between 2001 and 2008), through a planning that took under consideration the characteristics of the area. Archaeological and geo-archaeological data allowed us to perform a thorough diachronical and synchronical reconstruction of an area of about 170 hectares (fig. 1b).

For the roman period, with the exception of a dam built with 1400 *amphorae* and four walled channels (see Part. 4), the archaeological remains essentially consist of tracks that are difficult to identify: multiple cuts of channels, differing in shape and size, are found in clayey and silty sediments. As working method, each context and variation has been stored with the total station alongside the associated geospatial information. Continuous selective correlations between registered data, structures and stratigraphy graphically modelled, were the only option for a correct interpretation of field observations. A significant role was assumed by the systematic recording of type, size and quantity of shells, particularly helpful in determining changes between freshwater and saltwater environments. This correlation of layers, channel cuts and profiles, small height variations, allowed the reconstruction of the complex system that we ascribe to the production of salt, only readable through an extensive survey and closely connected to the geomorphological reconstruction of the lagoon. An accurate recording of the morphological aspects of vegetation

---

1   The fieldworks and data processing were managed by A. Facciolo, M. Gala, M.C. Grossi, M.L. Rinaldi, D. Ruggeri, S. Sivilli. The geoarchaeological research was carried out by C. Giraudi and A. Arnoldus-Huyzendveld; topographical survey by Geo Space s.r.l.; graphic models have been made by D. Citro and A. Tilia (Studio 3R); amphorae study is by S. Medaglia (Università degli Studi di Viterbo); sampling and study of the woods managed by E. Peverati; botanic remains were studied by A. Celant and D. Magri.

elements – exceptionally well-preserved in this anaerobic environment – allowed the reconstruction of the wooden structures supporting the extended production system. This systematic sampling of the wooden finds yielded, together with economic and paleo-environmental interpretations, dating information which confirm the occupation phases shown by the archaeological data.

Stratigraphy – Occupation

The stratigraphy encountered in the area was surprisingly constant (fig. 3). The base is marked by the presence of a peat layer at a depth of about 180-280 cm, which has been dated to 4000-3000 BC (Giraudi 2004; Bellotti *et al.* 2007). This stratum is covered, from bottom to top, by marshy, lagoonal and fluvio-lacustrine layers, which can be traced back to the Tiber floods. The lower layers of the sections contain freshwater malacofauna (*Lymnaea stagnalis, Planorbis corneus* and *Bithynia tentaculata)*, indicating the isolation of the lagoon from the sea, while the upper layers contain a brackish malacofauna, pointing to the occurrence of an ingression (*Cerastoderma sp., Cerastoderma edule, Abra alba,* and *Hydrobia acuta*).

The earliest part of the excavated area (dated at 10th-9th century BC) consist of archaeological remains of the Final Bronze Age, in a fresh water marsh sediment (Castelli *et al.* 2008; Arnoldus-Huyzendveld *et al.* 2009; Ruggeri *et al.* 2010).

The Protohistoric phases are covered and sealed by a fresh water marsh sediment, rich in plants remains. The small thickness of the layers indicates the stability of the swamp during this phase, both in extension and in depth.

The next layers suggest that the marsh evolved into a lagoon of brackish water, which fits in with the geological data indicating that between the 10th and 7th seventh century BC there has been a rupture of the coastal barriers, and the opening of one or more channels connecting the marsh to the sea (Giraudi 2004; Bellotti *et al.* 2007). These layers contain abundant archaeological features of the Roman period, showing a complex system related to salt exploitation, together with remains of medieval age.

We could identify the characteristics of the permanent shore of the lagoon bordering on the coastal terraces (to the NE), as opposed to the presumably seasonal shore between the lagoonal and peri-lagoonal areas (to the east and south). Traces of human occupation along the boundary of the marsh/lagoon has allowed us to reconstruct the shift of the shore line over time.

Proceeding from west to east, the layers show an increasing degree of weathering and pedogenesis.

In particular, the upper part of the stratigraphy shows a coloration tending to orange, and the peat and lagoon levels alternate with the gravelly layers of the terrace. These characteristics define the permanent shore, characterized by the overlaying of the lagoon sediments upon the sandy terrace sediments, with a slightly sloping escarpment. On the permanent shore, some channels belonging to the Roman period (1st century AD) were found at a short distance from the Protohistoric evidence; they seem to have followed the line of the shore. As a

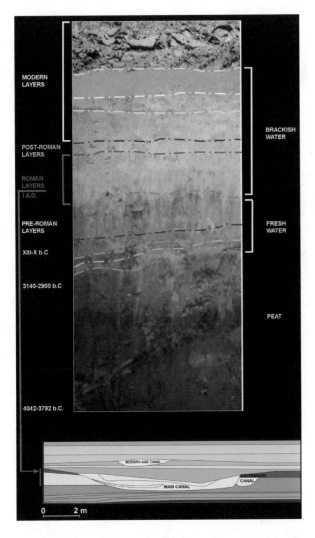

Figure 3. Stratigraphic section with showed layers dated.

matter of fact, the permanent shore seems to have been stable from prehistory to the 19th century AD.

A presumably seasonal shore was detected towards east and south, identified by thin, silty layers alternating with small fragments of brackish and fresh waters shells. This shore, related to both the Roman and Medieval age, is a geological formation of the northern lagoon sediments which lean against the terrace (fig. 4).

During Protohistoric phases, people exploited the area around the permanent shore as well as the lake itself. Evidence of Final Bronze Age suggests there were attempts to make the banks and the floodable areas, and consequently the water, more accessible. The finds come from various points of the marsh and suggest that on the bank there may have been an inhabited area, – although this was only partially explored – while in the areas that were submerged or dry, according to the season, there may have been manufacturing or other kinds of productive activity. In particular, we uncovered and identified a complex system of man-made mounds, with wooden supports at the base and on the sides, and layers of fine

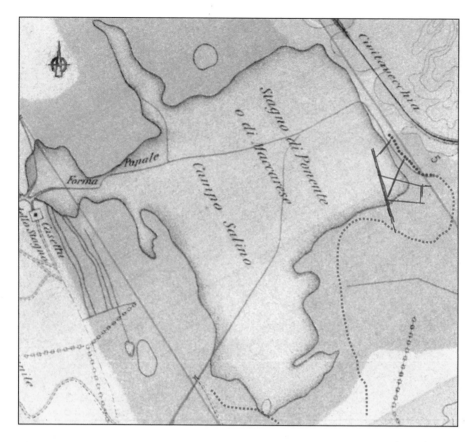

Figure 4. Hydraulic system (1ˢᵗ century AD) superimposed over Amenduni plan (1884). Permanent shore (blue broken line); presumably seasonal shore (red broken line) related to both the Roman and Medieval age.

sand from the terrace. On the mounds, we discovered a large number of items connected with cooking (ovens, cooking surfaces, fireplaces) and various other extremely heterogeneous materials. The absence of dwellings and the characteristics of the material suggest that the mounds were open-air areas, not designated for one specific activity but perhaps assigned to diverse functions.

The position and type of the Final Bronze Age finds produce interesting hypotheses regarding the way in which the marsh area may have been used and perceived. They suggest frequent incursions by humans into the marsh, and a determination to shape and adapt the landscape to their own needs. The contemporaneity and complementary nature of the site on the bank and the area of the mounds, suggest a type of settlement almost unknown in that period on the coast of *Latium*, involving the separation of the dwelling area from areas of production. From this point of view, the marsh might have been a kind of "off-site" zone, or in other words an area frequented daily, which was of paramount importance for the lives of the community[2].

During this investigation, the oldest clearly recognisable period that shows evidences of a system for making use of water, which was perhaps connected to salt production, is the first half of the 1st century AD (see Part. 4).

In late imperial period a different use was made of the area; the saltwork system did not work and a dense network of drainage channels of varying length and direction set itself. Later, during medieval times, a new plant arise in the area: channels were connected with sub-circular ditches and wooden poles or remains of wooden boards and tree trunks were found. All this would seem to be indicative of a system for activities other than salt production, such as fishing. These features of radial channels and large basins just are fishponds (Morelli *et al.* 2011b). In fact, during the medieval phases of occupation the saltworks were on the south side of the *Stagno di Maccarese*, beyond our investigated area (*ibid.*).

Unfortunately, the related archaeological evidence is undifferentiated, and does not provide evidence of a precise date. Even the stratigraphy does not show any differences from the one associated with the previous system; as a consequence, it is impossible to propose a precise date for this functional modification of the area. The exploitation of the system, although more and more infrequently, went on until modern time, when the ultimate reclaim of the area caused a drastic change in its use in favour of agriculture.

Roman Period: a 'probable' saltwork

Hydraulic system overview

The phase related to the salt production has been identified in a layer at -1.20 m above the sea level, which can be generally attributed to the Roman period. It was possible to determine that the whole area, a part of the Etruscan salt pans at first and of the Roman ones later (Giovannini 1985; 2001; Camporeale 1997), has been largely exploited through the years, especially due to the various short and medium range drainage works. This section of the Maccarese lagoon is about 1300 × 1200 m wide and reaches the Pleistocene terraces.

With special regards to the Roman Age, the excavations carried on at the ancient lagoon revealed a hydraulic structure which dates back to the first half of the 1st century AD. The system presents many elements referring to a complex, which worked in a specific direction and had a logical planning of the area.

On the plan (fig. 5) the system parts are marked with letters: A) *amphorae* dam and basins; B) 1st walled channel connected to 4th walled channel by a excavated in the ground channel; C) 2nd walled channel connected to 3rd walled channel by

---

2   In the wetland corresponding to the Maccarese Lake other archeological sites were discovered, dating from the Paleolithic to the Middle to Late Bronze Age (Arnoldus-Huyzendveld et al. 1998; Carboni 2002). In particular the Eneolithic settlement of Le Cerquete-Fianello, located on the north-west edge of the ancient lake, has been the subject of multidisciplinary investigations (Manfredini 2002). The lake-dwelling shows intensive pastoral and agricultural activity between 5370-4929 cal BP.

a second ground channel; D) single ground channel; E-F-G) ground channel in couple with poles alignment; H-I) single ground channel.

Amphorae

The archeological context has brought to surface a row of 1439 *amphorae*, vertically planted in the ground on their pointed tips and cut along the line of maximum expansion of the lower part of the belly (fig. 6).

No anthropic cut-marks during the installation of the *amphorae* were found. From several observations, they seem to have been placed in the ground by pressing and simultaneously rotating the pointed tip into the semi-solid sediment. In the area right around that row, at the foundation level as well as at the obliteration level, a layer rich in brackish shells and fragments of walls were also brought to light, along with handles and necks, all pertaining to the same type of *amphorae*.

It is reasonable to suppose that the *amphorae* were taller than the probable ground level, which corresponds to the base level of the wall structures and takes into consideration the estimated oscillations of the lagoon water level. It's important to highlight the *amphorae* were the inner structure of a bump and the dam was thus formed, though the real height is unknown.

Only in a few areas, almost aligned with the row, a concentration of *amphorae* fragments can still be found, which could be explained as a support to the consolidation of the level, while, on the inside, groups of wooden posts buttress the site. In many cases, the body of the *amphorae* is "flaked" vertically, probably due to the presence of brackish water, which, permeating, has "scaled" the container; conversely, the submerged pointed tips that were not exposed are well-preserved. The class is that of Dressel 6a and 6b and Dressel 20, in a chronological context

Figure 5. Hydraulic system (1ˢᵗ century AD) superimposed over aerial photograph.

of 1st century BC and early 1st century AD. On one *amphora* a stamp, bearing the consuls *Irtius* and *Pansa* names (43 BC), produces an important chronological element.

It is possible to find the same type of ceramic holders in similar contexts in Veneto, where the *amphorae* are used for water drainage (Pesavento Mattioli 1998), but with different functions and positions: when used for this purpose, *amphorae* are placed side by side and laid down, or placed vertically, but with their mouth

Figure 6. Amphorae dam. Details.

stuck in the ground; in other contexts, *amphorae* are placed vertically and in groups as for continuous foundations (Antico Gallina 2011). In our case it is clear that they are used as a water dam, because of the connection with building structures and because of their position higher than the basins.

The probable northern limit of the dam of *amphorae* was brought to light; where the *amphorae* end, after approximately 50 m, the consolidation is achieved by some sort of artificial cobblestones.

In some areas, and especially to the south, a double alignment of *amphorae* can be found, probably due to a need for greater stability or more intense maintenance of the dam, where the row was grafted to the ground.

Channels

The row of ceramic containers is about 1 km long, it follows a north-south direction and is perpendicularly interrupted by two walled channels (1st-2nd) (fig. 7), they are 300 m apart and counter forted with tuff bricks and lateritious belts (shard tiles small fins) (Grossi *et al.* 2008).

In plan, the walled channels have a characteristic funnel shape, with the opening to the west; this confirms their function as collectors of water incoming from the lagoon. They are characterized by the positioning of travertine marble blocks into the concrete bed, which present cavities that could be reconnected to sluices, as well. The architectural technique used (*opera reticolata* with bricks buttresses) dates back to the same phase of the dam's ceramic holders, that is to say the first half of 1st century AD. An organized working area related to the structure can be found close to the area of the II walled channel. Its location is strategic: at the crossroads between walled channels and ground channels, at the centre of the whole system.

Both walled channels (1st-2nd) with the sluices are connected to other walled channels (3rd-4th) by ground channel ('B' and 'C' in plan, fig. 5). On the wall structures, which have stone paving, but differ from the channels (1st-2nd) for the absence of sluices, the wooden formwork foundation is well-preserved. It has not been possible to identify a specific function for the walled channels (3rd-4th) without sluices, but they are likely to be interpreted as remains of structures that have disappeared, originally made to facilitate the distribution of water. That conclusion is supported by the discovery, not far from there, of a wooden element, probably a shovel for salt.

The entire described system is completed by two ground channels conventionally called "basins" ('A' in plan, fig. 5), placed parallel to both sides of the *amphorae* dam and therefore probably intended aswater collectors. The depth of the basins is not significant (max. 0.40-0.50 m), which coincides with the tidal range of these coastal plains. They have been identified in some trenches, and they appear like areas with a particular sediment, typical of later filled channels. The basins are reinforced with rows of wooden poles, adjacent to other channels too.

The '*amphorae* dam-walled channels – ground channel' system is completed by 4, maybe 5 couples of ground channels (E, F, G), of roughly constant size, more or less perpendicular to the main channels. Understanding the water flow direction within the reservoirs is difficult, but from the beginning along the *amphorae* dam

Figure 7. Aerial photograph of the 2ⁿᵈ walled channel.

to the end on walled channels 3 and 4 it has been possible to record a light slope from west to east. A mash of well-defined but not regular shapesemerges. The areas are quadrangular, measuring from 102 m to 150 m on their short side, and 202 m to 300 m on their long side; they are characterized by a sediment which underwent a post-depositional process of oxidation due to exposition. These are not tanks and storage ponds bordered by earth cords or barriers, but rather large areas limited by channels, which become evident it in the plan overview. This could possibly correspond to the description of salt production systems in *De Re Metallica* by *Georgius Agricola* (1556), where the author provides the details for the construction of marine saltworks in coastal, flat areas. He accurately describes how the water tanks should be – shallow, flat-bottomed, provided with earth banks – in a coastal area bordering a flat land. It is necessary to dig several main tanks, crossed by some channels provided with adjustable openings for the regulation of the water flow to the first tanks; the tanks themselves are inter-connected by other openings, which allow the water to flow from one to another. In fact, most of the known saltworks include different tanks, rigorously and specifically organized upon the quantity of water and the salinity degree: the salt water from the sea fells in consecutive tanks, allowing the sun activity to progressively increase its salinity and separate undesirable substances from the fine salt. In our case, it was not possible to identify 'different tanks' with 'specific openings'.

Poles

In correspondence with the convoy channelling of water, along the edges, alignments of vertically planted poles, from 10 to 15 cm, have been highlighted. They seem to have a role in the consolidation of parcels of land, between the paired channels and between the basins and *amphorae*. The repetition of this module suggests that such accommodations guaranteed the existence of a walkway. The chronology of poles is provided by ^{14}C dating: some elements are ascribed to the Roman Period (between 1st century BC and 1st century AD), other ones are later, probably due to different installation or use.

Some doubts remain for some channel 'branches' which are less aligned with the set, such as H and I, but above all L, of which we have a partial view. Most likely, H and I obey to a logic that diverges from the main module. In this area, in fact, the layers change, reflecting the presence of the terrace, which brings alluvial sediments, to prevent inflow of water from the high areas ('L' at north-east side, plan in fig. 5). Towards the southern border of the lagoon, where peri-lagoonal conditions exist, the series of parallel channels increase, presenting adjustments in time, to maintain the water control system efficient[3].

The area to the west of the *amphorae* dam has provided no archaeological structures, but there were some drainage channels later than the system of the Roman period. In fact, it seems that to the west of the dam there were no installations related to salt production system, but conceivably the area was affected by the presence of water, which passed through the closed channels in the controlled area.

To summarize, the system described above must have been a highly efficient way to convey water from the sea into a basin enclosing a portion of the lagoon: it included channels, flood zones and well-defined openings allowing for the regulation of water flow.

Although limited in space, this system may be put in relation to other evidences brought to light in the surrounding areas between the Tiber and the sea, such as the channels and other drainage structures from the Roman and later periods (for a general overview, see Morelli *et al.* 2011a, 261-285).

As to its function, production of salt through interconnected evaporation basins seems to be the most likely option, considering the placement of the whole system, the arrangement of the various elements, and the similarities with other establishments along the Tyrrhenian and Adriatic area (even if not chronologically related). Studies on ancient saltworks (La Trappola, Tuscany) (Citter and Arnoldus-Huyzendveld 2012); Pompei, Campania (Murolo 1995; Citter and Arnoldus-Huyzendveld 2012, to mention a few), deal generally with the site and its historical sources, since evidence of salt production is seldom identified in the archaeological record.

As a matter of fact, historical sources locate the so-called "*Portuensi*" saltworks in this same area, which was supplied by water from the brackish Maccarese lagoon, were in use during the entire Republican and Imperial periods (Nibby 1827; Nibby 1848; Tomassetti 1900; Ashby 1927), but no direct evidence was found thus far, with the only exception of an isolated inscription published by Lanciani (Lanciani 1888, CIL XIV 4285), dedicated to the "*genius saccariorum salarior(um)*

---

3   The southern area, immediately out of the plan in fig. 4, play the continuation of described system for about 200 m: amphorae do not continue and a long alignment of poles takes theirs place (unpublished data, C. Morelli pers. com.).

totius urbis camp(i) sal(inarum) rom(anarum)". Another inscription was found in an ancient building not far from our area: it reports a dedication to Neptune by *conductores* (contractors) *campi Salinarum Romanarum*, dated AD 135 (Morelli and Forte 2014). According to historical and bibliographic sources, the *Portuensi* saltworks have been exploited for a long time, as they are quoted in many different documents until the end of the XV century, under different names: *Campus Maior, Campus Salinarius*, and *Campus Salinus Maior* (Nibby 1827; Nibby 1848, 367-369; Tomassetti 1900, 52-58).

The described system, whose reconstruction emerged from the analysis of different interrelated elements, seems to have no direct comparisons in the ancient world – at least about published studies – but it shows parallels to several other Italian saltworks of ancient foundation and still in use today (Cervia, Emilia Romagna; Tarquinia, Latium; Margherita di Savoia, Puglia; Trapani, Sicily).

The aim of most of these systems is to gradually increase the degree of salinity of the water, from the periphery to the centre of the saltwork, by stepwise decantation through a series of basins (Agricola 1556).

Rutilius Namatianus, a Latin author who lived in the V sec. AD, described in *De Reditu Suo*, 475-484 the view before him during a trip: "a salty marsh, where sea water penetrates through tilted channels excavated in the ground (…); when the grass turns yellow, the landscape becomes dry, the dams are then closed, the sea does not enter and water becomes stagnant, it turns solid under the sea and the vivid influence of Phebus, so that elements become a thick crust".

The basins found along the *amphorae* dam, the channels and the areas among them are quite similar to the structures described by *Agricola (ibid.)*; however, real basins were not found and separators between the tanks could not be traced, while the spaces between the water supplying channels consist of open areas, not clearly defined.

Based upon the data collected, we have formulated the following hypothesis about the functioning of this system: one or more times a year, starting from the beginning of the dry season, the salt water was brought in through the walled channels, presumably during high tide, and eventually after having passed through a channel crossing the lagoon (which has not been found, since beyond the investigated area). Then the sluices were closed, thus isolating, together with the *amphorae* dam, the system temporarily from the main body of the lagoon. The salt water was distributed to the other channels, from which a shallow water surface could spread out over the intermediate flat areas. At the end of the evaporation cycle, the salt could be collected from the surface of the flat areas. This interpretation would imply that our saltworks produced unrefined marine salt.

During the evaporation cycle, an accessory control of the water level might have been attained through manipulation of the sluices.

The plan (fig. 5) shows a scattering of wide open areas, crossed by channels roughly perpendicular, regulating the water flow from the sea through two main channels interrupted by sluices. More specifically, the *amphorae* dam is assumed to have been working as a barrier and as a support for the walkway, since it was reinforced laterally in several points by poles. Also, the particularity density of the poles along the flow basins in the southern part of the system could indicate their function of consolidation of the walkway.

After all, long term archaeological research in the nearby areas have brought to light multiple remains of channels, basins, land arrangements and structures, revealing an intense exploitation, which was systematically subjected to anthropic control and specific functions. A large channel running from the hills to the Tiber, beyond the investigated area, had probably the function to deviate the surface water away for the saltworks (Morelli *et al.* 2011b).

The discovered structures seem to be part of a broader infrastructural development plan, carried out along the coastal area north of the Tiber river, and chronologically connected with the *Portus* plant and the achievement of the road line of the *Via Portuense* (Keay *et al.* 2005; Morelli *et al.* 2011a).

Acknowledgements

We would like to thank all those who collaborated to translate this paper: A. Grimaldi, F. Merighi, R. Ricco; mother tongue check by M.A. Tafuri. A special thought to Gastone Gala: we would like remember as one who first suggested that our system could be a saltwork.

References

Agricola, G. 1556. *De Re Metallica Libri XII*. Basilea: H. Froben.

Amenduni, G. 1884. *Sulle opere di Bonificazione della Plaga litoranea dell'Agro Romano che comprende le paludi e gli stagni di Ostia, Porto, Maccarese e delle terre vallive di Stracciacappa, Baccano, Pantano e Lago dei Tartari. Relazione del progetto generale 15/7/1880* (Ministero dei Lavori Pubblici). Roma: Ed. Eredi Botta, 1-36.

Antico Gallina, M. 2011. Strutture ad anfore: un sistema di bonifica dei suoli. Qualche parallelo dalle *Provinciae Hispanicae. Archivo Español de Arqueología* 84, 179-205.

Arnoldus-Huyzendveld, A., Mineo, M. and Pascucci, P. 1998. Il sito costiero dell'età del Bronzo di Le Cerquete-Olivetello (Fiumicino). *Bullettino della Commissione Archeologica Comunale di Roma* 99, 393-411.

Arnoldus-Huyzendveld, A., Citro, D., Facciolo, A., Gala, M., Grossi, M.C., Morelli, C., Rinaldi, M.L., Ruggeri, D. and Sivilli, S. 2009. The Lagoon of Maccarese (Rome-Fiumicino): environmental and archaeological developments over the last 3000 years. *Le Zone Umide, archivi del paesaggio culturale tra ricerca e gestione*. Seminario Internazionale - ZUM Genova 28-30 Gennaio 2009. Available at: http://www.dismec. unige.it/zum/atti.html.

Ashby, T. 1927. *The Roman Campagna in Classical Times*. London: E. Benn.

Bellotti, P. 2000. Il modello morfo-sedimentario dei maggiori delta tirrenici italiani. *Bollettino della Società Geologica Italiana* 119, 777-792.

Bellotti, P., Calderoni, G., Carboni, M.G., Di Bella, L., Tortora, P., Valeri, P. and Zernitskaya, V. 2007. Late Quaternary landscape evolution of the Tiber River delta plain (Central Italy): new evidence from pollen data, biostratigraphy and 14C dating. *Zeitschrift für Geomorphologie* 51/4, 505-534.

Bellotti, P., Calderoni, G., Di Rita, F., D'Orefice, M., D'Amico, C., Esu, D., Magri, D., Preite Martinez, M.,Tortora, P. and Valeri, P. 2011. The Tiber river delta plain (central Italy): Coastal evolution and implications for the ancient Ostia Roman settlement. *The Holocene* 2011/21, 1105-1116. DOI: 10.1177/0959683611400464.

Biglieri, A. 1896. La bonifica idraulica del delta del Tevere. *Giornale del Genio Civile* anno 1895, 1-56.

Camporeale, G. 1997. Il sale e i primordi di Veio. In: Bartoloni, G. ed. *Le necropoli arcaiche di Veio. Giornata di studio in memoria di Massimo Pallottino*. Roma: Università degli Studi di Roma "La Sapienza", 197-199.

Carboni, G. 2002. Trent'anni di ricerche preistoriche a Maccarese. In: Manfredini, A. ed. *Le dune, il lago, il mare. Una comunità di villaggio dell'età del Rame a Maccarese*. Firenze: Istituto Italiano di Preistoria e Protostoria, 39-47.

Castelli, R., Facciolo, A., Gala, M., Grossi, M.C., Rinaldi, M.L., Ruggeri, D. and Sivilli, S. 2008. Scavi e ritrovamenti. In: Caravaggi, L. and Carpenzano, O. eds. *Interporto Roma-Fiumicino. Prove di dialogo tra archeologia, architettura e paesaggio*. Firenze: Alinea Editore, 69-86.

Chiumenti, L. and Bilancia, F. 1979. *La campagna romana antica, medioevale e moderna. Edizione redatta sulla base degli appunti lasciati da Giuseppe e Francesco Tomassetti VI. Vie Nomentana e Salaria, Portuense, Tiburtina*. Arte e archeologia. Studi e documenti 16-17. Firenze: Olschki Editore.

Citter, C. and Arnoldus-Huyzendveld, A. 2012. New approaches to old issues: the application of predictive maps in archaeology. A case study: modelling the location of Grosseto's salt works from 900 BC to AD 1200. *Medieval Settlement Research* 26, 1-11.

Di Rita, F., Celant, A. and Magri, D. 2010. Holocene environmental instability in the wetland north of the Tiber delta (Rome, Italy): sea-lake-man interactions. *Journal of Paleolimnology* 44/1, 51-67. DOI: 10.1007/s10933-009-9385-9.

Di Rita, F., Celant, A. and Conati Barbaro, C. 2011. Interazioni tra clima, ambiente e uomo nell'evoluzione olocenica del delta del Tevere: dati e paleobotanici e ritrovamenti archeologici. *Rendiconti on line della Società Geologica Italiana*, 18/2011. DOI: 10.3301/ROL.2011.60.

Giovannini, A. 1985. Le sel et la fortune de Rome. *Athenaeum* 73, 373-387.

Giovannini, A. 2001. Les salines d'Ostie. In: Descoeudres, J.P. ed. *Ostia port et porte de la Rome antique*. Ginevra: Musée Rath, 36-38.

Giraudi, C. 2004. Evoluzione tardo-olocenica del delta del Tevere. *Il Quaternario-Italian Journal of Quaternary Science* 17 2/2, 477-492.

Goiran, J-P., Tronchère, H., Collalelli, U., Salomon, F. and Djerbi, H. 2009. Découverte d'un niveau marin biologique sur les quais de Portus: le port antique de Rome. *Mediterranée* 112, 59-67.

Grossi, M.C., Morelli, C., Citro, D., Facciolo, A., Gala, M., Medaglia, S., Rinaldi, M.L., Ruggeri, D. and Sivilli, S. 2008. Un'estesa struttura idraulica di prima età imperiale nel territorio di Maccarese (Fiumicino–Roma). In: *Meetings between Cultures in the Ancient Mediterranean.* AIAC XVII International Congress of Classical Archaeology, Rome 22-26 Settembre 2008. Available at: http://www.fastionline.org.

Keay, S., Millet, M., Paroli, L. and Strutt, K. eds. 2005. *Portus. An archaeological survey of the port of imperial Rome.* Archaeological Monographs of the British School at Rome 15. London: British School at Rome.

Lanciani, R. 1888. Il "Campus Salinarum Romanarum". *Bullettino della Commissione Archeologica Comunale di Roma* 16, 83-91.

Lugli, G. and Filibeck, G. 1935. *Il porto di Roma imperiale e l'Agro Portuense.* Bergamo: Officine dell'Istituto Italiano di Arti Grafiche.

Manfredini, A. ed. 2002. *Le dune, il lago, il mare. Una comunità di villaggio dell'età del Rame a Maccarese.* Firenze: Istituto Italiano di Preistoria e Protostoria.

Morelli, C. 2008. Tracce dei sistemi territoriali e ambientali antichi. In: Caravaggi, L. e Carpenzano, O. eds. *Interporto Roma-Fiumicino. Prove di dialogo tra archeologia, architettura e paesaggio.* Firenze: Alinea Editore, 27-41.

Morelli, C. and Forte, V. 2014. Il *Campus Salinarum Romanarum* e l'epigrafe dei *conductores*: il contesto archeologico. *Les Mélanges de l'Ecole Française de Rome – Antiquité* 126/1. Available at: http://www.mefra.revues.org/2059.

Morelli, C., Marinucci, A. and Arnoldus-Huyzendveld, A. 2011a. Il Porto di Claudio: nuove scoperte. In: Keay, S. and Paroli, L. eds. *Portus and its Hinterland: recent archaeological research.* Archaeological Monographs of the British School at Rome 18. London: British School at Rome, 47-65.

Morelli, C., Carbonara, A., Forte, V., Grossi, M.C. and Arnoldus-Huyzendveld, A. 2011b. La topografia romana dell'Agro Poruense alla luce delle nuove indagini. In: Keay, S. and Paroli, L. eds. *Portus and its Hinterland: recent archaeological research.* Archaeological Monographs of the British School at Rome 18. London: British School at Rome, 261-285.

Ministero Agricoltura e Foreste ed. 1947. *I Comprensori di Bonifica II. Italia Centrale.* Roma: Ministero Agricoltura e Foreste, 181-185.

Murolo, N. 1995. Le saline herculeae di Pompei: produzione del sale e culto di Ercole nella Campania antica. *Studi sulla Campania preromana* 2, 105-123.

Nibby, A. 1827. *Della Via Portuense e dell'antica città di Porto.* Roma: Angelo Ajami.

Nibby, A. 1848. *Analisi storica, topografica, antiquaria della carta de'dintorni di Roma.* Voll. I-II, second edition. Roma: tipografia delle Belle Arti.

Parisi Presicce, A. and Villetti, G. 1998. Le bonifiche: un ponte fra passato e futuro. In: Bagnasco, C. ed. *Il delta del Tevere. Un viaggio tra passato e futuro.* Roma: Palombi, 97-109.

Pesavento Mattioli, S. ed. 1998. *Bonifiche e drenaggi con anfore in epoca romana: aspetti tecnici e topografici.* Atti del seminario di studi, Padova 19-20 ottobre 1995. Modena: Franco Cosimo Panini.

Ruggeri, D., Gala, M., Facciolo, A., Grossi, M.C., Morelli, C., Rinaldi, M.L., Sivilli, S., Carrisi, E., Citro, D. and De Castro, F.R. 2010. Località le Vignole – Maccarese (Fiumicino–Roma): risultati preliminari dello scavo protostorico. In: Negroni Catacchio, N. ed. *L'alba dell'Etruria. Fenomeni di continuità e trasformazione nei secoli XII-VIII A.C. Ricerche e scavi.* Atti del Nono Incontro di Studi, Valentano e Pitigliano, 12-14 Settembre 2008, Preistoria e Protostoria in Etruria, 327-338.

Tomassetti G. 1900. Della campagna romana nel Medioevo. Illustrazione della via Portuense. *Archivio della Reale Società Romana di Storia Patria* 32/3, 5-86.

Ancient salt exploitation in the Polish lowlands: recent research and future perspectives

Józef BEDNARCZYK*, Joanna JAWORSKA**,
Arkadiusz MARCINIAK*
and Maria RUIZ DEL ARBOL MORO***

*Adam Mickiewicz University, Institute of Prehistory,
Collegium Historicum, ul. Św. Marcin 78, 61-809 Poznań, Poland
**Adam Mickiewicz University, Institute of Geology,
Collegium Geologicum, ul. Maków Polnych, 16, 61-606 Poznań, Poland
***CSIC (Spanish National Research Council),
Institute of History, c/ Albasanz, 26-28, 28037 Madrid, Spain

Abstract. Research on salt exploitation and production in Poland, in particular in Małopolska (Lesser Poland), has offered in the past a big amount of information and very interesting data for understanding of the role of salt in the articulation of the territory in prehistoric times. However, since the middle of the 1980s, Polish archaeology has not been very active and the research has not joined the recent renovations experienced in this field. Nevertheless, the very recent relevant findings related to salt exploitation and production in Polish lowlands – such as the important site 100/101 at Inowrocław – point to a renewal of this panorama. This paper aims to present an overview of the present state of the art on pre-medieval salt exploitation in the Polish lowlands, with a focus on Kujawy and Wielkopolska (Kujavia and Greater Poland) and to summarize the most relevant data integrated in their geo-historical context. The results of the excavations carried out at Inowrocław will be used as a paradigmatic example of the relevance of these new data to the explorations of salt exploitation in Central-Eastern Europe. The paper concludes with several considerations about future directions for research in this region.

Keywords. Roman Iron Age, Poland, Kujawy (Kujavia), Wielkopolska (Greater Poland).

Résumé. La recherche sur l'exploitation et la production du sel en Pologne, en particulier dans la Petite-Pologne, a offert par le passé une grande quantité d'informations et de données significatives pour la compréhension du rôle du sel dans l'articulation du territoire à l'époque préhistorique. Cependant, depuis le milieu des années 80, les archéologues polonais n'ont pas été très actifs. La recherche n'a pas rejoint les récents travaux appliqués dans ce domaine. Cependant, les tous derniers résultats liés à l'exploitation du sel et de la production dans les plaines polonaises – tel que l'important site de 100/101 à Inowrocław – laissent entrevoir un renouvellement de ce panorama. Cet article vise à présenter un aperçu de l'état actuel de la recherche sur l'exploitation de sel pré-médiévale dans les plaines polonaises (avec une spécialisation en Cujavie et de la Grande-Pologne) et de résumer les données les plus pertinentes intégrées dans leur contexte géo-historique. Les résultats des fouilles effectuées à Inowrocław seront utilisés comme un exemple paradigmatique de ces nouvelles données pour l'étude de l'exploitation de sel en Europe centrale et orientale. L'article conclut avec plusieurs considérations sur le futur de la recherche dans cette région.

Mots-clés. Age du Fer-Antiquité, Pologne, Kujawy (Kujavia), Wielkopolska (Grande-Pologne).

The study of salt exploitation in prehistoric and ancient times has re-emerged in the last years as one of the most promising and dynamic areas within current studies on the archaeology of resources exploitation and techniques. Good examples of this renovation are both the several interdisciplinary projects on prehistoric exploitation of salt that are being developed all over Europe (to cite but some examples: Ursulescu 1995; Chapman and Monah 2007; Gaydarska and Chapman 2007; Weller *et al.* 2011; Harding and Kavruk 2013; Harding 2013) and the celebration – and further publication – of several scientific meetings on the topic (such as Weller 2002; Morére Molinero 2006; Monah *et al.* 2007; Weller *et al.* 2008; Alexianu *et al.* 2011). All these outputs are producing very relevant data for the study of salt exploitation, salt production techniques and its integration in the organization of ancient territories (in particular the articulation of settlement and inter-regional exchange related to salt distribution and trade) in the Prehistory and Antiquity of Europe.

Surprisingly however is that Polish archaeology has hardly been active in these recent research endeavors, despite the fact that the study of salt production in Poland has a long history. Poland is very well known indeed for having one of the oldest documented salt exploitations in Europe. Moreover, intensive work by Polish scholars in the past has produced a large corpus of archaeological and geo-historical data on salt exploitation and production. A good example is the excellent work developed by scholars such as A. Jodłowski (see, for instance, 1971 and 1976) and Z. Bukowski (1963 and 1985).

Signs of salt production in prehistoric and ancient times can be found in Poland both in the uplands (eastern and western Małopolska) and lowlands (Kujawy)[1], where the remains of permanent salt manufacturing installations and tools connected with them have been recorded (Bukowski 1985, 44). Major excavations of the salt sites during the 1970s and 1980s showed that traces of salt production concern mainly three periods: the middle Neolithic, the Hallstatt period (750-450 BC) and the Roman Iron Age (from the turn of the Eras) (Jodłowski 1980; a summary of the main data can be found in Bukowski 1985). The archaeological finds confirming the Neolithic manufacture of salt have been found only in the uplands, near Kraków: at Barycz an important assemblage of installations and tools was excavated and analysed (Jodłowski 1971) and several vessels related to salt making from that period were found in sites such as Wieliczka, Bochnia-Chodzienice and Kraków-Pleszów. The production of salt is also attested during the Hallstatt period both in the uplands and in the lowlands though, to date, remains of production installations have not been recorded. The sole evidence are the large numbers of vessels possibly associated with salt production in the area of Kraków (at sites such as Barycz, Biskupice, Tyniec: see Bukowski 1985, 50 ff.) and in Kujawy (at sites such as Sobiejuchy, where a domed furnace possibly related to the evaporation of brine was recorded) (Bukowski 1985, 55). Salt production in the Roman Iron Age is attested for western Małopolska and Kujawy. In Wieliczka a salt manufacturing complex was excavated (Reguła 1969, cited by Bukowski 1985, 56 and 58). In the lowlands, in Otłoczyn (near Aleksandrów) and Zgłowiączka (near Wrocławek) two presumed salt furnaces from this period were also excavated (Jodłowski 1976), but the absence of other materials doesn't allow to relate them to salt exploitation.

With some exceptions, the work on these areas (see below) has not been systematically continued. Several papers on Wieliczka and the area of Kraków were published in the 1990s and later on, but these did not translate into more in-depth analyses of salt exploitation. Very recent contributions on the subject are rare. Among these is the unpublished work of A. Majchrzycka (2009) or the pages on Polish salt deposits in the book by Harding and Kavruk (2013, 180 ff.). The work of Bukowski (1985) remains the main and more complete published synthesis for salt production in Poland in prehistoric times.

Nonetheless, several studies and archaeological findings from the last years allow us to speak of a complete renovation of the panorama with the results of the new studies related to salt production in Kujawy and Eastern Wielkopolska. In fact, the recent research argues – contrarily to what has been thought so far – for the existence of significant pre-medieval salt exploitation in the Polish lowlands. The aim of this paper is to present these data integrated into their geo-historical context and to propose several lines for the future development of salt research in the Polish lowlands.

---

1   We have decided to use here the Polish original names of the regions cited in the text. Kujawy is normally translated to English as "Kujavia", though other widespread spellings are "Kujawia" or "Cuiavia". Wielkopolska is normally translated as "Greater Poland" and Małopolska as "Lesser Poland" or even "Little Poland".

Salt resources in the Polish lowlands: main characteristics and potential for exploitation in pre-medieval times

As stressed above, studies related to the subject of salt production in the Oder and Vistula basins in prehistoric and ancient times have shown that there are two main regions for the exploitation of salt in prehistoric and ancient times: the northern sub-Carpathian region, especially in the vicinity of Kraków, that is, the area of Małopolska; and Kujawy and Wielkopolska. As stated, the first area, the sub-Carpathian region and the area of Bochnia and Wieliczka, has been the subject of an intensive research, mainly in the 1970s and 1980s (see mainly Jodłowski 1971, 1976 and 1980), though some more recent work has already been published

Figure 1. Map of Poland including the main locations cited in the text.

(*i.e.* Kadrow 2003). The second area, Kujawy and Wielkopolska, has been less intensively studied (to date the main reference for this region is Z. Bukowski 1963 and 1985).

In both areas salt deposits are widespread: actually rock salts occur in Poland in two main evaporite formations: a Middle Miocene one (Badenian Stage) in southern Poland (*i.e.* the Wieliczka and Bochnia salt mines) and an Upper Permian (Zechstein) in northern and central Poland (*i.e.* the Mogilno, Wapno, Kłodawa, Góra, Inowrocław, Damasławek salt diapirs). Perhaps – and because their relation to the ancient and medieval exploitation – those of Małopolska are better known (the UNESCO World Heritage Site of Wieliczka is very well known throughout the world); however, today's production is articulated around Wielkopolska and Kujawy (Czapowski and Bukowski 2010 and 2012) (fig. 1).

It is important to differentiate, at this point, between two different issues to make the understanding of these salt resources easier: the first, their geological history; the second, the characteristics of their current form that made it available to people in the past. In relation to their geological history, Kujawy and Wielkopolska constituted the central part of the Polish basin at the end of Permian age (Zechstein). This basin became filled with four thick successions of evaporates – including salt rocks – nearly 2 km thick. The Zechstein rocks were covered by Triassic, Jurassic, Cretaceous and Cenozoic strata, while a complex system of salt structures evolved simultaneously in the Polish basin (a similar situation is noted in the adjacent German basin). Kujawy is a region affected by the most intensive salt tectonic and halokinetic activity: the effect of this activity was the formation of numerous salt structures, such as diapirs, pillows, *etc.*

These salt structures have various sizes and occur at a wide range of levels in the Mesozoic rocks on which the salt had intruded. Consequently, salt deposits in diapirs have very complicated internal structure: the layers of salt rocks have almost vertical arrangement, are folded, overthrust or reduced. Some of the salt diapirs (Mogilno, Wapno, Kłodawa, Inowrocław, Góra, Damasławek, see fig. 2) pierced the surface of the Mesozoic, and intruded into the Cenozoic cover (Czapowski and Bukowski, 2010, 513-514). It is these that have been exploited in modern, historical, and prehistoric times (Harding and Kavruk 2013, 25).

Today salt deposits have been documented in nine of the numerous diapirs that occur in central Poland. Two of the salt mines – Wapno and Inowrocław – have been closed already (Czapowski and Bukowski 2010); in the Kłodawa mine, salt exploitation is continued by underground working (fig. 3); Mogilno and Góra function as underground gas storage units and salt mining is carried out by leaching.

In relation to the second issue, the characteristics that made these salt sources available to people in the past (and today), it is important to understand that the salt mirror in most of the salt diapirs in Poland is located at depths below 1500 m.b.s.l., but, in some cases, (*i.e.* Mogilno, Wapno, Kłodawa, Inowrocław, Góra) at no more than 200-300 m.b.s.l., near surface of ground level and ground, sweet water. These salt structures are covered by the so-called cap-rock (usually gypsum/gypsum anhydrite cap-rock), protected by the upper part of salt bodies.

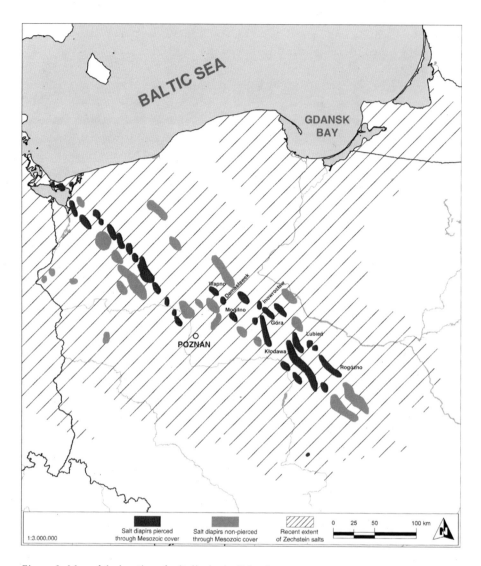

Figure 2. Map of the location of salt diapirs in Poland.

Cap-rock is formed as a result of the dissolution (by groundwater) of rock salt. All rock salt has some "impurities" (mostly anhydrite grains). Anhydrite is a less soluble material (*residuum*) which accumulates in the upper part of salt diapirs and is very easily altered into gypsum (Jaworska *et al.* 2010). The thickness of gypsum cap-rock varies: 70-160 m at Wapno, 100-190 m at Mogilno, 10-116 m at Góra and 50-180 m at Inowrocław. Cap-rocks are a sensitive system of circulation of groundwater near and around the diapirs; any erosion, fracturing in cap-rock creates natural hydraulic "windows" and changes the hydraulic conductivity in this body (Górski and Rasała 2008).

Figure 3. View of the outdoor facilities of the mine of Kłodawa (photo: María Ruiz del Árbol).

Salt structures are characterized by very complicated hydrogeological conditions resulting particularly from the lithological and structural differentiation of the sediments overlaying the cap-rocks and the different ways of hydraulic contact occurring within and above the cap-rock. Consequently, water characterized by the varied salinity – from fresh water to brine – occurs near the salt diapirs (Górski and Rasała 2008). The hydrodynamic conditions within the salt domes in Wapno, Mogilno and Góra reflect the natural groundwater flow from the upper parts of cap-rock in the direction of the salt mirror and simultaneously towards the edges. The cap-rocks of these salt domes (as well as in Inowrocław) are entirely saturated and create together with the overlaying layers the local groundwater recharge zones (Górski and Rasała 2008).

Outflow brines (or shallow retention brines) are also noted outside areas of salt domes. The salinization of groundwater in some areas of north-western Poland (including Kujawy and Wielkopolska) is caused also by brine ascending from the Mesozoic strata. In these places the groundwater salinization zones are mostly connected with the uplifted tectonic blocks, salts anticlines and fault zones (an important potential zone of brines migration), and where layers of impervious clay are reduced or absent (Kaczor 2005).

Salt domes and its immediate surroundings would have become in ancient times a place of obtaining salt from the brine, flowing on the surface or recognized in shallow wells. The archaeological evidence shows that in Poland, before medieval times, the only known method of obtaining salt was in fact the exploitation of saline springs[2]. As Z. Bukowski has already stressed, there is a complete lack of any traces of the use of mining methods of exploitation in the pre-medieval past. In fact this is due to the character of rock salt deposits, which would have required the use of complicated mining and deep drilling techniques (Bukowski 1985, 28).

Evidence for salt exploitation and production in Kujawy and Wielkopolska in prehistoric and ancient times

The subject of salt production in prehistoric and ancient times has been, as stressed in the introduction, intensively analysed by Polish scholars in the past. However, the studies published relate mostly to the uplands, the sub-Carpathian region. The work of Jodłowski and other researchers from the Salt Museum in Wieliczka (see the several volumes of the journal *Studia i Materiały do Dziejów Żup Solnych w Polsce*) shows that the oldest documented traces of salt production in the uplands date back to the middle period of the Neolithic (see above, introduction). The fact that during the Roman Iron Age, a distinct change in the salt-making technology is noticed by scholars, is very interesting. These changes comprise significant new solutions and improvements such as the use of ponds to purify the brine solution or the employment of huge evaporation vessels. However, the research has not got deeper with the issues such as the character and scale of production and its distribution.

Besides the uplands, the fact that Kujawy and Wielkopolska are based within a large saliferous zone made them very interesting for the analysis of ancient salt exploitation. However, not many scholars have referred to these regions. As already stressed, the most important published exceptions are the work of Bukowski (1963), related to the presumed exploitation of salt springs in Kujawy and Wielkopolska during the Hallstatt period; the paper of Cofta-Broniewska (1974); and the work of Burchard *et al.* (1966), in which the whole territory of Poland is analyzed.

The area has a privileged location: it lies within the area of exchange routes running from the south to the south-eastern Baltic coast, and has excellent soils and a well-developed hydrographic network (Bukowski 1985, 32). Stable settlements have been documented in the region during the entire Prehistory and Antiquity (Cofta-Broniewska and Kośko 2002). Although there is an abundant record of salt production since the medieval period, the ancient production in Kujawy and Wielkopolska has been, to date, based on indirect data. Z. Bukowski affirms that, presumably, salt springs have been exploited from the earliest times, "from the moment where a fairly stabilized settlement pattern developed and farming became widespread at the beginning of the Neolithic age" (Bukowski 1985, 44). Different Neolithic projects in the lowlands tried to address these issues, but no specific finds allow confirming that salt springs were exploited in the area of Kujawy

---

2   A description of the character of these salt springs can be found in Z. Bukowski (1985, 41-43). This author also refers to medieval and modern texts which mention numerous salt springs exploited on a large scale (1963, 263 ff.). The analysis of the many place names that proof the existence of salt springs (such as sól, solec, *etc.*) is very interesting (Bukowski 1985, 39; Majchrzycka 2009, 24 ff.), as the analysis of such places is the presence of halophytes (Wilkoń-Michalska 1963; Cofta-Broniewska and Kośko 1982; also a synthesis in Majchrzycka 2009, 18-23).

and Wielkopolska during the Neolithic and Bronze Ages. However, an indirect indication of such exploitation may be the large concentration of settlements in the saliferous regions.

Finds connected with the Lusatian culture in Kujawy and Wielkopolska date from the Hallstatt period. Bukowski (1963; a summary in 1985, 29 and 49 ff.) argued, on the basis of indirect data (toponymic data, geographical proximity of settlements to salt springs) and artefactual evidence (mainly clay objects similar in form to the so-called briquetage[3]) that salt production in Wielkopolska can be documented in some sites dating back to the Hallstatt period (c. 750-450 BC), such as Sobiejuchy. Such objects, however, came mainly from burial grounds, so the question is if the association of these objects with salt production has been sufficiently proved. Z. Bukowski relates other finds to salt exploitation, such as the large fireplaces found in open settlements – especially in fortified settlements in Kujawy and eastern Wielkopolska (Sobiejuchy, Izdebno) – which could have served to evaporate brine (Bukowski 1985, fig. 13 and page 55). In any case, in the archaeological literature (as stressed already by Bukowski 1985, 55) it is assumed that the development of Lusatian settlements in eastern Wielkopolska and Kujawy, and the rise of many fortified settlements of that culture in the Hallstatt C and D periods, was connected with the participation of the population in a long-distance exchange network in which salt produced in these regions could have played an important role (see also Harding *et al.* 2004). There is a remarkable tendency of settlements concentrated near Inowrocław. However, the location in this region of the so-called amber route and the excellent environmental conditions, should also be taken into account (Wielowiejski 1980; Bukowski 1988). As we will see below, in any case, the area of Inowrocław has demonstrated to be a linchpin for the study of ancient salt exploitation in the region.

Regarding the third period documented in the uplands by Jodłowski, the age around the turn of the Era, has the related archaeological evidence that allows confirming that organized salt production occurred in Kujawy. As stressed above, several studies on salt mining have shown a process of re-activation of salt exploitation during the 1st century AD in Małopolska, accompanied by the radically new solutions in salt-making technologies (*i.e.* new techniques for the evaporation of brine, cleaning and condensing it, refining and simmering it) that have been traditionally related to the presence of Celtic elements in the region. To date, for the case of Kujawy, apart from the above mentioned finds in Otłoczyn (near Ciechocinek) and Zgłowiączka (near Wrocławek) the assumptions relating to this period were mainly based on indirect data (such as the connection with the amber route, and the idea that salt would play an important role as a complement to the commerce of amber: Bukowski 1985, 60; Cofta-Broniewska 1979; Cofta-Broniewska and Kośko 2002).

---

3   Briquetage is the name given to the coarse ceramic specifically produced for the boiling of salt (Harding 2013, 10, note 2). For the history of the term see also: Olivier and Kovacik 2006, 559-560.

However, the results of the research in Kujawy during the last years have yielded the important and very relevant findings that will help to determine the role of the Kujawy as a significant salt production centre during the Roman Iron Age. Findings such as the industrial complex for salt extraction in the Przeworsk culture settlement documented in Chabsko (near Mogilno), that has been dated to the turn of the Era (Adamczyk and Gierlach 1998); and also, the important saltern excavated at Inowrocław (sites 100 and 101) by the Institute of Prehistory of the Adam Mickiewicz University in Poznań (Bednarczyk 2008).

Salt production in the Roman Iron Age in Kujawy: an example from Inowrocław, site 100/101

The saltern in Inowrocław is one of just a few such features in Poland. It was dated to the 2nd-4th centuries AD. The salt production centre has been recorded within two archaeological sites (named 100 and 101). The sites are situated at the bottom (a marshy zone) and slopes of the valley of the *Słony (Rąbiński) Rów* (that has been recently dried).

The information which led to the excavations was of various characters. Firstly, the geological context: the sites are located on the edge of the salt dome. The Inowrocław salt diapir (2.5 km long and 1 km wide) is one of the numerous salt bodies in the Polish lowlands (see fig. 2 above), formed as a result of the intrusion of the Late Permian (Zechstein) salt levels, from the depth of 6000 m into the Cenozoic cover. Its upper part protects the gypsum-anhydrite-clay cap-rock about 50-180 m thick; and the salt mirror occurs at the depth of 120-190 m (Ślizowski and Saługa 1996). The Inowrocław salt dome (the local highest point) is situated under the buildings of the city[4].

Secondly, the botanical information: in the area a significant concentration of halophilic plants has been recorded (Wilkoń-Michalska 1963; Piernik *et al.* 2005). Thirdly, hydro-geological evidence showed that this was the place where salted waters infiltrating layers over the top of the salt dome (located around 700 m from there) flow (Górski and Rasała 2008). And fourthly, the character of the ancient settlement documented there: the site appeared to be the key settlement of the micro-region of Inowrocław Rąbin – Solanki.

The excavations at Inowrocław were carried out by the team from Institute of Prehistory of the Adam Mickiewicz University in Poznań[5]. The excavation was integrated into a long-term program of studies of the region of Kujawy (Cofta-Broniewska and Kośko 2002, 172). The program covered the whole period of prehistory and Antiquity, but, for several reasons the territory covered was restricted to western Kujawy (the former districts of Inowrocław, Aleksandrów Kujawski and Radziejów). The results of the project allowed exploring the cultural development

---

4   In fact, the exploitation of salt in Inowrocław (Solno underground mine) has a long history: salt exploitation occurred there between 1875 and 1986. In 1991 the mine was liquidated by the planned sinking brine.

5   The excavations were directed by Prof. A. Cofta-Broniewska and Dr. J. Bednarczyk between 1982 and 2000 (with some interruptions).

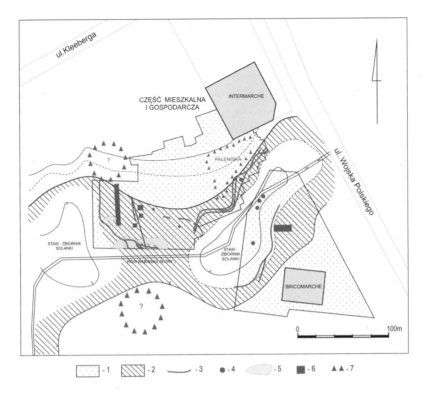

Figure 4. Distribution of the saline equipment in the area of Inowrocław. 1: explored area, 2: area of brine production installations (87.5-88 m.a.s.l.), 3: brine trenches, 4: brine wells, 5: brine reservoirs, 6: graduation towers, 7: furnaces (drawing: Barbara Bednarczyk).

of Kujawy societies and getting a complete multidisciplinary record of the area (a summary of the project achievements in Cofta-Broniewska and Kośko 2002)[6].

The saltern was documented in the area close to the supermarkets "Carrefour" and "Bricomarché". The whole investigated area, within both sites (100 and 101), covered about 4 ha (fig. 4). Almost the whole area of the saltern was excavated. Remaining unexcavated parts at the edges of the site are to be investigated. The research work has allowed the recording of a vast settlement (estimated to be of 6-7 ha) divided into two zones: a) the settlement area, in higher, dry parts of the slope and the edges of the valley. Several dwellings and structures (such as wells, furnaces and cellars) were documented there; b) the production area, within a wet and marshy bottom, and a lower part of the slope of the valley. The main part of the saltern was recorded there, including several trenches (see below), wells, reservoirs, graduation towers and hearths.

This is a unique production centre. Here, the different aspects of the production cycle – methods, equipment and tools, techniques, processes – have been recorded in a global and integrated way.

---

6   The knowledge of this area was also greatly expanded by the numerous rescue projects, for instance, along the curse of the transit gas pipeline Yamal-Western Europe, or planned expressways.

The recorded production process consisted of obtaining, purifying and enriching the brine, followed by the evaporation of the water from it and obtaining the crystalline salt. The features excavated in the saltern illustrate all the stages of the salt production cycle:

a   The brine was collected with the help of trenches and wells. At Inowrocław five wells and seven trenches were recorded. Wells were drilled to depths of 3-4.5 m; they were narrow, with their sides protected by braided wooden rods and poles (like a basket). In one of them, a part of a ladder made from the trunk of a pine tree was recorded (fig. 5). Trenches were also used to extract the saline solution from the marsh. These trenches are of various dimensions (from 7 to 140 m long; 30-120 cm wide; 20-70 cm deep)[7].

b   Ponds were used to collect, and to carry out a decantation process, as well as preliminary solar treatment of the brine. At Inowrocław these structures are vast, shallow ponds (0.5-1.5 ares) (fig. 6).

c   The process of increasing the concentration of salt was developed at Inowrocław by the use of graduation towers. This is the first site in which such wooden constructions are recognized, so we think they are a local innovation. The number of discovered ones is five. The largest has 37 × 6 m (the others are significantly smaller). Their reconstruction is hypothetical and made on the basis of the "negatives" of the pits (where the poles supporting the structure were placed) and the analogy of the modern graduation tower in Ciechocinek (19th century) (fig. 7). The pumping system is not known, so probably the brine solution was transported to the top of the graduation tower manually, using vessels.

d   The evaporation and drying of water from the saline solution was done employing hearths. At Inowrocław over 200 were recorded, distributed in groups in the area between the marshy and dry zones). Such structures are shallow pits (20-30 cm), usually rectangular, with burnt stones at the bottom.

The results of the excavations at Inowrocław show the innovative technological solutions (such as the graduation towers) unknown in other saline centres existing at that time in Central Europe. Also, the size and scale of the saltern complex shows that salt production there went beyond the needs of the local community and hence the produced salt must have been distributed over large distances. However, no distribution pattern has been recognized to date.

To date, Inowrocław is the only saline complex recorded and analysed in a global way in this area (other examples are more or less identified and on a fragmentary basis). This is a zone in which we should expect further discoveries related to the production of salt in the Roman Iron Age period as well as in earlier prehistoric periods.

---

7   Some trenches were recorded only partially.

Final considerations: future perspectives for the study of prehistoric salt production in Poland

Site 100/101 at Inowrocław opens up new perspectives on the study of ancient salt exploitation, production and distribution in Poland, as well as its role in the organization and shaping of the territory. The discovery of this large production centre is just the beginning of a potentially far reaching and complex project in which the distribution pattern and as well as the significance of this valuable resource for local community, the region and beyond is to be studied. In fact, to date, the character of the archaeological evidence in Poland, such as the apparent absence of any wooden installations in salt streams and springs, makes the recognition and recording of major prehistoric salt workings on the surface during fieldwork and field walking difficult (such as several colleagues have done in other regions, for instance the Carpathian zone: see, for example, Harding and Kavruk 2013). These new data (Inowrocław, but also Chabsko) offer the new valuable information on the understanding of the regional history.

It is therefore needed to re-examine the character and scope of salt exploitation in the local and regional scales in Kujawy and Wielkopolska in the light of the new data, as well as its integration in a wider context. In fact, our present research deals with the study of prehistoric exploitation, production and distribution of salt in north-western Poland, as well as the investigation of its role in shaping the social and economic character of Kujawy and Wielkopolska during the Roman Iron Age (1st-4th centuries AD) and its importance for the development of complex economic and social transformations of indigenous communities in the period of contacts with Rome.

We aim to expand the debates and new interpretations generated in archaeology and ancient history by revising the interpretations which have been proposed to explain the impact of the contacts with Rome in the *Barbaricum*. The current image is that of a superficial impact of Roman culture, restricted to the art and limited by local customs. In fact, some scholars argue that profound influences (such as production techniques or agricultural improvements and practices) were shunned, because of the fundamental differences between Roman and local indigenous social and economic organizations (Bursche 1996; Gralak 2012). We consider that there is a need of revising these interpretations, stressing the diversity of mechanisms and regional responses in the discussed period. We believe that it is possible to place the regional developments recorded in the Polish lowlands within the context of global transformations triggered by the Roman Empire. This makes it possible to put up materials of the Roman origin found in Kujawy in a hitherto unexplored perspective of the relations with the Roman Empire and go beyond the simplistic form of the so-called imports being a dominant mode of studying the Rome relations with the *Barbaricum* to date.

Accordingly, we believe that the systematic recording, analysis and interpretation of all forms of exploitation of salt can shed light on the diachronic character of changes in social formations and will make it possible to situate these changes in relation to the contacts with Rome: for example, to relate the processes of

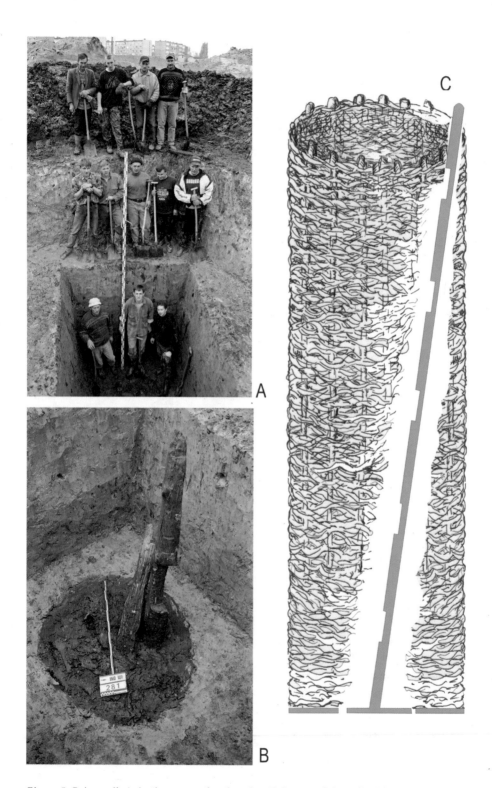

Figure 5. Brine well. A: in the course of exploration, B: bottom of the well with wooden ladder remains, C: reconstruction of the well (photographs: Józef Bednarczyk; drawing: Barbara Bednarczyk).

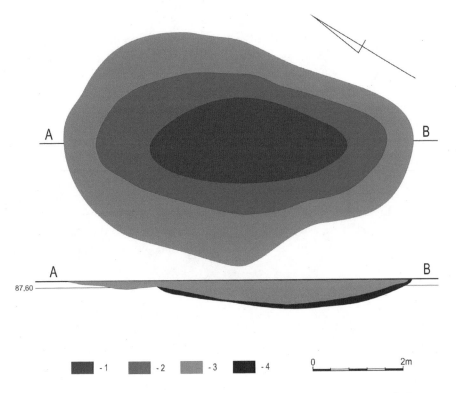

Figure 6. Layout of a brine reservoir at the depth of 1: 87.70 m.a.s.l, 2: 87.60 m.a.s.l., 3: 87.40 m.a.s.l., 4: layer of clay (drawing: Barbara Bednarczyk).

Figure 7. Photograph of the graduation tower of Ciechocinek (photo: Annette Bolaños).

reactivation of salt exploitation, or the new solutions in salt making technologies, to the impact of Rome in the Barbaricum. This relation between Rome's imperialist interests and salt resources is further corroborated by the abundant accumulation of Roman coins in the saline areas surrounding the amber route in Polish territory (Kowalenko 1952, 71; Gumowski 1958; Cofta-Broniewska 1979).

We would argue that the future investigations must be related to several intertwined issues: a) the analysis of the character of salt resources and their techniques of exploitation including the documentation and analysis of the characteristic features of salt mining in the area of Kujawy and Wielkopolska through different and complementary datasets, including geological, archaeological, technological and paleoenvironmental data; b) the distribution, trade and exchange patterns (destination of salt exchange, main routes involved, including the amber routes); c) the analysis of the role of salt mining within changes in social, political and territorial realities, at the local and regional scales; and d) the understanding of the impact of salt in the processes of appropriation and control of vast regions and areas.

Acknowledgements

The authors would like to thank Lucyna Leśniak and Michal Krueger for their help during the preparation of the paper. They are also grateful to Anna Majchrzycka, for sharing her work on the prehistoric salt works of Wielkopolska and Kujawy. Thanks are due also to Brais Currás, who made figures 1 and 2, and to Annette Bolaños, who took the nice photograph of the Ciechocinek graduation tower included in figure 7. Also to Monika Porubanova, who kindly revised the English translation and to Laure Manver, who revised the French abstract.

References

Adamczyk, K. and Gierlach, M. 1998. The Archaeology of the Transit Gas Pipeline: Idea – Concept – Practice. In: Chłodnicki, M. and Krzyżaniak, L. eds. *Pipeline of Archaeological Treasures. Exhibition Catalogue, Palais d'Europe Strasbourg, 14-26.9.1998.* Poznań: EuRoPol GAZ, 11-17.

Alexianu, M., Weller, O. and Curcă, R.-G. eds. 2011. *Archaeology and Anthropology of Salt. A diachronic approach.* Proceedings of the International Colloquium, 1-5 october 2008. British Archaeological Reports (International Series) 2198. Oxford: Archaeopress.

Bednarczyk, J. 2008. Pracownia obróbki bursztynu w osadzie z okresu rzymskiego w Inowrocławiu stanowisko 100, woj. kujawsko-pomorskie. In: Bednarczyk, J.; Czebreszuk, J., Makarowicz, P. and Szmyt, M. eds. *Na pograniczu światów. Studia z pradziejów międzymorza bałtycko-pontyjskiego ofiarowane profesorowi Aleksandrowi Kośko w 60 rocznicę urodzin.* Poznań: Wydawnictwo Poznańskie, 21-30.

Bukowski, Z. 1963. O możliwości wykorzystywania solanek w okresie halsztackim na terenie Wielkopolski i Kujaw. *Archeologia Polski* 8, 246-273.

Bukowski, Z. 1985. Salt production in Poland in prehistoric times. *Archaeologia Polona* XXIV, 27-71.

Bukowski, Z. 1988. Critically about the so-called amber route in the Odra and Vistula river basins in the Early Iron Age. *Archeologia Polona* XXVIII, 71-122.

Burchard, H., Keckowa, A. and Leciejewicz, L. 1966. Die Salzgewinnung auf polnischen Boden im Altertum und im frühen Mittelauer. Ergon V. *Appendix to Kwartalnik Historii Kultury Materialnej* XIV/4, 745-760.

Bursche, A. 1996. Contacts between the Late Roman Empire and North-Central Europe. *The Antiquaries Journal* 76, 31-50.

Chapman, J. and Monah, D. 2007. A seasonal Cucuteni occupation at Siliste-Prohozesti, Moldavia. In: Monah, D., Dumitroaia, G., Weller, O. and Chapman, J. eds. *L'exploitation du sel à travers le temps*. Piatra Neamt: Editura Constantin Matasa, 71-88.

Cofta-Broniewska A. 1974. Wczesnośredniowieczna warzelnia soli w Inowrocławiu. *Ziemia Kujawska* IV, 5-13.

Cofta-Broniewska, A. 1979. *Grupa kruszańska kultury przeworskiej*. Poznań: Wydawnictwo Naukowe UAM.

Cofta-Broniewska, A. and Kośko, A. 1982. *Historia pierwotna społeczeństw Kujaw*, Warszawa-Poznań.

Cofta-Broniewska, A. and Kośko, A. 2002. *Kujawy w pradziejach i starożytności*. Inowroclaw-Poznań; Fundacja Ochrony Dziedzictwa Kulturowego Społeczeństw Kujaw.

Czapowski G. and Bukowski K. 2010. Geology and resources of salt deposits in Poland: the state of the art. *Geological Quarterly* 54/4, 509-518.

Czapowski G. and Bukowski K. 2012. Salt resources in Poland at the beginning of the 21st century. *Geology, Geophysics & Environment* 38/2, 189-208.

Gaydarska, B. and Chapman, J. 2007. Salt research in Bulgaria. In: Monah, D., Dumitroaia, G., Weller, O. and Chapman, J. eds. *L'exploitation du sel à travers le temps*. Piatra Neamt: Editura Constantin Matasa, 147-160.

Górski J. and Rasała M. 2008. Hydrogeologia wybranych wysadów solnych regionu kujawskiego – aspekty poznawcze i utylitarne. *Geologos* 13, 1-153.

Gralak, T. 2012. *Influence from the Danubian Zone of the Barbaricum on the territory of Poland in Late Antiquity*. Wrocław: Wydawnictwo Uniwersytetu Wrocławskiego.

Gumowski, M. 1958. Moneta rzymska w Polsce. *Przegląd Archeologiczny* X, 87-200.

Harding, A. 2013. *Salt in Prehistoric Europe*. Leiden: Sidestone Press.

Harding, A. and Kavruk, V. 2013. *Explorations in Salt Archaeology in the Carpathian Zone*. Budapest: Archaeolingua.

Harding, A., Ostoja-Zagórski, J., Palmer, C. and Rackham, J. 2004. *Sobiejuchy: A fortified site of the Early Iron Age in Poland*. Warsaw: Polish Academy of Sciences.

Jaworska, J., Ratajczak, R. and Wilkosz, P. 2010. Definicja i elementy budowy tzw. czapy gipsowej na przykładzie badań czap struktur solnych Wapna i Mogilna (Definition and structure of a cap-rock base on the investigations of Wapno and Mogilno salt Domes). *Kwartalnik Akademii Górniczo-Hutniczej, Geologia* 36/4, 492-505.

Jodłowski, A. 1971. *Eksploatacja soli na terenie Małopolski w pradziejach i we wczesnym średniowieczu.* Studia i materiały do dziejów żup solnych w Polsce 4. Wieliczka: Muzeum Żup Krakowskich, 1-316.

Jodłowski, A. 1976. *Technika produkcji soli na terenie Europy w pradziejach i we wczesnym średniowieczu.* Studia i materiały do dziejów żup solnych w Polsce 5. Wieliczka: Muzeum Żup Krakowskich.

Jodłowski, A. 1980. *Periodyzacja dziejów solnictwa na ziemiach polskich do końca XIII wieku.* Studia i materiały do dziejów żup solnych w Polsce 9. Wieliczka: Muzeum Żup Krakowskich, 7-32.

Kaczor, D. 2005. Zasolenie wód podziemnych kenozoiku Polski północno-zachodniej w wyniku ascenzji solanek z mezozoiku. *Przegląd Geologiczny* 53/6, 489-498.

Kadrow, S. 2003. Charakterystyka technologiczna ceramiki kultury łużyckiej. In: Kadrod, S. ed. *Kraków-Bieżanów, stanowisko 27 i Kraków-Rżaka, stanowisko 1, osada kultury łużyckiej.* Via Archaeologica. Źródła z badań wykopaliskowych na trasie autostrady A4 w Małopolsce. Kraków: Zespół do Badań Autostrad, 205-220.

Kowalenko, W. 1952. Przewłoka na szlaku żeglugowym Warta-Gopło-Wisła. *Przegląd Zachodni* 11/5-8, 46-100.

Majchrzycka, A. 2009. *Warzelnictwo soli w pradziejach i we wczesnym średniowieczu w Wielkopolsce i na Kujawach. Stan badań. Możliwości poznawcze.* Unpublished Thesis, Poznań University.

Mohah, D., Dumitroaia, G., Weller, O. and Chapman, J. eds. 2007. *L'exploitation du sel à travers le temps.* Piatra-Neamt: Editura Constantin Matasa.

Morére Molinero, N.E. ed. 2006. *Las salinas y la sal de interior en la historia: economía, medioambiente y sociedad.* Sigüenza: Universidad Rey Juan Carlos.

Olivier, L. and Kovacik, J. 2006. The Briquetage de la Seille (Lorraine, France): proto-industrial salt production in the European Iron Age. *Antiquity* 80, 558-566.

Piernik, A., Hulisz, P. and Nienartowicz, A. 2005. Wpływ użytkowania na wartość ekologiczną śródlądowych łąk halofilnych. *Zeszyty Problemowe Postępów Nauk Rolniczych* z. 507, 415-423.

Ślizowski, K. and Saługa, P. 1996. *Surowce mineralne Polski. Surowce chemiczne.* Kraków: Wyd. Centrum PPGSMiE PAN.

Ursulescu, N. 1995. L'utilisation des sources salées dans le Néolithique de la Moldavie (Roumanie). In: Otte, M. ed. *Nature et culture. Colloque de Liège (13-17 décembre 1993).* Liège: ERAUL, 487-495.

Weller, O. ed. 2002. *Archéologie du sel : Techniques et sociétés dans la Pré- et Protohistoire européenne.* Rahden/Westfalie: Verlag Marie Leidorf.

Weller, O., Brigand, R., Nuninger, L. and Dumitroaia, G. 2011. Prehistoric salt exploitation in Eastern Carpatians, Romania. A spatial approach. *Studia Praehistorica* 14, 197-219.

Weller, O., Dufraisse, A. and Pétrequin, P. eds. 2008. *Sel, eau et forêt. D'hier à aujourd'hui*. Cahiers de la MSHE Ledoux 12. Besançon: Presses Universitaires de Franche-Comté.

Wielowiejski, J. 1980. *Główny szlak bursztynowy w czasach Cesarstwa Rzymskiego*. Wrocław: Polska Akademia Nauk.

Wilkoń-Michalska, J. 1963. *Halofity Kujaw*. Studia Societatis Scientiarum Torunensis, sectio D (Botanica), vol.VII, Nr 1, Toruń.

Part Three

The rise of salt exploitation

Prehistoric salt production in Japan

Takamune KAWASHIMA

Archaeological Museum, Yamaguchi University, Yoshida 1677-1, Yamaguchi 753-8511, Japan

Abstract. In the Kantō region of the Late Jōmon period, it is clarified that salt was produced because of the existence of a special pottery. Salt production is widely performed in the Pacific Coast of eastern Japan. In northern Japan, the tradition of salt production continues to the Middle Yayoi period, in which agriculture is introduced to western Japan. While the agriculture spreads eastwards, salt is produced only in northern Japan at the first stage of the Yayoi period. It is controversial from the point of view that a demand of salt increases with the introduction of agriculture. There is neither direct relation of the salt production technique nor the trace of exchanging salt between both regions. In the Middle Yayoi period, salt production occurred in the Inland Sea, which continued to the later periods. While the development of salt production after the Kofun period in the Inland Sea area was largely depending on the political power, it is still unknown why salt production of the Yayoi appeared in this region and period. In this paper, I will try to examine the origin of the salt production in the Inland Sea area and the difference between both regions, as well as the meaning of salt in the prehistoric period.

Keywords. Salt production, Jōmon, Yayoi, hunter-gatherers, Japan.

Résumé. Dans la région de Kantō durant le Jōmon tardif, la production du sel est prouvée par l'existence d'une poterie spécifique. C'est sur la côte pacifique de l'est du Japon que le sel est largement produit. Dans le nord, la tradition de la production du sel se poursuit jusqu'au Yahoi moyen, période pendant laquelle l'agriculture est introduite à l'ouest du Japon. Alors que les pratiques agricoles diffusent depuis l'ouest, le sel est seulement produit au nord du Japon durant la première phase du Yahoi. L'hypothèse que les besoins en sel augmentent avec l'introduction de l'agriculture demeure controversée. Entre ces deux régions, aucun indice d'échange de sel ni de transfert de techniques n'est documenté. Pendant le Yahoi moyen, la production de sel se développe dans la Mer Intérieure et ce jusque dans des périodes plus récentes. Dans la mesure où l'essor de la production du sel autour de la Mer Intérieure après le Kofun est largement dépendant des pouvoirs politiques, la question de l'apparition de la production du sel dans cette région pendant le Yahoi demeure toujours une inconnue. Cette contribution examine aussi bien l'origine de la production du sel dans la Mer Intérieure que les différences régionales et les enjeux du sel pendant la Préhistoire.

Mots-clés. Production du sel, Jōmon, Yayoi, chasseurs-cueilleurs, Japon.

While most prehistoric salt production was performed by agricultural societies (Kawashima 2010; 2012a), there is an example of pottery salt production by hunter-gatherers in prehistoric Japan (Kondō 1962; 1984; 1994). In the Kantō region of the Late (*c.* 2500-1250 BC) and the Final Jōmon period (*c.* 1250-950/400 BC), salt was produced by boiling brine with specially-made pottery, a technique which has a different technical origin from the salt production that occurred in western Japan. Salt production was widely conducted in the Jōmon period along the Pacific Coast of eastern Japan (Takahashi 2008). In northern Japan, the tradition of salt production continued to the Yayoi period (*c.* 950/400 BC-AD 250)[1] when agriculture was introduced to Japan. While agriculture spread from the west, salt was produced only in northern Japan in the first stage of the Yayoi period. This fact is controversial from the point of view of the assumption that demand for salt increases with the introduction of agriculture. There are no direct connections in the salt production techniques or traces of the exchange of salt between western and northern Japan at this time. In the Late Yayoi period, salt production occurs around the Inland Sea and was conducted on a larger scale than in the Jōmon. Using comparisons with salt production after the Jōmon, in this paper I will describe the characteristics of Jōmon salt production and consider its origins.

Archaeologists have contributed to a number of topics related to salt, including clarification of whether coarse pottery was used for salt production (Kondo 1962), the typology of salt-making pottery in various regions (Tsunematsu 1994), the salt making process itself (Nakamura 1996; Takahashi 2007), and so on. However, there is scarce discussion about the gap between Jōmon and Yayoi salt production, and also about the appearance of salt-making pottery in the Middle Yayoi period.

Jōmon

In Japan, there is no rock salt and salt lakes are also absent (Kondō 1975). While springs which contain salt are known and salt was produced from such salt springs in early modern and modern times, no prehistoric site near such springs has been found to contain a large quantity of salt-making pottery. Salt production around inland salt springs may have operated after the introduction of large earthenware cooking pots or iron vessels for boiling brine. Basically, in Japan seawater was the main source for salt production since the Jōmon period.

---

1   AMS dating for the beginning of the Yayoi period has been controversial (see Kaner and Ishikawa 2007, 3-4).

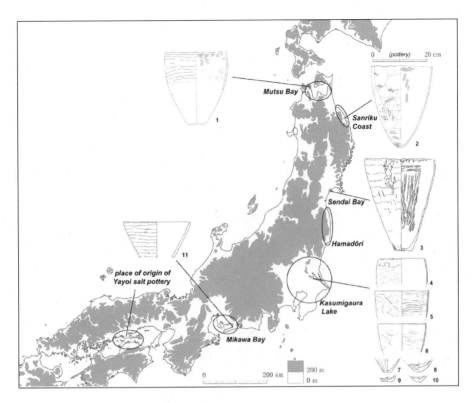

Figure 1. Distribution of Jōmon salt-making pottery and the place of origin of Yayoi salt production. 1: Imazu (after Fujinuma et al. 2005, fig. 68), 2: Ōashi I (after Takagi 1999, fig. 69), 3: Satohama (after Kimishima 1999, fig. 2), 4-10: Hirohata (after Kondō 1962, fig. 3), 11: Ōnishi (after Iwase 1994, fig. 4).

Salt-making pottery of the Jōmon period has been known since the 1960s (Kondō 1962). Salt production in the Jōmon period is recognized only on the Pacific coast side of eastern Honshū Island (Iwase 1994; Koikawa and Katō 1994; Kimishima 1999; Kitabayashi 1994; Kondō 1962) (fig. 1).

Figure 1 shows the distribution of Jōmon salt-making pottery. Except in the Kantō region, salt-making pottery was mostly found at coastal sites. There are some regional differences in pottery shape, but all the area retain the same basic pottery form, the deep pot. Along the Mutsu Bay area, wavelike rims, which can be seen on other local pottery, and flat bottoms are dominant (Kitabayashi 1994). While this type of rim is finished carefully in contrast to the salt-making pottery in other regions, the outside surface treatment remains coarse. On the Sanriku Coast, the base of salt-making pottery is pointed or has a very small flat shape (Kimishima 1999). On most rims, finger imprints can be seen, so that the rim is not smoothed flat. While some rims are smoothed, the rim profile shows pointed tips like other coarse rims. The salt-making pottery of the Sendai Bay area also keeps its coarse finishing for the outside wall like the former two areas. It is known that the base shape in this area changes from flat to pointed after the end of the Final Jōmon period (Koikawa and Katō 1994). The diameter of the flat base is centered at between five to six centimeters, which is larger than those in any other area. There are approximately 50 sites from which salt-making pottery was found. Since salt production continued until the Middle Yayoi period in this area, this should be one of the most important places for Jōmon salt production. In the Kantō district, salt pottery sherds were distributed not only on the coast, but also in the inland area (Takahashi 2007; Tsunematsu 1994). Some salt-making pottery sherds found from inland sites also have the same characteristics such as traces of heat and exfoliation of outside walls. While the distribution of salt-making pottery has been thought to indicate exchange networks (Suzuki and Watanabe 1976), no direct evidence of the transportation of salt-making pottery has been found. The difference of the rim shape of salt-making pottery between the production sites and the inland sites has been pointed out by Kawashima (2010; 2012a), and this could be a key to investigate the exchange networks of salt.

Jōmon salt-making pottery as well as those from later periods has some characteristic features, such as reddish color from heat, possible scales attached to the pottery, and exfoliation of outside walls, all of which could be caused by use in salt making (Kondō 1962; Kawashima 2008). The surfaces of exterior walls are exfoliated up to near the rim, which could happen because of the crystallization of salt in the wall of the pot. These facts suggest that the pottery was heated from the bottom, and that the pottery was filled almost to the top with brine. Basically, the fire could not have been strong, but it is also possible to suppose that the fire could have reached the pottery rim because some rim sherds were reddish. Salt pottery has no decoration, in contrast with the normal Jōmon pottery which has cord-marks, incisions, and other attached ornaments on the outside wall; even coarse pottery has incisions or simple attachments. Both salt and normal pottery share thin walls with similar shapes from the bottom to the upper part, but the rim of salt pottery remains thin. While the inside of salt pottery is well smoothed, the outside is finished roughly. Cracks of clay strings can be seen on the outside walls of salt pottery from Sendai Bay and other northern areas. This coarse finishing and thin walls could be created because of the large-scale consumption of salt pottery. The technical change of salt pottery making could imply emerging specialization (Kawashima 2008). The base shape shows a tendency to become smaller in the later period (Kawashima 2012b).

According to archaeological experiments (Kondō 1984), it is reported that the salt pottery used for boiling brine was easily broken, sometimes even in one operation. The boiling process is still unclear, but the trace of heat can be seen clearly on the base sherds. The fact that the salt pottery was heated with fire shows that it could be related to the accumulation of salt pottery sherds in particular sites. Some sites are known for their large amount of pottery sherds and are thought to have been production sites.

The appearance of salt production with pottery may have been based on pre-existing salt-making techniques. According to several ethnological examples in New Guinea, it is not necessary to use pottery to produce salt. It is reasonable to assume that before Jōmon salt production using pottery become common, there had been a simpler method of salt production without pottery. Kanō (2001) analyzed small shells found from an ash layer in a Jōmon site. The shells were types

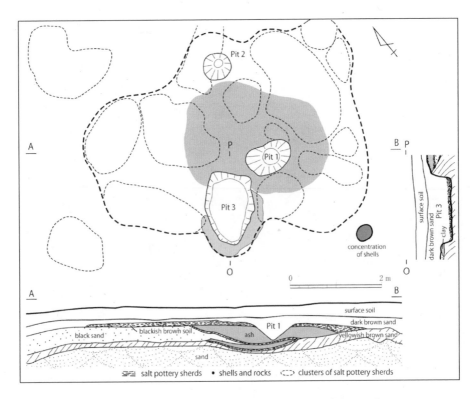

Figure 2. Possible hearth at Hōdō (after Tozawa and Handa 1966, figs. 15-16).

that lived on sea grasses, such as *Zostera marina*. As the small shells were burned, he concluded that the ash was used for making salt. Small shells were also found attached to salt pottery (Abe *et al.* 2013).

The salt production process and facilities

There are some structures connected to the salt production process in the Jōmon, which are mostly recognized as hearths and working spaces (Nakamura 1996, Terakado 1983). On the southern shore of Lake Kasumigaura, a possible working space was found at Hōdō, in which three pits were dug (Tozawa and Handa 1966) (fig. 2). A dark brown sand layer filled with salt pottery sherds covered an irregular oval shape of more than 6 by 4 meters, under which ash layers were found in pits. The bottom of the pits are covered with salt pottery sherds. According to the accumulation of salt pottery sherds, ash, and carbon rich soil, this place must have been connected to salt production, especially to brine boiling.

Pit 1 was dug through the dark brown sand, and two other pits were also dug from the same level. Under Pit 1, two layers of ash were found under which salt pottery sherds were accumulated. As shown in the profile, ash accumulation around Pit 1 may have contained several salt pottery sherd layers, which suggests that this place was repeatedly used in boiling process over many years. It is noted that the grayish white material, which was often observed on salt pottery, was found in the ash layer. This should be the same material which is reported by

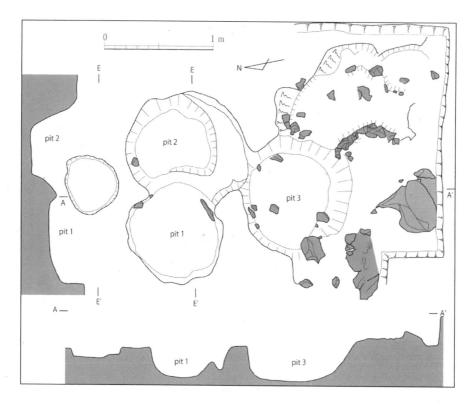

Figure 3. Pits found at Nigade (after Miyagi Prefectural Shiogama Girls' High School history club 1972, fig. 18).

Kondō (1962) and which is thought to have been strongly connected with the boiling process. The upper ash layer had a reddish colored part which could have been fired. In the bottom of Pit 3, a thin layer of salt pottery sherds, shells and stones was found, which had a trace of fire on the northeast side.

This kind of working area is also found at Nigade, northern Japan. This site is located on a low hill, 10-15 m above sea level, facing a small cove. At Nigade shell mound, a working space was found with a concentration of salt pottery sherds, orange-red ash, and three pits which were partially dug into a tuff repository (Miyagi Prefectural Shiogama Girls' High School history club 1972) (fig. 3). These pits belong to the same period, the end of the Final Jōmon. Over the pits, two clusters of salt pottery sherds and dark soil were observed, under which clusters of salt pottery sherds and orange-red ash were alternately deposited. As the walls of the pits consisted of loamy soil which was not burnt at all, in the site report it is suggested that these pits were not used for the boiling process, but for condensing seawater, since there is no trace of fire on the loamy soil of the pits (*ibid.*, 29). Although it is not clear that the orange-red ash was deposited primarily in the pits, as layers of salt pottery sherds and orange-red ash were alternately observed, it is also possible to think that the pits were used for the boiling process. In the case that the pits were used as a disposal site, such alternating layers would not have been observed. The fire for boiling brine could be very small, but it should have been maintained continuously during the operation. Repeated use of fire in one place could have produced the ash layer and made its color orange-red. Since other features which could have been hearths were not found and the location of the pits is almost 15 m above sea level, there is a space for discussion to presume the existence of a condensing facility in the Jōmon.

Other hearths in the Sendai Bay area consisted of stones, at Shinhama B (Miyagi Prefecture Board of Education 1986) and Kinokamiyama (Tokita and Sakurai 1982). At Shinhama B, two hearths were found, and both consisted of stones. One was obviously paved with flat stones in a shallow pit, which were 10-30 cm in diameter. The other also had a shallow pit, and was surrounded by heated stones. At Kinokamiyama, 11 hearths with heated rocks were found constructed on the beach. Salt pottery was mostly found on the beach closer to the sea. These were examples of hearths constructed by stones, but there were other types of hearth in the same period in the Sendai Bay area. At Satohama, 11 hearths were constructed on the beach at the Nishihatakita area of Satohama (Koikawa and Katō 1988; 1994; Suzuki 1992). The hearths consisted of a plaster-like material which was thought to be made by shell. Some of them were constructed in shallow pits.

All the hearths at Satohama and one of hearths at Shinhama B belong to the middle of the Final Jōmon, and the other at Shinhama B and the hearths at Kinokamiyama belong to the end of the Final Jōmon like those at Nigade. Suzuki (1992) assumes that the hearth changed from the pit type to the type consisting of rocks. While the salt pottery retained a similar shape over a wide area, for example the base was flat in the middle of the Final Jōmon and changed to be pointed at the end of the Final Jōmon, there was a diversity in the shape of hearths among salt production sites around Sendai Bay. This could suggest that the salt was produced by different groups who monopolized the production site and could use the site continuously, probably every summertime (Koikawa and Katō 1988, 31).

After the Yayoi period in western Japan

Although some level of specialization of salt production is observed in the Jōmon (Kawashima 2008; 2010; 2012b), as noted above, the Jōmon salt production continued to the Middle Yayoi period only in the Sendai Bay area. It is still unknown why the Jōmon type of salt pottery disappeared. If the agricultural society demands salt, salt production around the Sendai Bay area could have continued into the later periods. There must have been a fundamental social change during the transitional period from Jōmon to Yayoi.

In order to clarify the deference between Jōmon and Yayoi salt production, I will focus on the salt-making pottery in the eastern Inland Sea area, where this pottery first appeared. The most significant difference between Jōmon and Yayoi salt-making pottery is that Yayoi salt pottery has a pedestal (fig. 4). While a similar style of pottery already existed in the local ceramic types in Okayama Prefecture, this pedestal could be attached especially for the boiling process of brine. However, it is known that this pedestal became smaller and finally the vessel shape changed to a bowl in the Middle Kufun period. In this region, hearths are found in the

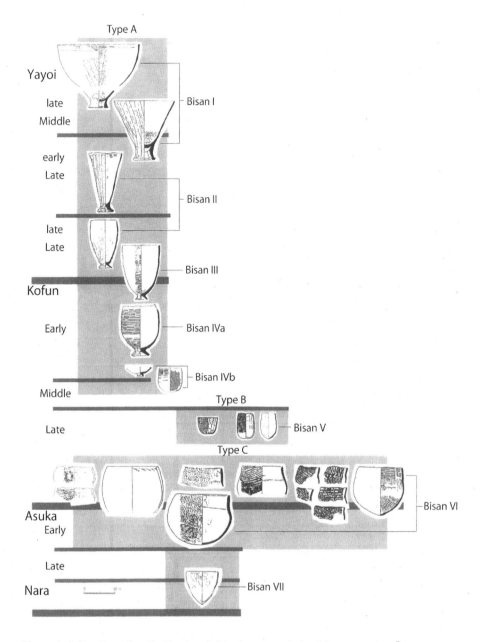

Figure 4. Salt pottery after the Yayoi period in the eastern Inland Sea area (after Ōkubo 2010, fig. 1).

Late Yayoi period (fig. 5). As approximately 70 salt-making pottery base sherds were found from the hearth at Jōtō, and there were some accumulations of 60-80 base sherds outside the hearth, with 70 vessels thought to have been used for one operation (Yanase 1986). The structure of hearths seems to have been connected with the boiling technique and the arrangement of salt-making pottery. In the Middle Kofun period, hearths, usually shallow oval pits with rocks, appeared in the eastern Inland Sea area (Ōyama 1991). Since rocks found in the hearths could be

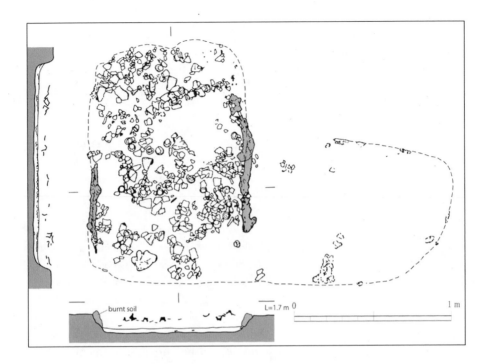

Figure 5. Hearth in the Late Yayoi period at Jōtō (after Yanase 1986, fig. 167).

used to stabilize salt-making pottery, pedestals probably did not have an important role in the boiling process. After the Late Kofun period, when the shape of salt-making pottery changed to a bowl shape, the bottom of hearths was generally paved with rocks.

The fact that the size of the hearths in the Yayoi is not larger than the Jōmon ones indicates that the scale of the Yayoi salt production could be similar to that of the Jōmon. As the Yayoi society was economically based on rice agriculture, the scale of salt production should have been larger than that of the Jōmon salt production. However, hearths for boiling brine have not been found from the beginning of Yayoi salt production. This implies that Yayoi salt production started in a small scale, and that salt production was not introduced from somewhere as an established technique. There is no clue why pottery salt production in western Japan appeared first in the eastern Inland Sea area in the Middle Yayoi period. Kondō (1984, 110-111, 1994, 10-11) presents three possible reasons for the appearance of salt production in western Japan.

1. Diffusion of the salt production technique from the Sendai Bay area, Tōhoku: he is suspicious of this scenario (Kondō 1984), because there is no evidence of the diffusion of the technique, such as pottery.
2. Invention of salt production on Kojima Island: This island is a relatively large island in the Inland Sea, and has Yayoi settlements where agriculture was conducted. The island is located in the central area which could have been important for maritime trade. These conditions fit the appearance of salt production, but as Kondō himself notes, it does not explain why salt production appeared on this island.

3. Diffusion of the salt production technique from the Korean Peninsula: In the Middle Yayoi period, many material items were introduced to Japan from the Korean Peninsula, including bronze weapons, metallurgy, and glasswork. Kondō (1994) thinks this is the most probable explanation, but evidence of pottery salt production in Korea is still unknown.

Compared to the salt-making pottery of the Jōmon and the Yayoi in northern Japan, the Yayoi salt-making pottery that appeared in the Inland Sea area (fig. 1) has some differences, especially in the shape of the base. The outside walls of salt-making pottery in the Inland Sea area are well scraped, which is different from the Yayoi salt-making pottery in the Sendai Bay area which keeps Jōmon tradition. Basically, this vessel shape and the way of making salt pottery are same as the local Yayoi pottery of the Inland Sea area. First, the outside wall is made from the rim to the pedestal, and then the base is attached. In this sense, the Yayoi salt-making pottery could not have been directly introduced or diffused to the Inland Sea area from the northern region where the last salt production of Jōmon style was still carried out. Since the origin of salt making in the Inland Sea area is still unclear, it is important to find traces of the initial stage of salt production in this area, for example the evidence of non-pottery salt production, similar features shared by salt-making and regular pottery which indicate the boiling of brine, and so on.

Emergence of salt-making pottery in the Jōmon period and in the Yayoi period

In order to investigate the difference of the appearance of salt pottery between the Jōmon and the Yayoi period, the use of salt could be an important topic. In the Yayoi period, systematic wet field rice agriculture was introduced in northern Kyūshū in the 10th century BC. Salt-making pottery in this period has not been discovered, so this implies that a large amount of salt was not required until the Middle Yayoi (c. 400/200 BC-AD 50). Rather, salt production occurred later (at the end of the Yayoi or the beginning of the Kofun) in northern Kyūshū which has the longest tradition of wet field rice agriculture, since agriculture was introduced at the beginning of the Yayoi period in this area. Regarding this fact, it seems difficult to assume that the physiological need for salt associated with increasing carbohydrate intake was behind the appearance of pottery salt production in western Japan. Also, it is difficult to suppose that the salt production occurred for herding cattle or horses. Horses were introduced to Japan at the end of fourth century, in the Middle Kofun period (Ozaki 2012). On the other hand, it is thought that the oldest examples of cattle were found in the Middle Yayoi period. As the evidence of cattle and horses before the fourth century is scarce when the salt production occurred (Kubo and Matsui 1999), it is difficult to conclude that such large domestic animals were raised in a specialized way which required salt.

Another alternative is for preserving food. However, there is no radical change in fishing tools and evidence of fishing activity in the Middle Yayoi period. Later, in the Late Yayoi, it is said that clay net-sinkers for net fishing increased along with the development of salt production (Manabe 1994). The same kind of argument can be seen for the Kofun period, regarding the relationship with octopus pots (Sekiyama 2012). Although this kind of theory which interprets the emerging salt production in connection with fishery is attractive, it seems insufficient to explain the emergence of salt production. There are no ethnographic examples of simple societies where salt was initially used for preserving food (Kawashima 2010; 2012a).

After the Kofun period, the scale of salt production developed rapidly and the production area expanded to most parts of the main islands of Japan. In this stage, it is reasonable to conclude that salt was used for wider purposes, such as for herding cattle and horses, leather tanning, industry, preserving food, and so on (Kondō 1994, 23). With the rise of state level society in the Asuka, Nara, and Heian periods, salt making became politically controlled. It is clear from records written on wooden strips (*mokkan*) that salt was produced in many places as tax in kind (*yō*) or tribute (*chō*) and then brought to the capital.

In a previous paper (Kawashima 2012a), I used ethnographic data from highland New Guinea to argue that Jōmon salt could have been used for exchange and ritual, and also as a status symbol. Like the Jōmon, the appearance of Yayoi salt production could not have been strongly connected with other technology or production. From the view point of Jōmon salt production, there is still a space for debating the reason why salt production started in the Middle Yayoi period in a particular place.

After the Yayoi period, there are some examples of salt-making pottery found in ritualized contexts. There are examples of salt pottery found in ditches and pits with other ritual objects. In the early Kofun period, salt-making pottery was found with fine pottery, and after the Middle Kofun, with horse teeth and bones as well as other ritual objects (Ōbayashi 2005). Later, clay horses were added to this kind of ritual. In the case of mortuary ceremonies, salt pottery was found with normal pottery from grave mounds, for example on Kiheijima Island where production sites were found (Kondō 1984). In contrast to production sites, salt pottery from grave mounds tends to be found as complete vessels, which could have been used as offerings. There is a tendency that in the earlier part of the Kofun period, salt pottery could have been more important for rituals, as in the later part other ritual objects increased.

While the relationship between salt and horses can be seen in ritual contexts in the Kofun period, it is notable that salt was used for rituals even before herding horses became important in the fifth century. This implies that salt retained ritual meanings since the beginning of salt production. Compared with Yayoi salt production, which has been continuously conducted until the contemporary period, Jōmon salt production was temporally and geographically limited and seems to have had a different social meaning. However, at the beginning of Yayoi salt production, there is little evidence for a strong connection between salt production and other activities. It cannot be assumed that the social meaning of salt has been the same from the beginning of Yayoi salt production, even if after the Kofun period salt production became important for industry.

Acknowledgement

I would like to offer my special thanks to Prof. Fujinuma Kunihiko, Masahiro Chida, and Atsushi Mori who gave me the opportunity to observe salt pottery from the Mutsu Bay and the Sanriku Coast area. I also would like to thank all the session organisers, Dr. Robin Brigand, Prof. Olivier Weller, Prof. Marius Alexianu, and Dr. Roxana-Gabriela Curcă, for their acceptance of my paper at 19th EAA conference in Pilsen in 2013. I am deeply grateful to Prof. Mark J. Hudson for his useful corrections and comments on the manuscript.

References

Abe, Y., Kawanishi, M., Kurozumi, T. and Yoshida, K. 2013. Jōmon jidai ni okeru seien kōi no fukugen: Ibarakiken Hirohata kaizuka saishū no hakushoku kekkakutai no seiseikatei to dokiseien [Reconstruction of Salt Production Process in Prehistoric Jomon Period Japan]. *Sundaishigaku* 149, 137-159.

Fujinuma, K., Sekine, T., Tsutagawa, T., Mukaide, H., Komukai, R., Fukami, R., Yokoyama, H. and Akiyama, S. 2005. *Aomoriken Tairadakemura Imazu iseki hakkutsu chōsa hōkokusho* [Report of excavation at the Imazu site, Tairadate, Aomori Prefecture]. Hirosaki: Hirosaki University.

Iwase, A. 1994. Tōkaichihō ni okeru Jōmon banki dokiseien no kanōsei: Ōnishikaizuka shutsudorei wo dō toraeruka [The possibility of salt production in the Final Jōmon period in the Tōkai district: focusing on the pottery at Ōnishi shell mound]. *Mikawakōko* 7, 21-38.

Kaner, S. and Ishikawa, T. 2007. Reassessing the concept of the 'Neolithic' in the Jomon of Western Japan. *Documenta Praehistorica* 34, 1-7.

Kanō, T. 2001. *Bishō dōbutsu izontai no kenkyū* [A study of micro faunal remains]. Tokyo: Kokugakuindaigaku daigakuin (Collection of Studies at Graduate School of Kokugakuin University).

Kawashima, T. 2008. Salt Production and social complexity in the Jōmon period. In: *Living with Diversity*. Proceedings of 1st Slovenia Japan University Cooperation Network Graduate Student Forum. Tsukuba: Department of Humanities and Social Sciences, University of Tsukuba, 87-98.

Kawashima, T. 2010. Jōmon jidai doki seien ni okeru rōdōkeitai [Labor Organization in Salt Production of the Jōmon Period]. *Tsukuba Archaeological Studies* 21, 1-34.

Kawashima, T. 2012a. Reconsideration of the use of salt in the Jōmon period. *Inter Faculty* 3. Available at: https://journal.hass.tsukuba.ac.jp/interfaculty/article/view/54.

Kawashima, T. 2012b. Emerging craft production and local identity: a case of the Late Jōmon period. *Documenta Praehistorica* 39, 263-268.

Kimishima, T. 1999. Tōhoku chihō no seiendoki: Sanriku hokubu wo chūshin ni [Salt Pottery in Tohoku Region]. *Kitakamishiritsu maizōbunkazai sentā kiyō* 1, 11-22.

Kitabayashi, Y. 1994. Aomoriken [Aomori Prefecture]. In: Kondō, Y. ed. *Nihon doki seien kenkū* [Studies of Pottery Salt Production in Japan]. Tokyo: Aokishoten, 103-121.

Koikawa, K. and Katō, M. 1988. *Satohama kaizuka 7* [Satohama Shell Mound Site 7]. Tagajō: Tohoku Museum of History.

Koikawa, K. and Katō, M. 1994. Miyagiken Iwateken [Miyagi Prefecture and Iwate Prefecture]. In: Kondō, Y. ed. *Nihon doki seien kenkyū* [Studies of Pottery Salt Production in Japan]. Tokyo: Aokishoten, 72-102.

Kondō, Y. 1962. Jōmon jidai ni okeru doki seien no kenkyū [The Study of the Jōmon Salt Production]. *Okayama daigaku hōbungakubu gakujutu kiyō* 15, 1-28.

Kondō, Y. 1975. The salt industry in ancient Japan. In: de Brisay, K. W. and Evans, K. A. eds. *Salt: The Study of an Ancient Industry*. Colchester: Colchester Archaeological Group, 61-65.

Kondō, Y. 1984. *Doki seien no kenkyū* [Studies of Pottery Salt Production in Japan]. Tokyo: Aokishoten.

Kondō, Y. ed. 1994. *Nihon doki seien kenkyū* [Studies of Pottery Salt Production in Japan]. Tokyo: Aokishoten.

Kubo, K. and Matsui, A. 1999. Kachiku sono 2 [domestic animals 2]. In: Nishimoto, T. and Matsui, A. eds. *Kōkogaku to Dōbutsugaku* [Archaeology and zoology]. Kōkogaku to shizenkagaku 2. Tokyo: Dōseisha, 169-208.

Manabe, A. 1994. Yayoijidai ikō no Setouchi chihō no gyogyō no hatten ni kansuru kōkogakuteki kōsatsu [Archaeological study on the development of fishery in the Inland Sea after the Yayoi period]. *Setonaikai rekishi minzoku siryōkan kiyō* 7, 19-42.

Miyagi Prefecture Board of Education 1986. *Shinhama B*. Sendai: Miyagi Prefecture Board of Education.

Miyagi Prefectural Shiogama Girls' High School history club 1972. *Nigade II*. Shiogama: Miyagi Prefectural Shiogama Girls' High School history club.

Nakamura, A. 1996. Jōmon jidai dokiseien ni kansuru ichishiron: Ikō niyoru seien kōtei no hukugen [An Attempt on the Salt Production Using Pottery in the Jōmon Period: Restoration of the Salt Making Process from Archaeological Features]. *Shikan* 135, 82-94.

Ozaki, T. 2012. Nihon zairaiba no rekishiteki hensen to genjō [Historical change and current condition of Japanese native horse]. *Kadaishigaku* 59, 15-28.

Ōbayashi, H. 2005. Seiendoki wo tomonau saishi no kigen to tokushitsu [The origin and characteristics of rituals using salt pottery]. In: Ōsaka daigaku kōkogaku kenkyūshitsu ed. *Machikaneyama kōkogaku ronshū* [Machikaneyama archaeological studies]. Toyonaka: Ōsaka daigaku kōkogaku kenkyūshitsu, 789-806.

Ōkubo, T. 2010. Setouchi no Yayoi Kofun jidai dokiseien: seisan ryūtsū no hensen [Salt production with pottery in the Inland Sea: Transition of production and sidtribution]. In: Shikoku kōkogaku kenkyūkai dokiseien kenkyū bukai ed. *Seiendoki no bunpu jōkyō kara mita shio no seisan ryūtsū no kentō: Shikokuchiiki no Yayoi Kofun jidai wo reini* [Studies on salt production and its distribution: examples of Yayoi and Kofun salt production on Shikoku island]. Tokushima: Shikoku kōkogaku kenkyūkai dokiseien kenkyū bukai, 1-12.

Ōyama, M. 1991. Seien [Salt production]. In: Ishino, H., Iwasaki, T. Kawakami, K., Shiraishi, T. eds. *Seisan to ryūtsū* I [Production and distribution]. Kofunjidai no kenkyū 4. Tokyo: Yūzankaku, 147-163.

Sekiyama, H. 2012. Engyō to gyogyō [Salt production and fishery]. In: Hirose, K. and Wada, S. eds. *Kofunjidai* [Kofun period]. Nihon no kōkogaku 8. Tokyo: Aokishoten, 34-62.

Suzuki, M. 1992. Dokiseien to kaizuka [Pottery Salt Production and Shell Mounds]. *Quarterly the Archaeology* 41, 47-51.

Suzuki, M. and Watanabe, H. 1976. Kantō chihō ni okeru iwayuru Jōmon shiki "doki seien" ni kansuru shōkō [An Essay on So-called Pottery Salt Production in the Jōmon period in the Kanto Region]. *Jōsōdaichi* 7, 15-46.

Takagi, A. 1999. Ōashi I iseki hakkutsu chōsa hōkokusho [Report of excavation at Ōashi I]. Morioka: Iwate Prefecture Center for Archaeological Operations.

Takahashi, M. 2007. Dokiseien to kyōkyū: Kantō chihō no 2 iseki wo chūshin ni [Salt production with pottery and its supply: Focusing on the two important sites in the Kantō district]. In: Kosugi, Y., Taniguchi, Y., Nishida, Y., Mizunoe, K. and Yano, K. eds. *Monozukuri: dōguseisaku no gijutu to soshiki* [Production: techniques and organization for producing tools]. Jōmon jidai no kōkogaku 6. Tokyo: Dōseisha, 274-286.

Takahashi, M. 2008. Seien doki [Salt Pottery]. In: Kobayashi, T. ed. *Sōran Jōmon doki* [Handbook of Jōmon Pottery]. Tokyo: UM Promotion, 1082-1085.

Terakado, Y. 1983. Seien [Salt Production]. In: Katō, S., Kobayashi, T., and Fujimoto, T. eds. *Jōmon jidai no kenkyū*, vol.2. Tokyo: Yūzankaku, 57-67.

Tokita, K. and Sakurai, Y. 1982 *Kinokamiyama Shell mound / Noyama site*. Shichigahama: Shichigahama Town Board of Education.

Tozawa, M. and Handa, J. 1966. Ibarakiken Hōdō iseki no chōsa: Seienshi wo motsu Jōmon jidai banki no iseki [Hōdō Site, Ibaraki: A Final Jōmon Site with Salt Workshops]. *Sundaishigaku* 18, 57-95.

Tsunematsu, S. 1994. Kantō kakutoken [The Kanto Region]. In: Kondō, Y. ed. *Nihon doki seien kenkyū* [Studies of Pottery Salt Production in Japan]. Tokyo: Aokishoten, 28-64.

Yanase, A. 1986. Jōtō iseki [Jōtō site]. In: Okayama Prefecture history editorial board ed. *Okayama kenshi* [History of Okayama Prefecture], vol.18. Okayama: Okayama Prefecture, 168-169.

New data and observations related with exploitation and transport of salt in Transylvanian prehistory (Romania)

Gheorghe LAZAROVICI*
and Cornelia-Magda LAZAROVICI**

*"Lucian Blaga" University of Sibiu, 55 Grigore Alexandrescu, Cluj-Napoca, Romania
** Iaşi Institute of Archaeology, 6 Codrescu Street, Pavilion H, Iaşi, Romania

Abstract. Starting with the Neolithic and up until Middle Ages, the access roads to areas with salt sources and then those used for its transport to the west and south were carefully controlled by communities of different eras. We have analysed several areas with salt sources and roads that start from these areas. Then, we will present some axes and hammers that can be used as crushing tools for minerals (salt, copper). We will draw attention to an anthropomorphic idol seated on a throne and carrying a knapsack discovered at Turdaş (Turdaş culture).

In the Turda-Tureni-Miceşti-Cheile Turzii area there are several tumuli (from the end of Copper Age) that we believe marks ridges nearby the roads leading to salt sources. The basins of the Someşul Mic and Someşul Mare rivers provide the best connection to the Panonian Plain. Some settlements such as Iclod and Ţaga have very impressive fortifications. The site from Ţaga controls the way to central Transylvanian plain. The location of Cojocna salt sources allows the connection through Cluj-Napoca and Huedin to the Crişul Repede basin. In the Someşul Mare basin, there have also been discovered two menhirs. This area ensures the connection to Maramureş region where there are similarly salt resources (but lower than the Transylvanian ones), as well as copper.

Keywords. Control of salt resources, salt roads, mining tools, prehistoric sites.

Résumé. Du Néolithique au Moyen Age les routes d'accès aux zones d'extraction du sel et celles utilisées pour son transport à l'ouest et au sud ont été soigneusement contrôlées par les communautés de différentes époques. Nous examinons plusieurs secteurs de Transylvanie riches en sel ainsi que les routes qui y débutent. Sont ensuite présentés plusieurs types de haches, de marteaux ou de broyeurs pouvant être considérés comme des objets utilisés pour écraser les minéraux (sel et cuivre). Une référence est faite à l'idole anthropomorphe au sac à dos découverte à Turdaş, de la culture homonyme.

Dans la zone de Turda-Tureni-Miceşti-Cheile Turzii, plusieurs tumuli de la fin de l'Age du Cuivre marqueraient les crêtes qui encadrent les routes menant aux exploitations de sel. Quant aux bassins des rivières Someşul Mic et Someşul Mare, ils fournissent la meilleure connexion à la Plaine Pannonienne. Quelques sites (*e.g.* Iclod et Ţaga) y possèdent des fortifications impressionnantes. Ţaga contrôlait par exemple la route menant au centre de la plaine transylvaine. Dans ce secteur, deux menhirs sont documentés. Les sources salées de Cojocna sont situées dans la région qui relie le bassin du Crişul Repede par Cluj-Napoca et Huedin. Cette zone se connecte à la province de Maramureş, où on connait des exploitations de sel (moins qu'en Transylvanie), mais aussi des exploitations de cuivre.

Mots-clés. Contrôle des ressources, routes du sel, outils miniers, sites préhistoriques.

Due to new projects related to salt in Moldavia or Transylvania (Weller and Dumitroaia 2005; Alexianu *et al.* 2011; Harding and Kavruk 2013), we reactivated our older interest related to salt in prehistory (Lazarovici *et al.* 1982-1986; Lazarovici and Maxim 1995) and collected information for this topic. In several recent studies we have underlined the role of salt in the Neolithisation process (Lazarovici and Lazarovici 2006, 74; 2011), proved by recent excavations in Transylvania – the sites from Miercurea Sibiului and Cristian (Luca *et al.* 2012a; 2014). Other topics were related with devices involved in salt transportation (knapsack or vessels used for brine transport in areas were salt is missing: *i.e.* Neolithic asymmetric amphora with several handles suitable for transporting liquids on long distance (Kitanovski *et al.* 1990, 107-108, fig. 1, Vrbianska Cuka) or tools used for salt exploitation in Neolithic context (axes, hammers). Both tools and knapsacks are used during Bronze Age, at the end of this period, salt exploitations reaching the highest level as is shown by Figa site (Harding and Kavruk 2013) or other areas less investigated.

The Romanian subsoil contains large salt deposits (especially in the sub-Carpathian areas of eastern and south Carpathians, as well as in Transylvanian Plateau and seldom in Maramureş or Banat) compared with Hungary or the regions south of the Danube (except Provadia, Bulgaria, for prehistoric era). During prehistoric times, the roads from Transylvania to Pannonian Plain, and especially through the Banat to the central and south Balkans Mountains that today represent the border between Serbia and Bulgaria, played an important role for generalization processes of migration and diffusion during the Neolithic (Lazarovici 2006; Luca and Suciu 2005; 2007), Copper Age, and even in the beginning of the Bronze Age (tumuli related with salt areas: Lazarovici and Lazarovici 2011). The geological rise of the Balkan and Carpathian mountains brought up several mineral resources such as salt, copper and gold, which were exploited extensively in prehistory.

Our theme now refers to artefacts related to transport of liquids (Lazarovici 1988, fig. 2/6) and minerals at great distances. We will discuss about the "knapsack" and tools for crushing minerals (salt, copper, gold). These artefacts originate from

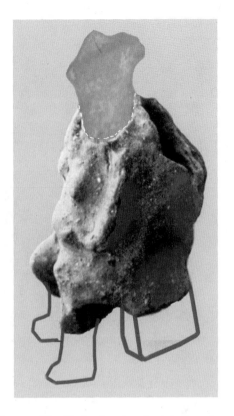

Figure 1. Turdaş, idol seated on a throne with a knapsack or vessel on its back (photo Gh. Lazarovici).

Turdaş (figs. 1 and 2) and *Ocnele Mari*-Govora (fig. 3), both related with the salt sources, exploitation and control of salt.

New research on the Sibiu-Deva highway route led to the discovery of several Early Neolithic settlements proving once again that Neolithisation process was closely linked with salt; this product was absolutely necessary for communities entering the territory of today's Romania (Lazarovici 1976, 228-232; 1977, XIX, 1, 6, 9, 11; 1983, 13-14; 1996; Lazarovici and Maxim 1995, 200; Lazarovici and Lazarovici 2006, 74f.) whose main occupations were shepherding and agriculture. In the last years in the Sibiu area several sites belonging to the Early Neolithic have been investigated, such as Miercurea Sibiului (four sites), to which are added those from Cristian and Ocna Sibiului (Luca *et al.* 2014).

In all ages (starting with the Neolithic and until the Middle Ages) salt roads are related to the main communication routes, particularly the valleys of major rivers and mountain' passes (Lazarovici 2009, 179-180; Schuster *et al.* 2010, 261-270; by animal transport, Angeleski 2012, 109, fig. 6/29-30). In some areas, large sites exercised control roles. For the Early Neolithic, a salt road is scored in the region of Oltenia along the Olt Valley by the discoveries from Copăcelu/Valea Răii (Nica 1995, 47, fig. 1/30) with materials from Starčevo-Criş (SC) IC, IIIB-IVA, Early Bronze Age and other (Petre-Govora 2001), (fig. 3); this road continues along the Middle Olt basin in Transylvania.

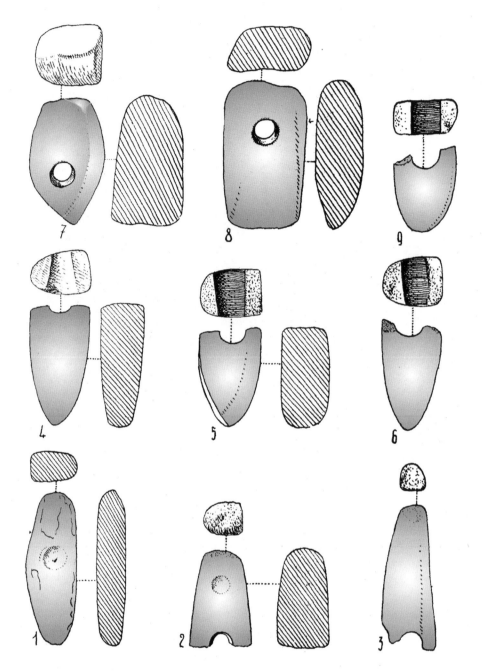

Figure 2. Hammer axes from Turdaş site (Gh. Lazarovici, processing after Roska 1941).

The Olt Valley

The Govora area (lower Olt)

Sites of Govora area control sources of salt and minerals from the lower part of Olt River. The area is known for Govora bathes, such as other bathes at Ocna Sibiului,

Figure 3. Axes, hammers and crushing tools from the Govora Museum (photos Gh. Lazarovici).

Miercurea Sibiului, Figa and other not investigated, like Cojocna (Kalmar 1984, 392, 403, fig. 7.1, shoe shape ax). Salt and metals exploitation in Govora area is marked by a series of hammers suitable for crushing mineral containing salt, copper, and gold. Dated on Early Neolithic are perforated axe with a high nape (fig. 3.1), and broken mouth suitable for salt exploitation; this damage area may be a result of its use but it is difficult to prove. This axe has analogies in the famous salt mines in Hallstatt (Kowarik and Reschreiter 2009, 44) to give one of the most significant examples, but also in other sites of salt areas from Transylvania (Uioara de Sus, Cojocna *etc.*, see below).

The Middle Olt area

Ocna Sibiului. Another important settlement related with the Neolithisation is Ocna Sibiului (medieval name confirms the main occupation: *Salzburg, Salzbrich, Salisfodium, and Salisburgum*). Here salt baths (fig. 4) and salt exploitation are related with different periods. The Early Neolithic site dominates the valley with salt baths, and on the other side of the valley is a settlement of the Petreşti culture (Copper Age). In this area there are traces of several periods but most of them are from the Paleolithic (Paul 1995; Ciută 2005). Starčevo-Criş pottery discovered in pit house 1 of this site, as well as radiocarbon data, place it among the earliest, and salt sources from the area play an important role in the Neolithization process.

Figure 4. Salty lake at Ocna Sibiului, 2007 (photo Gh. Lazarovici).

The Middle Mures area

Turdaş

The Turdaş settlement controls the access roads during the Late Neolithic and early metal era (due to gold and copper deposits in the Apuseni Mountains), as well as the valleys that lead to salt sources in Miercurea Sibiului (four sites of Early Neolithic) and on the Mureş River area (Ocna Mureş) and Cojocna (in Someşul Mic basin).

From Cojocna start the salt sources of western Transylvania. If we follow the range area of Turdaş culture, we clearly see that it embraces the salt and copper sources. From Turdaş site comes a fragment of a clay idol seated maybe on a throne (legs are broken). This idol carries in its back side some sort of rucksack with a wide mouth. The figure represents a female divinity, the Great Mother, keeping the hands on the belly, and having a bracelet on the right hand. Association of idol that sits on the throne and the backpack is very interesting and in our opinion reflects the transport of a sacred liquid.

The idea of staying on the throne is frequent in the Late Neolithic, in the Tisza (Hegedűs and Makkay 1987, Abb. 3-4, 9; Gimbutas 1991, 3-23.1, unpublished idol and a throne from Brănişca, Popescu collection) and the Precucuteni culture (Makarević 1960, 282; Marinescu-Bîlcu 1974, fig. 102/7, 113/14; Monah 1982, 11, fig. 12; Ursulescu 2001, 53-54, fig. 7/3, 6), but especially in Copper Age when several idols are associated with thrones. We have also to remind throne representations of *Danube script,* rendered on the bottoms of containers (Zorlenţu Mare: Winn 1981, Zorlenţ 2) or on Tărtăria tablets (Lazarovici *et al.* 2011, fig. VIIC. 6b, 8a-8c). But such thrones are known from other cultural areas, first of all in Romanian territory, in Precucuteni, Cucuteni (Gimbutas 1984, 73, fig. 26; Monah 1997, 35-36, 39, fig. 261/2, 5, 262/1-2, 7; Lazarovici and Lazarovici 2007, 143; 2012, 338, fig. VIII. 66, 75-78) and Gumelniţa (Andreescu 2002, 24, pl. 14/1, pl. IV).

The Turdaş seating idol belongs to the Turdaş culture (4950-4450 cal BC: Lazarovici and Lazarovici 2006, 568-570; 2007, 35-37) that is contemporary with Vinča B2/C-C2, both mentioned civilizations underlying the first elements of the Copper Age in Transylvania, but also in Serbia, Bulgaria, Hungary and other, embodied by *Vinča C shock* term (comprising cultures/groups: Turdaş, Foeni, and Vinča C1; Lazarovici 1994).

The best known is the eponymous settlement of Turdaş located on the Mureş Valley. We refer to both collections and old excavations, but especially to the new ones, coordinate by S.A. Luca (Luca *et al.* 2012; Luca 2012). All these three civilizations (Turdaş, Foeni group, Vinča C1) are located in Transylvania in areas that control the passage of Mureş River, copper and gold sources of Apuseni Mountains, but especially the salt sources on Mureş River from Ocna Mureş and to the Middle Olt basin. The contact between these civilizations will stop or determine some changes of the Zau culture in the central and western areas of Transylvania (Lazarovici 2009), where then arises the Petreşti culture (Copper Age). The Turdaş culture continues the control and movement towards northern Transylvania and to Oaş-Maramureş area (also containing copper and salt sources: Kacsó 2006).

Between the many pieces of the Zsofia Torma collection, there are several perforated axes with long and thick necks, suitable for crushing, broking or blunting. Of course the use of the axe, as today is multifunctional because of its active principle (broken, chipped, beaten, and crushed). We desire to draw attention that these artefacts could be used in mining (for salt and gold) not only for cutting, beating or as hoes. We also mention some copper axes found in areas of salt with traces of intensive use. A traceological study on these types of artefacts is needed to confirm the hypothesis.

In a previous study we supposed that asymmetric amphora with four-five handles could be used to transport salt (some of these also have human attributes: *i.e.* the one from Dudeştii Vechi – old name Beşenova Veche or Óbessenyő in Hungarian – where on the belly a navel suggesting human womb and pregnancy can be seen: Bognár-Kutzián 1944, pl. XXV/6a). With the same occasion we have presented such artefacts from Hungary and Macedonia (Madzari, fig. 5, Stence and others). Some Macedonian colleagues consider that water was transported with these amphorae (many such types of amphorae are known in the Neolithic sites from Macedonia).

Uioara-Ocna Mureş

This area is very rich from an archaeological point of view. From Uioara de Jos (previous name Ciunga) come a perforated axe with blunt tip and thick neck (Lazarovici and Cristea 1979, 435, fig. 3.5, 1 = 5/10; 4.10) suitable for breaking

Figure 5. Amphorae for liquid transport, Madzari Archaeopark, Skopje (photo Gh. Lazarovici).

up blocks of salt. Here were discovered materials related to the Starčevo-Criş, as well as with other periods (Copper Age, Coţofeni culture, Bronze Age, Roman, Middle Ages).

At Uioara originates the largest repository of bronze objects of Central Europe discovered in a workshop for bronze processing (Petrescu-Dîmboviţa 1977, Uioara); here have been found mining tools that could be also used for other sort of minerals (copper), not only for salt.

Turda-Tureni-Miceşti-Cheile Turzii

The Arieş River and its streams flow into Mureş River at Sănduleşti. At Turda there are lakes and salt mines of ancient times, extensively commented on by V. Wollmann (1996) and others.

Our recent or older investigation in the Miceşti salt spring area (Tureni commune, Cluj County) have shown in surroundings discoveries of Copper Age and especially many tumuli, in the area also being discovered an axe hoard of Banyabic/Vâlcele type (Maxim 1999, no. 622 *s.v.* Miceşti; copper artifacts analyzed by Beşliu *et al.* 1995, 133, L27-L33; Lazarovici and Lazarovici 2011 and bibliography).

In the Copăceni-Vâlcele boundary there are traces of exploitation, quarries of different periods, not yet investigated. In the same area there are known places for washing auriferous sand or toponyms related to this activity (Maxim 1999, nr. 629, at Mihai Viteazu village on *Aranyas Hill*).

Figure 6. Left: Someşul Mic-Mureş area. Right: tumuli agglomerations (end of the Copper Age and beginnings of the Bronze Age) and Neolithic settlements (red circles) in the area of the Miceşti salt spring (yellow star), Landsat image 2002, © USGS.

During the Copper Age and Bronze Age, salt spring from Miceşti is associated with the copper and gold workshop of Cheile Turzii-Peştera Ungurească.

Not far away from Cheile Turzii, at Tureni, there is a large tumulus and nearby a small necropolis consisting of several flattened tumuli (fig. 6). The big tumulus guards the ridge path to Miceşti salty spring and passes between the Hăşdate Valley and the Arieş River, respectively Turda area, as well as ridge and footpaths that lead to the Cheile Turzii/Turda Gorges (that it is also a place for sacred rituals). The western part of the Miceşti Valley is guarded by another large tumulus (having an internal pillars structure), maybe related with the Early Bronze Age, partially investigated by Zoia Maxim and Mihai Wietemberger during the Câmpia Turzii-Gilău highway project. This tumulus guards the peak between the Miceşti Valley and Şeuşa (*So,* salt in Hungarian) Valley.

Some Early Bronze Age tumuli are associated with ethno-cultural movements from the east, mainly related to shepherds' tribes. During Coţofeni III and Early Bronze Age, shepherds of those times raised mounds and mortuary facilities in the Miceşti area where it is an important salt spring as well as in other Transylvanian areas (Câmpia Turzii, Răscruci, Dăbâca-Borşa, area of Cheile Aiudului-Cheile Turzii-Cheile Turenilor *etc.*) (Lazarovici and Kalmar/Maxim 1987). But there is clear evidence that burials' necropolis continues the same ritual, starting with Coţofeni III, until pottery evolves to the Early Bronze Age (Vlassa *et al.* 1987).

A big tumulus at Petreştii de Jos (information and excavations by Zoia Maxim and Mihai Wietemberger) guards the roads to salt sources from the upper basin of the Hăşdate Valley that comes from the Miceşti salt spring and Şeuşa Valley. This tumulus has an internal wooden structure similar to mound with catacombs.

Someşul Mic Basin

Two important river basins of Northern Transylvania, Someşul Mic and Someşul Mare represent the best way of connecting with east Panonian Plain. Settlements located in this area could control the salt roads.

Cluj-Napoca – Polus Center

This area on the western exit of Cluj-Napoca was inhabited since Starčevo-Criş period, during the Zau and Coţofeni cultures, Bronze Age, La Tène, Roman and migration periods (Gepid graves), as well as Early Middle Ages (Alicu 2008, 6-13).

Tumuli and menhir from Cluj-Napoca – *Polus Center* related with the Early Bronze Age are located in the valley in contrast to many other situations when we find it marking the ridge roads. But a similar location is attested in the Someşul Mic Valley at Răscruci, Jucu and other.

The Early Bronze Age tumuli from *Polus Center* and others belonging to different phases of the Bronze Age mark the path to the Miceşti salt spring through the Făget valley, to the peak leading to Miceşti-Tureni-Sănduleşti. We believe that the Roman *burgus* identified at *Polus Center* also controlled the way to Miceşti, where another Roman checkpoint was located. In the forest that guarded the road along the Făget valley we have discovered several unpublished tumuli.

Iclod

On the Someşul Mic Valley there are many salt sources at Sic, Coasta, Buneşti, with roads to the west to Lona valley (Dăbâca, in Early Middle Ages cleared customs on salt that passed westward: Pascu *et al.* 1968; Rusu 1977). Iclod (fig. 7) and Fundătura settlements have strong fortification systems from the Middle to Late Neolithic (Lazarovici *et al.* 1996a; 1996b; Mischka 2008).

Ţaga

In the border of Ţaga village are mentioned salty areas or salt lakes (Mârza 2009, 62, fig. 3.15) not yet investigated. The Late Neolithic site from Ţaga is intensively fortified (three defensive ditches and three or four palisades, gates with bastions and towers for the control of enclosures: Lazarovici *et al.* 1996c; 1997; 2009) and controlled the roads to the central high Transylvanian Plain, materials discovered here proving contacts and imports from the Precucuteni and Petreşti cultures. Salt sources from Gherla-Buneşti to central part of Transylvanian Plain were likewise controlled.

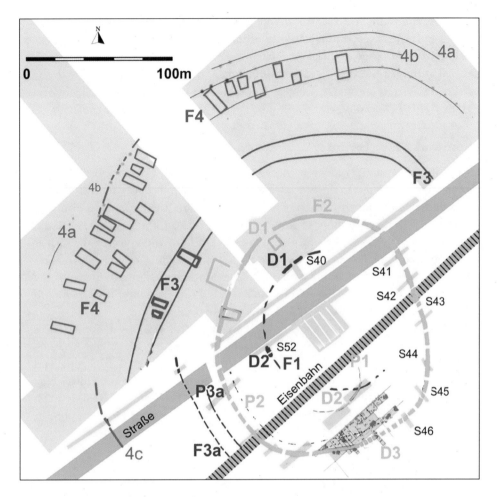

Figure 7. The site from Iclod (Transylvanian Plain): the fortification systems (and some dwellings). The site controls the salt roads to the Central Transylvania and the Pannonian Plain.

In the vicinity, at Sântioana there are salty lacks related with salt sources on the right side of Someșul Mic from Coasta to Sic. Salty lands appear in the mill channel and in the mill foundations, wood of such buildings being very well kept.

Cojocna

The Cojocna salt sources area are connected through Huedin to the Crișul Repede River. An important settlement from the Early Neolithic, Gura Baciului (6000-5300 cal BC), is located 25 km from Cojocna, and the largest Middle Neolithic settlement of Cluj-Napoca is at only 17 km from the same salt source. The Cluj-Napoca settlement belongs to the Zau culture (5400-4800 cal BC) and is the largest site (over 30 ha) of this period in Transylvania. We have written on other occasions about the sites density in these areas across different periods (Lazarovici and Lazarovici 2011). Research on this topic has not been made although the area is extremely rich. In the area of Cojocna, there are two Neolithic sites, one controlling the road to Middle Mureş basin, and another the road to the Someş and Arieş rivers through Valea Florilor. Here are also traces related with salt industrial exploitation of metal eras (Copper Age and Hallstatt, both unexplored), as well as in relation with the Zau culture (when it is noticed a synthesis with the emerging Petreşti culture of Copper Age spread in the Transylvanian Plain and Transylvanian Plateau).

Someşul Mare Basin

The Ciceu and Corabia menhirs marks the way to the east, to Figa (c. 17 km in straight path), but also to the north where there are salt and copper sources, the last ones in the northern part of the Târgu Lăpuş depression (the Maramureş historical province: Strâmbu Băiuţului 45 km NW and Cavnic 50 km N) (Lazarovici and Lazarovici 2012). The Ciceu menhir was collected from courtyard of the former CAP (Agricultural Production Cooperative), but according to the information available it was discovered in a field of the Someşul Mare Valley. To the east is the salt road on the Someş Valley and to the north is a ridge, an interfluve leading to the mentioned copper sources of Strâmbu Băiuţului, Maramureş.

The Figa site and many other sources belonging to the Upper Someş Basin are investigated by a Romanian-English team, led by Valer Cavruc and Anthony Harding; research made here is very important for manner of collecting and recording, as well as for data and material interpretation (Cavruc and Chiriacescu 2006; Monah et al. 2008; Harding and Cavruc 2006; Cavruc and Harding 2008; Alexianu et al. 2011; etc.). Here were found axes, hammers made by stone, bone or wood. These wooden artifacts are preserved only in salt lakes zones.

In the neighborhood, in the Săsarm village, in a bed of a small river were found some monumental stones, one of it rendering a human head (inf. Adela Kovacs); reserves for such an interpretation would be justified because of the discovery place. Generally there are reservations about such stone human heads, as was in Gura Baciului case. But in our opinion such stones should not be neglected.

In the area there are not large Neolithic sites; they are located over 10-30 km far, on the roads that control the paths to the salt sources. The nearest site is at Coldău, partially investigated by Vlassa and Glodariu (Vlassa 1973); the settlement, located on the banks of the Someşul Mare River could control the water transport and the land one from the valley of mentioned river. The area of the site is about 3 ha and is fortified with a defensive ditch (now -1 m difference from the current level of soil). Pottery indicates an early level of the Petreşti culture (with preserved fingernail pinched decoration).

For sure there are many other data related to the tools and objects involved in salt exploitation, possibilities of salt transportation or control of these activities. Objects and sites don't have a single function, and pending advancement of assumptions.

References

Angeleski, S. 2012. *The Early and Middle Neolithic in Macedonia: Links with the Neighbouring Areas.* BAR International Series 2332. Oxford: Archaeopress.

Andreescu, R. 2002. *Plastica antropomorfă gumelnițeană. Analiză primară.* Muzeul Național de Istorie a României, Monografii III. Bucharest: Muzeul Național de Istorie a României.

Alexianu, M., Weller, O., Curcă, R.-G. eds. 2011. *Archaeology and Anthropology of Salt: A Diachronic Approach.* Proceeding of the International Colloqvium, 1-5 october 2008, Al. I. Cuza University (Iași, Romania). BAR International Series 2198. Oxford: Archaeopress.

Alicu, D. ed. 2008. *Polus istorie pierdută, istorie regăsită.* Cluj-Napoca: Muzeul Național de Istorie a Transilvaniei.

Beșliu, C., Olariu, A., Lazarovici, Gh. and Olariu, A. 1995. O piesă de cupru din Sălaj și câteva probleme teoretice privind analizele de cupru preistoric aflate în Muzeul din Cluj. *Acta Musei Porolisensis* XVI, 97-128.

Bognár-Kutzián, I. 1944. *A Körös Kultura.* Dissertationes Pannonicae ex Instituto Numismatico et Archaeologico Universitatis de Petro Pazmany Nominatae Budapestinensis Provenientes, 2, nr. 23. Budapest: Királyi Magyar Pázmány Péter Tudományegyetem Éremés Régiségtani Intézete.

Cavruc, V. and Chiriacescu, A. eds. 2006. *Sarea, Timpul și Omul, Catalog de expoziție.* Sfântu Gheorghe: Editura Angustia.

Cavruc, V. and Harding, A.F. 2008. Noi cercetări arheologice privind exploatarea sării în nord-estul Transilvaniei. Raport preliminar. In: Monah, D., Dumitroaia, G. and Garvăn, D. eds. *Sarea de la Prezent la Trecut.* Bibliotheca Memoriae Antiquitatis XX. Piatra Neamț: Editura Constantin Matasă, 149-178.

Ciută, M. 2005. *Începuturile neoliticului timpuriu în spațiul intracarpatic Transilvănean.* Bibliotheca Universitatis Apulensis 12. Alba Iulia: Aeternitas.

Gimbutas, M. 1984. *The Goddesses and Gods of Old Europe 7000-3500.* London: Thames and Hudson.

Gimbutas, M. 1991. *The Civilization of Goddess. The World of Old Europe.* San Francisco: Harper.

Harding, A.F. and Cavruc, V. 2006. Băile Figa (or. Beclean, jud. Bistrița Năsăud). In: Cavruc, V. and Chiriacescu, A. eds. *Sarea, Timpul și Omul, Catalog de expoziție.* Sfântu Gheorghe: Editura Angustia, 56-59.

Harding, A.F., Kavruk, V. 2013. *Explorations in Salt Archaeology in the Carpathian Zone.* Budapest: Archaeolingua.

Hegedűs, K., Makkay, J. 1987. Vestő – Mágor. A settlement of the Tisza culture. In: Tálas, L., Raczky, P. eds. *The Late Neolithic of the Tisza Region: A Survey of Recent Excavations and Their Findings: Hódmezővásárhely-Gorzsa, Szegvár Tűzköves, Öcsöd-Kováshalom, Vésztő-Mágor, Berettyóújfalu-Herpály.* Szolnok, 85-103.

Kacsó, C. 2006. *Date cu privire la exploatările timpurii de sare din Maramureș.* In: Cavruc, V. and Chiriacescu, A. eds. *Sarea, Timpul și Omul, Catalog de expoziție.* Sfântu Gheorghe: Editura Angustia, 97-121.

Kalmar, Z. 1984. Materiale neo-eneolitice intrate în colecția Muzeului Național de Istorie a Transilvaniei I. *Acta Musei Napocensis* XXI, 391-403.

Kitanovski, B., Simoska, D. and Jovanović, B. 1990. Der Kulplatz auf der Fundstätte Vrbjanska Čuka bei Prilep. In: Srejović, D. and Tasić, N. eds. *Vinča and its World. International Symposium. The Danubian Region from 6000 to 3000 B.C.* Serbian Akademy of Science and Arts, Centre for Archaeological Research, Faculty of Philosophy, Volume LI, Book 14. Belgrade.

Kowarik, K. and Reschreiter, H. 2009. The earliest traces. In: Kern, A., Kovarik, K., Rausch, A.W. and Reschreiter, H. eds. *Kingdom of Salt. 7000 years of Hallstatt.* Wien: Natural History Museum, 44-46.

Lazarovici, C.-M. and Lazarovici, Gh. 2006. *Arhitectura Neoliticului și Epocii Cuprului din România. I. Neoliticul.* Bibliotheca Archaeologica Moldaviae IV. Iași: Trinitas.

Lazarovici, C.-M. and Lazarovici, Gh. 2007. *Arhitectura Neoliticului și Epocii Cuprului din România. II. Epoca Cuprului.* Bibliotheca Archaeologica Moldaviae, VI. Iași: Trinitas.

Lazarovici, Gh. 1976. Fragen der neolithischen Keramik im Banat. In: Mitscha-Märheim, H., Friesinger, H. and Kerchler, H. eds. *Festschrift für Richard Pittioni zum siebzigsten Geburtstag.* Archaeologia Austriaca 13-14. Wien: Berger, 203-234.

Lazarovici, Gh. 1977. *Gornea-Preistorie.* Caiete Banatica, Seria arheologie 5. Reșița: Muzeul de Istorie al Județului Caraș-Severin.

Lazarovici, Gh. 1983. Neoliticul timpuriu din zona Porțile de Fier (Clisură). *Banatica* 7, 9-34.

Lazarovici, Gh. 1988. Venus de Zăuan. Despre credințele și practicile megico-religioase (Partea I-a). *Acta Musei Porolisensis*, 25-70.

Lazarovici, Gh. 1994. Der Vinča C – Schock im Banat. In: Roman, P. and Alexianu, M. eds. *Relations Thraco-Illyro-Helléniques.* Actes du XIVᵉ symposium national de Thracologie. Băile Herculane (14-19 septembre 1992). Bucharest: Institut Roumain de Thracologie, 62-100.

Lazarovici, Gh. 1996. The Process of the Neolithisation and the Development of the first Neolithic Civilisations in the Balkans. In: Grifoni Cremonesi, R., Guilaine, J. and l'Helgouach, J. eds. *The Neolithic in the Near East and Europe.* Colloqvium XVII, 9, XIII ICPPS, Forli, Italia, 4-14, september, 1996. Forli: Abaco, 21-38.

Lazarovici, Gh. 2006. The Anzabegovo – Gura Baciului Axis and the First Stage of the neolithisation Process in the Southern – Central Europe. In: Tasić, N. and Grazdanov, C. eds. *Homage to Milutin Garašanin.* Belgrade: Serbian Academy of Science and Arts, Macedonian Academy of Science and Arts, Special Editions, 111-158.

Lazarovici, Gh. 2009. Cultura Zau. In: Drașovean, Fl., Ciobotaru, D.L. and Maddison, M. eds. *Ten years after: The Neolithic of South-east of Balkans, as uncovered by the last decade of Research.* Proceedings of the Conference held at the Museum of Banat on November 9th-10th 2007. Timișoara: Marineasa, 179-217.

Lazarovici, Gh. and Cristea, N. 1979. Contribuții arheologice la istoria străveche a comunei Uioara de Jos, Ciunga, jud. Alba. *Acta Musei Napocesnsis* XVI, 431-446.

Lazarovici, Gh. and Kalmar/Maxim, Z. 1987. Șantierul arheologic Iclod. Campania din 1985. *Apulum* 24, 9-39.

Lazarovici, Gh. and Lazarovici, C.-M. 2011. Some Salt Sources in Transylvania and their Connections with the Archaeological, Sites in the Area. In: Alexianu, M, Weller, O. and Curcă, R.-G. eds. *Archaeology and Anthropology of Salt: A Diachronic Approach.* Proceeding of the International Colloqvium, 1-5 october 2008, Al. I. Cuza University (Iaşi, Romania). BAR International Series 2198. Oxford: Archaeopress, 89-110.

Lazarovici Gh. and Maxim Z. 1995. *Gura Baciului.* Bibliotheca Musei Napocensis XI. Cluj-Napoca.

Lazarovici, Gh., Nandris, J. and Maxim, Z. 1982-1986. Etnoarheologia zonelor înalte din România, 1982-1986 ms. Romanian-English Project (London Institute of Archaeology, National History Museum of Tansilvanya – Ministry of Culture).

Lazarovici, Gh., Maxim, Z., Meşter, M., Bulbuc, A., Radu, S. and Crişan, V. 1996a. Şantierul arheologic Iclod. Campania din 1995. *Acta Musei Napocensis* 32/1, 267-299.

Lazarovici, Gh., Maxim, Z., Meşter, M., Bulbuc, A., Radu, S. and Crişan, V. 1996b. Şantierul arheologic Fundătura-Poderei. *Acta Musei Napocensis* 33/1, 301-321.

Lazarovici, Gh., Wietenberg, M., Meşter, M., Radu, S., Ilieş, I. and Bodea, M., 1996c. Şantierul arheologic Ţaga. *Acta Musei Napocensis* 33/1, 323-352.

Lazarovici, Gh., Meşter, M., Radu, S. and Maxim, Z. 1997. Şantierul arheologic Ţaga. Campania din 1996. *Acta Musei Napocensis* 34/1, 691-702.

Lazarovici, Gh., Maxim, Z. and Meşter, M. 2009. Ţaga. Istoria societăţii. In: Mârza, I. ed. *Monografia comunei Ţaga.* Ţaga: Primăria Comunei, 220-272.

Lazarovici, Gh., Lazarovici, C.-M. and Merlini, M. 2011. *Tărtăria and the sacred tablets.* Cluj-Napoca: Mega.

Lazarovici, Gh., Lazarovici, C.-M. and Constantinescu, B. 2012. Despre analizele pieselor de aur din atelierul de bijuterii de la Cheile Turzii-Peştera Caprelor/Peştera Ungurească. *Apulum* XLIX/1, 1-21.

Luca, S.A. and Suciu, C. 2005. The Beginning of the Early Neolithic in Transilvania. In: Spinei, V., Lazarovici, C.-M. and Monah, D. eds. *Scripta praehistorica. Miscellanea in honorem nonagenarii magistri Mircea Petrescu- Dîmboviţa oblata.* Iaşi: Trinitas, 139-156.

Luca, S.A. and Suciu, C. 2007. Migration and Local Evolution in the Early Neolithic of Transylvania, the Typological-Stylistic Analysis and the Radiocarbon Data. In: Spataro, M. and Biagi, P. eds. *A short walk throught the Balkans: the first farmers of the Carpathian basin and adjacent regions.* Quaderno XII. Trieste: Società per la Preistoria e Protostoria della Regione Friuli-Venezia Giulia, 77-88.

Luca, S.A., Georgescu, A., Munteanu, C., Niţoi, A., Bocan, I. and Neagu, C.M. 2012. *Cercetările arheologice preventive de la Cristian (jud. Sibiu). Campania 2011-2012.* Bibliotheca Brukenthal LX, Sibiu: Muzeul Naţional Brukenthal.

Luca, S.A. ed. 2012. *Cercetările arheologice preventive de la Turdaş-Luncă (judeţul Hunedoara): Campania 2011.* Bibliotheca Brukenthal LIX. Sibiu: Muzeul Naţional Brukenthal.

Luca, S.A., Suciu, C. and Şeulean Tudorie, A. 2014. O schemă evolutivă a celui mai vechi val de neolitizare din sud-vestul Transilvaniei. Studiu de caz. In: *Satu Mare. Studii şi comunicări 2013-2014.*

Makarević, M.L. 1960. Ob ideologičeskih predstavlenijah u trâpolâskih plemen. *Zapiski Odesskogo arkheologičeskogo obščestva* I/34. Odessa, 290-301.

Marinescu-Bîlcu, S. 1974. *Cultura Precucuteni pe teritoriul României.* Bucureşti: Academiei R.S.R.

Mârza, I. 2009. Resursele naturale. In: Mârza, I. ed. *Monografia comunei Ţaga.* Ţaga: Primăria Comunei, 60-63.

Maxim, Z. 1999. *Neo-eneoliticul din Transilvania.* Bibliotheca Musei Napocensis XIX. Cluj-Napoca.

Mischka, C. 2008. Geomagnetische Prospektion neolithischer und kupferzeitlicher Siedlungen in Rumänien. *Eurasia Antiqua, Zeitschrift für Archäologie Eurasiens* 14, 101-116.

Monah, D. 1982. O importantă descoperire arheologică. *Arta* 7-8, 11-13.

Monah, D. 1997. *Plastica antropomorfă a culturii Cucuteni-Tripolie.* Bibliotheca Memoriae Antiquitatis III. Piatra Neamţ: Ed. Constantin Matasă.

Monah, D., Dumitroaia, Gh. and Garvăn, D. eds. 2008. *Sarea de la Prezent la Trecut.* Bibliotheca Memoriae Antiquitatis XX. Piatra Neamţ: Editura Constantin Matasă.

Nica, M. 1995. Descoperiri ale complexului cultural Boian V – Gumelniţa în Oltenia. *Arhivele Olteniei* 10, 35-46.

Paul, I. 1995. *Vorgeschichtliche Untersuchungen in Siebenburgen.* Bibliotheca Universitatis Apulensis I. Alba Iulia: Imago.

Petre-Govora, Gh. 2001. *Govora de la primii oamenii la contemporani.* Râmnicu Vâlcea: Petras.

Petrescu-Dîmboviţa, M. 1977. *Depozitele de bronzuri din Romania.* Biblioteca de arheologie, XXX, Institutul de istorie şi arheologie „A.D. Xenopol" Iaşi. Bucharest: Academiei R.S.R.

Pascu, Şt., Rusu, M., Edroiu, N., Iambor, P., Gyulai, P., Wollmann, V. and Matei, Şt. 1968. Cetatea Dăbâca. *Acta Musei Napocensis* V, pp. 153-199.

Rusu, M. 1977. Transilvania şi Banatul în secolele VI-IX. *Banatica* 4, 169-213.

Schuster, Ch., Ţuculescu, I. and Dumitrescu, I. 2010. Câteva gânduri cu privire la exploatarea sării în Nord-Estul Olteniei. Din preistorie şi până în epoca modernă. *Angustia* 14, 261-270.

Ursulescu, N. 2001. Dovezi ale unei simbolistici a numerelor în cultura Precucuteni. *Memoria Antiquitatis* XXII, 51-70.

Vlassa, N. 1973. Săpăturile arheologice de la Coldău (jud. Bistriţa-Năsăud). *Acta Musei Napocensis* X, 11-38.

Vlassa, N., Takacs, M. and Lazarovici, Gh. 1987. Hügelgräber in Banat und Siebenbürgen in der Späten Jungsteinzeit. In: Srejović, D. and Tasić, N. eds. *Hügelbestattung in der Karpaten-Donau-Balkan-Zone Während der Äneolithischen Periode: Internationales symposium, Donji Milanovac 1985.* Belgrad: Balkanološki Institut SANU, 107-119.

Weller, O. and Dumitroaia, Gh. 2005. The earliest salt production in the world: an early Neolithic exploitation in Poiana Slatinei-Lunca, Romania. *Antiquity* 79, 306. Available at: http://antiquity.ac.uk/projgall/weller/index.htlm.

Winn, S. 1981. *Pre-writing in Southeastern Europe: The Sign System of the Vinča Culture ca. 4000 BC.* Calgary, Alberta: Western Publishers.

Wollmann, V. 1996. *Mineritul metalifer, extragerea sării și carierele de piatră în Dacia romană/ Der Erzbergbau, die Salzgewinnung und die Steinbrücke in römischen dakien.* Muzeul Național de Istorie a Transilvaniei, Deutsches Bergbau-Museum Bochum. Cluj-Napoca.

Spatial analysis for salt archaeology: a case study from Moldavian Neolithic (Romania)

Robin BRIGAND and Olivier WELLER

UMR 8215 *Trajectoires*, Université Paris 1 Panthéon-Sorbonne, Maison de l'Archéologie et de l'Ethnologie, 21 allée de l'Université, F-92023 Nanterre cedex, France

Abstract. This paper presents the results of a spatial analysis project in Romanian Moldavia focused on the dynamics of salt exploitation in the longue durée. Spatial and statistical measures are used to investigate the relationship between salt resources distribution and settlement patterns from the Early Neolithic to Chalcolithic (6000-3500 BC). This work combines methodologies used in landscape archaeology with the potential of the Geographic Information System to mobilise archaeological artefacts in a large-scale setting and for many thematic purposes. General goal is to evaluate how salt resources were a driving factor for these farming groups of eastern Romania.

Keywords. Moldavia, Neolithic, settlement pattern, GIS.

Résumé. Cette contribution présente les résultats des analyses spatiales menées en Moldavie roumaine autour de la dynamique des exploitations préhistoriques du sel dans la longue durée. Des études statistiques et spatiales sont menées afin d'explorer les relations entre la distribution des ressources en sel et la trame des peuplements néolithique et chalcolithique (6000-3500 BC). Ce travail combine les méthodologies de l'archéologie du paysage avec un outil puissant comme les Systèmes d'Information Géographique afin de mobiliser les découvertes archéologiques dans le cadre d'une approche multi-scalaire et ouverte à différentes entrées thématiques. L'objectif général est d'évaluer comment les ressources en sel ont été largement intégrées aux territoires des premières communautés agricoles de l'est de la Roumanie.

Mots-clés. Moldavie, Néolithique, système de peuplement, SIG.

The aim of the present work is to study prehistoric settlement patterns, as well as the nature and distribution of salt resources. In salt archaeology, the territorial dimension related to its production has been traditionally put forward for the more recent periods of the Bronze Age and especially for the Iron Age. More recently, many studies have focused on understanding the forms of territorial organisation inherent to the colonisation of saliferous regions, and the contexts of emergence of fortified settlements, stable and directly linked to the control and exploitation of salt springs or rock-salt deposits. In this respect, the Subcarpathian region of eastern Romania (Moldavia) is particularly interesting, since it displays a unique density of saline-water springs, reflected by the discovery of the first forms of salt exploitation recorded for the earliest Neolithic (Criş) and, thereon, the emergence of a cultural centre of an unparalleled richness and importance during the Chalcolithic (Precucuteni and Cucuteni). A decade of research concerned both with the nature and with the use of the salt resources, as well as the establishment of an archaeological database covering the timespan from *c.* 6000 BC to *c.* 3500 BC, allowed us to advance a first archaeological assessment of the territorial strategies employed by these societies in the eastern-Carpathian regions. Several questions frame this endeavour: is salt a structuring resource, attracting and fixating human populations for nearly 3000 years? Is the control of salt able to attract massively, objects and materials that are socially valued and thus to indirectly stimulate a strong local dynamics capable of fuelling long-distance trade circuits? Can salt, by itself, explain the remarkable trajectory of the prehistoric societies from Moldavia? To provide some answers to these fundamental questions on the place of salt in these ancient societies, we relied on an integrated study of the social and environmental facets involved. A major tool like a Geographic Information System (GIS) completed the archaeological and ethnographic approaches around the salt springs, in order to modelize the forms and dynamics of land occupation. It also served to enrich the discussion on the territorial organisation and resource management, now the centre of an emerging approach dealing with several key objects of prehistoric archaeology: supply, accessibility and availability of mineral, lithic or agronomic resources; distribution of raw materials; inter-site relationships; territorial delimitation and construction of territories. The work presented in these pages adds rigour to this approach: it seeks to improve our view of the diachronic relations and interactions between society and the environment.

The Moldavian Salt

Romania has the most abundant and accessible salt resources in the whole of Europe (fig. 1). Connected to the Carpathian orogenesis, the saliferous deposits of lagoonal origin from the Aquitanian and the Tortonian appear as halite formations or saliferous clays, and are distributed both along the outer and inside edge of the Carpathian range (Moldavia, Muntenia, Oltenia, Transylvania) (*e.g.* Merutiu 1912; Velcea and Savu 1982, 239-243). In Moldavia, the halite deposits are distributed along a north-south axis and generally mark the transition between the Oligocene-Eocene formations and the more recent ones of the Miocene. South of

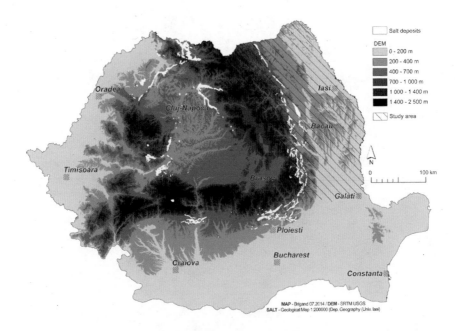

Figure 1. Salt deposits, study area and main agglomerations.

Bacău, near the Curvature Carpathians, the tectonic dynamics and the interplay of differential erosions contributed to the low depths of these deposits and their recurrent outcrop (fig. 2).

Halite outcrops, found particularly in the area of the Curvature Carpathians, are located high up between 300 m and 700 m above sea level, on steep slopes of minor waterways which are often torrential. As for the salt springs, fed by the groundwater that washes the saline bedrock, they are found at variable hights (from 135 m to 936 m) and generally on two types of topographic contexts: at the top of a little secondary valley, more or less deeply cutting through the substrate; and at the bottom of a valley and close to the thalweg, on modest terraces that protect them from alluvial processes. Those above 700 m are, for the most part, found north of Piatra Neamț (fig. 3), along the minor tributaries of the Bistrița or Suceava rivers, or on the first chain of the Carpathian foothills. Those below 300 m are found near the middle courses of the Siret and Bistrița rivers, save for one spring, located much further east in the Moldavian Plain (Iași County).

Apart from the latter, to which we will return later on, the availability of the salt resources puts the Subcarpathian region in direct opposition to the Moldavian lowlands. This fundamental difference may however seem contrived, since we have also recorded east of the Siret almost a hundred saline soils (and many more remain unrecorded) of which less than half are emerging waters that are very little or slightly brackish. Their reduced salinity, often difficult to determine, results *a priori* of the dissolution of salts contained by the marl and clay of the geological substrate, followed by their capillary movement to the surface. The use of these saliferous resources is not well documented, either by ethnography or archaeology.

Figure 2. Salt springs and rock-salt outcrops in Moldavia. A. Solca-Slatina Mare (Suceava), B. Cucuieți-Slatina Veche (Bacău), C. Hangu-Slatina (Neamț), D. Oglinzi-Poiana Slatinei (Neamț), E. Coza-Grochile (Vrancea), F. Coza-Alghianu (Vrancea). Photos RB and OW.

Still, very specific customary uses by pastoral communities are not excluded. Since we have only very limited data on these soils and saline waters, and their role in the clustering of settlements cannot be demonstrated for the time being, we have not dwelled on them.

State of the art

We know that the first forms of salt exploitation, whether in liquid or solid form, should be put in connection with the emergence of the first agro-pastoral communities and the emergence of complex economies from the Neolithic onwards (Weller 2002). In addition, the earliest traces of salt production in Europe have been found in the eastern Carpathians (Ursulescu 1977; 1995; Dumitroaia 1987; Weller and Dumitroaia 2005; Weller *et al.* 2010a). Concurrently with these first archaeological evidences, which complete our systematic surveys conducted since 2004 (Weller *et al.* 2007; 2010b), the rise and flourishing of ethnographic research (Alexianu *et al.* 1992; 2011)[1] emphasised the fundamental role of this resource in human and animal alimentation, in the preparation and preservation of food, as well as in the consolidation and socio-economic development of the human communities.

The spatial relations between the Moldavian salt springs and the Neolithic and Chalcolithic settlement patterns (6000-3500 BC) were first underlined by a geographer from the University of Iași in the late 1950s (Șandru 1952; 1961). For the first time ever in Moldavia, this researcher advanced the hypothesis that salt was a resource that fostered stability and development among the Cucuteni communities. At the same time, the discovery and excavation of the Chalcolithic settlement from Poduri-*Dealul Ghindaru* in Bacău County (*e.g.* Monah *et al.* 2003), in a region that abounds in salt springs, stimulated approaches of a spatial standpoint, initially focused on Neamț County (*e.g.* Weller and Nuninger 2005; Weller *et al.* 2011; Brigand and Weller 2012). We present in these pages a first study conducted for the entire region of Moldavia (fig. 3).

Ethnoarchaeological Background

The specificity of the Moldavian landscape is a unity of place seldom found in European ethnoarchaeological studies, in terms of both traditional practices still very much alive, and in archaeological remains attesting the antiquity and continuity of these salt extraction points for almost 8000 years. Of the nearly 189 salt springs surveyed in Moldavia by the French-Romanian team, 21 have yielded traces of Neolithic or Chalcolithic exploitation. Less than half (8) require confirmation through archaeological soundings and radiocarbon dating (fig. 3). The 19 rock-salt outcrops, found almost exclusively in Vrancea County and along the Carpathian curvature, have not yet provided evidence of ancient exploitation.

Salt exploitation generally comes with large amounts of fragmentary coarse pottery in the immediate proximity of the sodium chloride waters. Some are intensively exploited during the first Neolithic, for instance the springs from

---

1   Research carried out within the framework of a French-Romanian collaboration, conducted in Romania through two CNCS (Romanian National Research Council) research projects (2007-2010; 2011-2014) managed by M. Alexianu (for a presentation of the goals and the most recent results, see Alexianu *et al.* 2012), and an archaeological mission of the French Ministry of Foreign and European Affairs overseen by O. Weller after 2004.

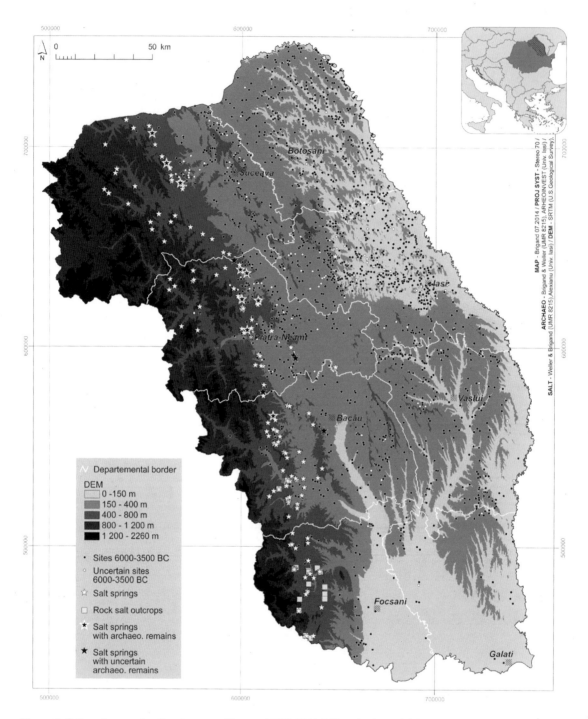

Figure 3. Salt springs, rock-salt outcrops, settlement (6000-3500 BC) and salt-exploitation sites.

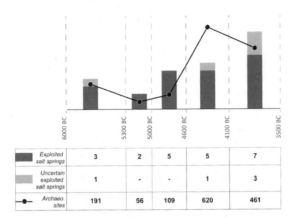

	6000 BC	5300 BC	5000 BC	4600 BC	4100 BC	3500 BC
■ Exploited salt springs	3	2	5	5	7	
▦ Uncertain exploited salt springs	1	-	-	1	3	
●— Archaeo. sites	191	56	109	620	461	

Figure 4. Chart of the evolution of salt springs exploitation and of the population dynamics during the Neolithic and Chalcolithic of Moldavia. The sites for which the chronology has not been established or questionable are not taken into account. 6000-5300 BC: Criş, 5300-5000 BC: Linear Pottery, 5000-4600 BC: Precucuteni, 4600-4100 BC: Cucuteni A, 4100-3500 BC: Cucuteni A-B and B.

Ţolici-*Hălăbutoaia* (Neamţ)[2], Oglinzi-*Băi* (Neamţ) and Oglinzi-*Poiana Slatinei, zona A* (Neamţ). Almost a thousand years later, following the demographic growth and population expansion of the Cucuteni A period (fig. 4), the first briquetage appeared. Of standardised shapes and weights, they mark the inclusion of salt into the long-distance trade networks (Weller 2002) and are linked to the large-scale exploitation of the salt springs, despite the conspicuous demographic fall from the dawn of the 4th millennium BC.

The absence of briquetage and salt pans probably reflects a less-established exploitation procedure, more seasonal and often less conspicuous to archaeologists. In this sense, the research of P. Pétrequin and O. Weller on the present-day methods of exploitation of salt resources in Papua (the Indonesian New Guinea) have filled the repository on the production of crystallised salt by stressing the importance of techniques which do not use recipients, nor fired clay (Pétrequin *et al.* 2001). These observations led to interpretative models which, applied on the field to the putative exploitations of salt springs from eastern France (Pétrequin and Weller 2008), have demonstrated the use of more rudimentary techniques during the Neolithic, namely the direct salt water sprinkling of fireplace.

Also, research on the first exploitations of salt faced a major hurdle: only the production sites that produced abundant ceramics and/or accumulations of charcoal were able to be identified; those that display less intensive production practices are not identifiable, this for taphonomic (sedimentary dynamics of the slopes, leaching of springs often found near watercourses, *etc.*) as well as technical reasons (the direct use of the saline waters, without crystallisation, collecting and transportation in organic containers, *etc.*). In order to go beyond the mere representation of salt exploitation provided by field archaeological surveys, inherently limited, we have also implemented a statistical approach aimed at classifying the salt springs not only according to their salinity, but in terms of a set of typological (the nature and complexity of the catchments, depth, water flow), chemical (salinity) and ethnographic (uses) descriptors that have been systematically registered.

---

2   First mentioned by S. Marinescu-Bilcu (1974, 20), this spring was discovered by O. Weller *et al.* in 2005 (2007, 143-146). The archaeological deposit has a stratigraphy estimated at around 8 m, and extends from the Early Neolithic to the Bronze Age (Weller *et al.*, in press).

Exploratory Statistical Approach

The goal of this approach is to outline a typology of salt springs grouped in homogeneous classes, in order to focus on those that display the essential characters of an ancient exploitation.

This undertaking is based, from the outset, on the finding that the salt springs exploited during prehistoric times as well as today, have always a series of distinct characteristics: a high salinity, an important water flow, a generally complex catchment structure, a current or sub-current production of crystallised salt[3]. A factor analysis is conducted to reveal inter-data relationships. This comes prior to an HAC hierarchical ascendant classification that aims to sort the series into homogenous groups. For the construction of the space factor, it will be required to differentiate the active variables from the illustrative ones, which do not affect the analysis, but which nevertheless help for the interpretation of the groups. The qualitative variables are the following:

- Catchment: simple (dugout trunk, wells in square wooden fittings or assembled planks), complex (composite wells, cistern-wells, platform), stone or concrete, pit, not available;
- Depth: reduced (below 1 m), medium (1-3 m), high (over 3 m), not available;
- Water flow: none, weak, moderate, strong, not available;
- Salinity: slightly saline (10-30 g/l), moderately saline (30-80 g/l), very saline (80-110 g/l), exceptionally saline (over 110 g/l);
- Use: ignigenous salt and common use, common (domestic) use, therapeutic, not used, not available;
- Archaeology: presence of pre- and proto-historic, medieval, modern and contemporary vestiges.

Because our aim is to identify the springs likely to have been exploited in the past by human communities (high salinity, strong water flow, *etc.*), the 'archaeology' variable will not be used, so that it does not influence the construction of the factorial axes. It is, nonetheless, kept as an illustrative variable. The results of the factorial analysis and of the HAC of the salt springs are presented in figure 5; excluded from the statistical analysis are the undetermined salt springs (generally those not surveyed), the mineral (sulphurous) springs, and the rock-salt outcrops, nevertheless present in the final document. The number of classes (2) is determined from reading the dendogram generated by the automated classification.

Class 1 (37 entries, 19.6%) is formed by a coherent group of springs. It comprises foremost springs with extremely or very saline waters, captured in complex structures, with high (to medium) depths. The contribution of the descriptor 'ignigenous salt' is particularly important because almost all the springs where production of *huscă* is attested are part of this class, despite the absence of some

---

3 Practically, some of these springs have been used for the production of ignigenous salt (Rmn. *huscă*) distributed on a local as well as regional scale (*e.g.* Alexianu *et al.* 2011).

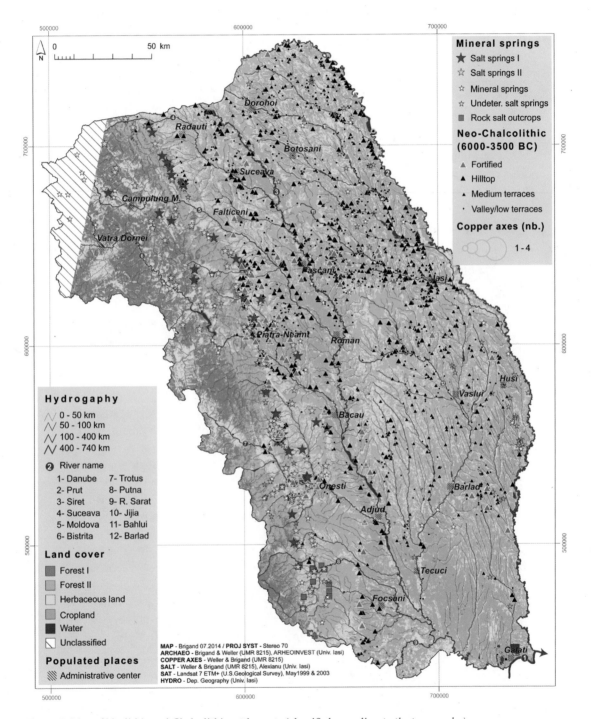

Mineral springs
★ Salt springs I
☆ Salt springs II
☆ Mineral springs
☆ Undeter. salt springs
■ Rock salt outcrops

Neo-Chalcolithic (6000-3500 BC)
▲ Fortified
▲ Hilltop
▲ Medium terraces
· Valley/low terraces

Copper axes (nb.)
1 - 4

Hydrogaphy
0 - 50 km
50 - 100 km
100 - 400 km
400 - 740 km

River name
1- Danube   7- Trotus
2- Prut   8- Putna
3- Siret   9- R. Sarat
4- Suceava 10- Jijia
5- Moldova 11- Bahlui
6- Bistrita 12- Barlad

Land cover
Forest I
Forest II
Herbaceous land
Cropland
Water
Unclassified

Populated places
Administrative center

MAP - Brigand 07.2014 / PROJ SYST - Stereo 70
ARCHAEO - Brigand & Weller (UMR 8215), ARHEOINVEST (Univ. Iasi)
COPPER AXES - Weller & Brigand (UMR 8215)
SALT - Weller & Brigand (UMR 8215), Alexianu (Univ. Iasi)
SAT - Landsat 7 ETM+ (U.S.Geological Survey), May1999 & 2003
HYDRO - Dep. Geography (Univ. Iasi)

Figure 5. Map of Neolithic and Chalcolithic settlements (classified according to the topography), copper axes, salt resources (sorted by their typological, chemical and ethnographic descriptors), and land occupation (supervised classification of Landsat images).

variables. The salt springs exploited in prehistory are well represented in this class[4]. Some are not, because of typological or chemical descriptors (*i.e.* catchment and salinity) not consistent with the group in its whole.

Class 2 (152 entries, 80.4%) is mostly made up by rudimentary and unspecified catchments, with variable water flow (practically absent, weak and medium), and where the uses are domestic or not specified, sometimes therapeutic and hardly ever for the production of ignigenous salt. Their depth varies, it is generally low to medium and unspecified. The salinity likewise varies, from weakly to very saline. This class also gathers the entries for which a number of descriptors are missing, basically for taphonomic reasons (lost, clogged or replaced springs).

Geo/Archaeological Database & Dynamics

The elaboration of the archaeological map of Moldavia, limited to the Neolithic (*c.* 6000-5000 BC) and the Chalcolithic (*c.* 5000-3500 BC), was made possible by the development of a georeferenced database comprising all information available from inventories and contributions published since the 1970s. It only contains the definite sites and those for which the georeferencing is certain; the database has information on 1641 sites dating between 6000 BC and 3500 BC, of a total of 1989 sites. The database on 'copper axes', populated by 57 entries, is built starting from various articles and inventory records published by I. Mareş (2002), updated and enhanced in 2012.

Owing to this wealth of information, it was possible to develop an exhaustive archaeological database, precise in terms of the discovery contexts, the nature of the artefacts, the quality of the geographical position in the GIS, *etc.* A major problem arose when it came to qualifying the nature of the archaeological sites. A first important criterion is the presence or absence of anthropic fortifications. We acknowledge that on account of the sometimes elusive character of defensive works as the sites taphonomy, it is possible that many habitations were fortified and because of land levelling, due to agricultural work or erosion, the still-standing vestiges or the ditches have disappeared and are perceivable only through extensive digging. Despite this limitation, the presence/absence of defensive structures constitutes the first level of hierarchy that we took into account (fig. 5).

The nature of the artefacts discovered during field surveys or excavations should help define another level. Nevertheless, considering the fact that a large majority of sites remain poorly defined, insufficiently prospected and unequally documented, how should one elaborate a typology of sites using unspecified descriptors?

---

4   For the most important: Țolici-*Hălăbutoaia* (Petricani, Neamț), Oglinzi-*Poiana Slatinei* (Răucesti, Neamț), Voitinel-*Slatină* (Gălănesti, Suceava), Solca-*Slatina Mare* (Solca, Suceava), Cucuieți-*Slatina Veche* (Solont, Bacau), Ghindăoani-*Slatină* (Balțătești, Neamț), Negritești-*Slatina Mare* (Podoleni, Neamț). The springs that have traces of Neolithic exploitation and which have not been included into this class are the following: Balțătești-*Slatina A* (Balțătești, Neamț), Garcina-*Slatina C* & *Slatina III* (Garcina, Neamț), Oglinzi-*Băi* (Răucești, Neamț), Tazlău-*Slătioara* (Tazlău, Neamț).

A classification of sites has therefore been attempted by taking into account their topographic situation. We will follow in this regard a paradigm of Romanian archaeological research, which, after the 1970s, used topographic criteria to distinguish between different types of habitats. As such, we find in the old registries of N. Zaharia *et al.* (1970, 32-34), D. Monah and Ş. Cucoş (1985, 42-43), or in the more recent ones of M.-C. Văleanu (2003, 49-51) and D. Boghian (2004, 56), a more-or-less elaborate classification between high, medium and low positioning of archaeological sites. The GIS and the morphometric analysis applied to a DEM (Digital Elevation Model) with a medium resolution (SRTM, corrected, refined and resampled at 50 m) allows to control multiple natural processes (such as the slope, solar exposure, *etc.*) by automating this procedure (Wilson and Gallant 2000; Conolly and Lake 2006; Rodier 2011).

In this line of thought, we used the 'topographic position index' (TPI), which allows a comparison of the elevation of each cell with the average one of a given surrounding: a negative value represents the lowest areas in relation to their immediate environment (valley, thalweg), while a positive one corresponds to an area much higher than its vicinity (peak, ridge, headland). The archaeological database is therefore enhanced by this value, which is then used to classify the sites according to their position within the landscape. The classification proposed (fig. 5) according to 3 classes (HAC) thus distinguishes the elevated sites, the valley ones, and those located in intermediary positions, generally on slopes. A note should be made that this is by no means a ranking of archaeological sites, since only a single descriptor has been considered (TPI). It will be necessary to introduce further variables, starting with the cultural ones (duration of habitation, richness of the settlement, *etc.*).

Two other descriptors derived from topography are used: the 'topographic openness' and the 'total viewshed'. The former is a basic morphometric analysis, which provides an adequate apprehension for the main models (Yokoama *et al.* 2002). It consists in considering, for each pixel, the line of sight over 8 azimuths, and in measuring both convexity and concavity. The second descriptor determines the total viewshed (Llobera 2003). It defines, for each pixel, the number of pixels that can see it. Considering that this analysis produces for the entire landscape a visibility potential, it can be compared to the topographic openness, which, depending on a different computation, will determine if a pixel is located in an open or closed visual landscape. Particularly time-consuming and requiring computer resources which are rarely available, this particular computation was performed for a dense set of points (every 2 km, nearly 130,000 points) and an 8 km viewshed radius.

The scaled values of the topographic index, the landscape openness and the total visibility of each site were converted into statistics in order to evaluate, from 6000 BC to 3500 BC, the evolution of the contexts of the sites (fig. 6). We similarly established shares per class of soils (pedological map, at a 1:200,000 scale, reclassified): class 1- valley soils, little or moderately fertile, generally young and weakly developed, sometimes waterlogged; class 2- very fertile soils with high contents of organic matter (chernozems); class 3- soils of high plateaus often under

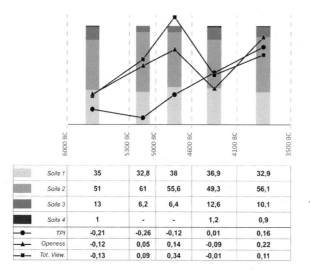

		6000 BC	5300 BC	5000 BC	4600 BC	4100 BC	3500 BC
	Soils 1	35	32,8	38	36,9	32,9	
	Soils 2	51	61	55,6	49,3	56,1	
	Soils 3	13	6,2	6,4	12,6	10,1	
	Soils 4	1	-	-	1,2	0,9	
—●—	TPI	-0,21	-0,26	-0,12	0,01	0,16	
—▲—	Openess	-0,12	0,05	0,14	-0,09	0,22	
—■—	Tot. View.	-0,13	0,09	0,34	-0,01	0,11	

Figure 6. Diagram of the evolution of the sites contexts between 6000 and 3500 BC (for the chronology of the different cultural phases, see fig. 4). The values represent the percentage of habitation sites by soil class and for the topographic index, openness and total visibility, to the average scaled values set for chrono-cultural phase.

forest covering, of limited productivity for agriculture and suitable for livestock farming; class 4- altitude soils unsuitable for agriculture.

Salt attractivity

Starting from the GIS-based tools and an abundant dedicated literature, the objective is to propose a map cost-distance of salt resources in the pre-Carpathian area, expressed in time units (fig. 7). The computation of the anisotropic distances is particularly useful for our study, since it takes into account various elements of the landscape, starting with the slope and the land occupation. The determination procedure first consists in defining a friction surface, which sets the degree of constraint affecting movement. Its energy cost is primarily dependent on the value of the slope, but also of the vegetation cover, although it is difficult to evaluate for the targeted periods. We believe, nonetheless, that the elevated forests bordering the study area to the west were similarly a hindrance to human movements during the recent prehistory. Also, the resulting friction surface (or cost) takes into account a 20% forest covering. It is therefore 80% of the friction surface that the topographic surface alleges.

The rest of the procedure uses the 'path distance' function in ArcMap to obtain an estimation of the anisotropic time, which means that the direction of movement (to the springs, in our case) is taken into account. The Reciprocal Tobler's Hiking Function consists in an anisotropic distance calculation largely distributed. The values of the slope is used for augmenting or reducing the cost incurred by the crossing of each pixel; a 0-slope gradient has the lowest cost and, conversely, a value over 70 degrees has the highest cost. The speed of movement used in this study is 5 km/h. These values are subsequently converted into time slots representing the distance-time expended to reach a salt spring (fig. 7). They are determined through the use of a vertical factor taking into account the relation between the value of the

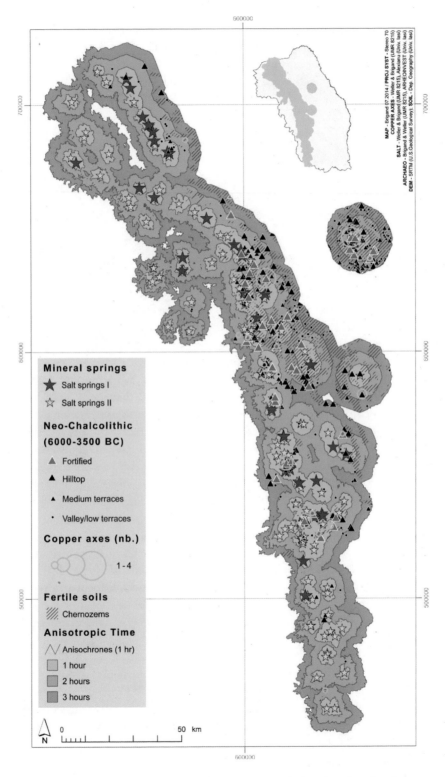

Figure 7. Anisochrones representing the travel distances to the salt springs (one hour interval).

slope and the cost incurred[5]. The map of distances-times is stopped at three hours. Within this radius and according to a one-hour interval, we have measured the number of fortified settlements, unfortified sites, and copper axes (fig. 8), as well as the dynamics of the attractiveness of salt springs between 6000 and 3500 BC (fig. 9).

Final Discussion

The analyses presented in these pages allow us to draft a synthesis on the forms and dynamics of settling in the Moldavian Neolithic and Chalcolithic, in interaction with the natural resources and the landscape.

Regional Distribution

The archaeological sites are distributed to the east of the Carpathian range; the salt springs form the western limit of settling area, especially in the pre-Carpathian depression delimited by the Bistriţa and the Moldova rivers (fig. 5). The main area of settling is found at heights of about 200 m on average: the lowest sites are found on the Moldavian Plain and the low alluvial valleys of the Siret, Prut and Bârlad rivers; the highest ones on the first plateau (pre-Carpathian depression – the Suceava Plateau), the Central Plateau and the Curvature Carpathians. The highest sites (over 500 m) are distributed homogeneously in the narrow and deeply furrowed valleys that characterise the Carpathian piedmont; they are all linked to saliferous areas – particularly where there are springs with a strong attraction value (class 1), save for the site from Agăş-În *Spatele Gării* (Agăş, Bacău County) located in the high valley of the Trotuş River, and Hangu (Chiriţeni, Neamţ County).

These sites in high altitude are nevertheless rare. Could this be a consequence of the level of archaeological investigation and thus an effect related to the exhaustiveness of archaeological map? As a matter of fact, since these pre-mountainous environments are largely occupied by dense tree vegetation, the archaeological surveying is quite difficult. It is nevertheless possible to suggest that the climate, the elevation and the scarcity of agronomic resources contributed to a low density of occupation, which in these sectors remain almost exclusively focused on the saliferous resources. We bet that future research focused on the pre-Carpathian forested areas, ever more so thanks to the recent tools of remote sensing (LIDAR), will allow us to document even more precisely the occupation of the Carpathian foothills.

Where contemporary anthropic pressure is most important, the archaeological density is consistent. This is particularly true for the sectors south of the Moldavian Plain (the valleys of the Bahlui, Bahluieţ and Jijia valleys). Elsewhere, particularly in Botoşani and Vaslui counties, occupation is widespread and does not seem to be particularly concentrated, with a few exceptions (notably east of Bârlad or between

---

5   For three salt springs found in distinct topographic sectors – the Carpathians: Ceahlău-*Slatină* (Ceahlău, Neamţ); Moldavian Plateau: Ţolici-*Hălăbutoaia* (Petricani, Neamţ); Moldavian Plain: Balş-*Arcaci* (Târgu Frumos, Iaşi) – field walking tests conducted on the occasion support the results presented here.

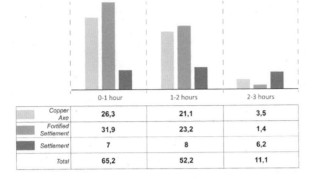

	0-1 hour	1-2 hours	2-3 hours
Copper Axe	26,3	21,1	3,5
Fortified Settlement	31,9	23,2	1,4
Settlement	7	8	6,2
Total	65,2	52,2	11,1

Figure 8. Percentages of copper axes, fortified and unfortified settlements, within less than one, two and three walk hours from a salt spring.

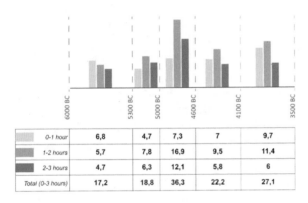

6000 BC   5300 BC   5000 BC   4600 BC   4100 BC   3500 BC

	6000 BC	5300 BC	5000 BC	4600 BC	4100 BC	3500 BC
0-1 hour	6,8		4,7	7,3	7	9,7
1-2 hours	5,7		7,8	16,9	9,5	11,4
2-3 hours	4,7		6,3	12,1	5,8	6
Total (0-3 hours)	17,2		18,8	36,3	22,2	27,1

Figure 9. Percentages of habitation sites within less than one, two and three walk hours from a salt spring.

the Prut and Dorohoi; also note that where the land occupation is largely comprised of herbaceous or forest surfaces, the Neolithic and Chalcolithic population density is low or even absent): the Tutova hills, the central plateau south of Iaşi and, generally speaking, the piedmont area between Rădăuţi and Fălticeni or south of Piatra Neamţ.

Does that mean that the distribution map does not objectively reflect ancient occupation, but rather a reflection of the intensity of archaeological surveys, as in the nature of the land cover? Let us consider for instance the weak prehistoric occupation of the area delimited by the Focşani-Bârlad-Galaţi triangle. Does it reflect a modest occupation pattern, or just limited archaeological prospecting? It is difficult to decide, and it is possible that the conjunction of these two factors contribute to an apparent shortcoming on the archaeological map. Nevertheless, despite this limitation, it is possible to provide a summary of the key characteristics of settling, particularly by focusing on the population dynamics between the Criş and the Cucuteni A-B and B periods.

General Dynamics

Figure 4 provides a pertinent image of the evolution of the number of sites between 6000 and 3500 BC. A significant decline occurred between the Criş (*c.* 6000-5300 BC) and the Linear Pottery (*c.* 5300-5000) periods, perhaps due to a difficulty in identifying sites in eastern Romania. From the Precucuteni (*c.* 5000-4600) onwards, we observe a manifest increase in the number of sites that reached their peak during the Cucuteni A (*c.* 4600-4100). This particularly high value reflects, without a doubt, an unprecedented demographic outburst, as well as a very strong territorial investment. It also indicates a reorganization of the settling processes, based on structuring of the territories clearly distinct from the previous periods. This is how the establishment of new agro-pastoral practices, based on an increased mobility of the domestic units, could equally explain the notably large number of sites from the Cucuteni A phase (Lazarovici and Lazarovici 2003, 413).

In what concerns the Cucuteni A-B, researchers have already noticed that the relatively low number of sites for this period (148 sites calibrated with certainty) is more a reflection of the research linked to difficulties in identification, than a sign of demographic retraction (Zaharia *et al.* 1970, 33; Boghian 2004, 57; Petrescu-Dîmbovița and Văleanu 2004, 335). For example, in Moldavia, around 60 sites assigned to the Cucuteni A-B were the result of a planned archaeological action. As we are more interested in the settling forms and dynamics, it seems opportune to regroup the Cucuteni A-B sites with the Cucuteni B ones, since the distinguishing elements of the two periods are, in the absence of extensive archaeological investigations, almost impossible to define only on the ground of surface material. This chronological simplification within a single chrono-cultural period is also based on the fact that more than 40% of the sites assigned to the Cucuteni A-B continue during the Cucuteni B phase. Thus, in general, we note between Cucuteni A on the one hand, and Cucuteni A-B and B (*c.* 4100-3500 BC) on the other, a demographic relapse marked by a notable reduction in the number of habitations, generally well reflected in the literature (*e.g.* Boghian 2004, 55)[6].

Soils and settling

From 6000 to 3500 BC, the lands occupied are more or less the same (fig. 6): foremost the fertile soils of the chernozem type, followed by the less fertile soils of the great alluvial valleys, and then, of marginal share, the high-altitude soils with very limited agricultural output. However, changes in the occupation shares according to the soil typology deserve clarification. During the Criş period, we observe that the high-elevation soils (classes 3 and 4) are occupied to an unprecedented level throughout the entire time span, not much so during the Cucuteni A, and to a lesser extent during the Cucuteni A-B and B. This occupation shows a more diversified occupation strategy than it would be during the Linear Pottery and Precucuteni periods, during which the very fertile soils of the chernozem type were favoured. This finding profiles the first settling wave associated to the exploration of the different types of terrains. We observe this dynamics in the Cucuteni A period, during which the demographic growth is reflected in the occupation of a very varied range of ecosystems. Nevertheless, regardless of the area and period

---

6   Also observe that almost 45% of the Cucuteni A-B sites are located in Botoşani county. Here, the number of Cucuteni A-B sites in relation the number of Cucuteni A or B ones is relatively equal, which contrasts sharply with what has been ascertained for other counties in Moldavia. We consider that this reflects a research bias depending on the different scientific strategies and competencies across the territory, rather than a prehistoric reality.

considered, the archaeological sites are spread in ecotone contexts, that is to say in the proximity of different pedological contexts, so that the types of accessible resources are varied.

Topographic contexts

The Criş sites are found in low areas and on terraces near minor watercourses characterised by modest hydrographic regimes, those that emerge from low values of the topographic index, topographic openness and total viewshed (fig. 6). With the Linear Pottery period, the topographic index decreases significantly: it reflects a continuing tendency to settle valleys and in the proximity of watercourses. However, the increase in the openness value as well as that of total visibility leads to crucial observations: although in their majority valley ones, the sites are henceforth established in more open environments and where the visual field is noticeably wider. This finding, which corroborates the increase in visibility observed in Iaşi and Neamţ counties (Brigand *et al.* 2012; Brigand and Weller 2013, 202-203), supports the idea that this period witnessed the emergence of the first coherent territorial pattern that was based on important establishments likely to exert an efficient control of the territory.

The first half of the 5th millennium BC saw a radical evolution of the topographic contexts. Right away, we observe that the high and middle terraces are preferred, reflecting a tendency to establish habitations on widely opened promontories, where the degree of submission to the view factor is particularly high. Accordingly, habitations are founded in large alluvial valleys – beginning with that of the Bistriţa, downstream from Piatra Neamţ – and directly involved in the control of the main communication routes. Apart from the value of the topographic index, which continues to increase during the Cucuteni A – reflecting the surge in the number of hilltop habitations – the value of landscape openness, as that linked to the total visibility, drops drastically. This is a result of the diversification of forms of occupation observed during the second half of the 5th millennium BC. Although most of them were perched on headland, the settlements of the Middle Chalcolithic now occupy a wide variety of valleys, both large and visually very wide, or very narrow and with very reduced visibility. This trend reversed again at the end of the Cucuteni: the high values of all the topographic index values seem to underline a territorial reorganisation resulting in a shift towards habitations located in the wide alluvial valleys and, in fact, the abandonment of the marginal areas occupied during the Cucuteni A.

Salt attractiveness

Proximity analyses are common in prehistoric archaeology, especially when it comes to measuring the distance between a source of raw materials and the objects from which they come. In the archaeology of salt, this method is proposed in order to highlight the correlation between objects that were socially valued and salt, the assumption being that the elites who had abundant reserves of salt were likely to similarly acquire other prestige goods. F. Harding (2013, 99-109) has engaged in this exercise and tried to establish a spatial connection between salt resources – as well as the copper and gold ones – and bronze swords. It is this methodology that we hereby take further, through the use of four data sets (the salt springs; the fortified settlements; the unfortified habitations; and the copper axes) and the presentation of the results in the time units (limited to three hours of walk from a salt spring), rather than in Euclidean distances (fig. 8). The proposed diagram eloquently presents several important results.

The percentage of unfortified sites located within a three-hours-walk radius from a salt spring remains modest (*c.* 21%) and shows no significant variations. Still, the highest value is in the time range between one and two hours (8%). A look at the archaeological map (figs. 3 and 5) clarified these results and reminds us that the majority of sites are found east of the Siret River, or much more than three hours away from a salt spring. In contrast, the percentage of fortified habitations located within a 3-hours radius around a salt spring is particularly high (*c.* 55%), and suggests a strong attractiveness of these resources and an eagerness of the prehistoric communities to control both their exploitation and the distribution of finished products. This hypothesis seems fully confirmed by the very high percentage of fortified sites located less than one hour (*c.* 32%) and between one and two hours walk (23.2%). With respect to the percentage of long copper axes, our observations are in the same line: a concentration of wealth in an area near the salt resources, at less than one hour walk (*c.* 26%), and between one and two hours (*c.* 21%).

It is as if the exploitation of salt and the distribution of salt cakes were heavily invested and controlled activities, which attracted towards these centres rare and sought after objects. The significant and gradual reduction in the number of fortified sites and copper axes, as the distance to the salt spring increases, is a paramount argument: it illustrates the attraction role of the salt resource; its capacity to stimulate the exchange of goods and to attract objects of very high social value, such as massive copper axes; its control across a very dense network of fortified settlements. Nevertheless, these results call for a series of comments on some particular areas.

- The first comment concerns the presence of the spring from Balş-*Arcaci* (Târgu Frumos, Iasi) located near the eponymous site from Cucuteni and therefore in an extremely rich archaeological environ (Petrescu-Dîmboviţa and Văleanu 2004; Brigand *et al.* 2014). The integration of this ancient spring, whose uses are well documented by ethnography (Weller *et al.* 2007, 175-177)[7] is legitimate even though it is not without some questions as to its marginal position in relation to other salt springs from the pre-Carpathian area.

---

7   This source of salt water marked on the territory of the village of Băiceni, identified thanks to the decisive intervention of V. Cotiugă from the University of Iaşi and the former Cucuteni mayor (I. Tun), is located in an area of salty soils characterised by abundant halophile vegetation. Though abandoned in the 1960s, we were able to obtain a series of precious information both on the nature of the catchment system (in stone wells of *c.* 1 m in depth) and on the uses made by the locals (preserving food and as fodder, production of crystallized salt, *etc.*).

- The second comment is about the existence, to the east of Piatra Neamț and of Cracău, of soils that have a very high agronomic potential. The intensity of archaeological occupation in this area can be explained both by the presence of very rich soils (fig. 7) – see the chernozem peninsula vaunted by P. Enculescu (cf. Lupaşcu 1996, 83) – and also by the abundance and accessibility of very saline springs that display all the characteristics of a prehistoric exploitation (fig. 5).

What about the settlement dynamics close to sodium chloride springs? Figure 9 provides some answers, showing a steady increase in the number of sites within the three-hours radius around a salt spring, between 6000 and 3500 BC. Only the Precucuteni seems singular, with a share of 36% of sites. This increase in the vicinity of salt during the first half of the 5th millennium BC occurs simultaneously with the intensification of the salt springs exploitation, especially starting with the Linear Pottery (fig. 4). This enhanced occupation of the areas near the salt springs seems nonetheless to favour areas found between one and two hours walk (*c.* 17%), or even two and three hours walk (*c.* 12%), over those at less than one hour walk (*c.* 7%).

This dynamics reflects a characteristic of the Precucuteni occupation that we have already observed elsewhere (Brigand and Weller 2013, 203-204): the immediate vicinity of a salt spring is rarely settled; on the contrary, the control of the access to the salt and of the main waterway outlets seems to be a priority of the Chalcolithic communities. The very high values of the total viewshed and of the landscape openness (fig. 6) clearly show that it is the control of the communication and exchange routs which is at the centre of the territorial strategies of the Precucuteni period. During the Cucuteni A, but especially during the Cucuteni A-B and B, there is a strengthening of the occupation of areas located at less than one hour from the salt spring, despite a notable decline in the population (fig. 4); we witness an escalation of the process of appropriation of the salt resources, concurrently with a heightened and reorganised territorial control (fig. 6).

In general, the habitation sites appear to favour the areas found between one and two hours walk from the salt spring (fig. 8). There is nevertheless an exception, the Criş period, during which the largest share is taken by sites located between two and three hours walk from the source. This observation supports the idea outlined after having examined the context of the settlement – especially the agronomical ones (fig. 6): a less structured settling front involved in exploring different terrain types.

This exploratory research aimed to characterise the forms of human settling between 6000 and 3500 BC. The use of the GIS allowed us to shed light on the place of salt in the territorial and economic organisation of human societies from recent prehistoric times. This contribution stresses that the salt resources, probably as well as its circulation, were subject to an increased interest. Multiple periods emerge from the analyses presented in these pages. The Early Neolithic (Criş) appears as a first phase of colonisation during which the salt resources are explored, though without being integrated into any particularly structured form of territorial organisation. The Precucuteni appears as an experiment expected to last, which witnesses the emergence of a coherent population network sustained by elevated settlements, and of a control of the access to the salt and of its transportation. As for the Cucuteni, it is marked by the flourishing of the Chalcolithic cultures of Moldavia, as evinced by the extremely dense network of settlements involved in a manifold exploitation of various resources, be they saliferous, agronomic or pastoral.

It has sometimes been stated that the development of the Neolithisation process in Eastern Europe and the Balkans rested on the availability of salt resources and the availability of rich and fertile soils. The conjoined study of a consistent archaeological database, of an exhaustive registry of salt resources, and of the geographic contexts, allowed us to expound our assertions and to provide a solid baseline for understanding the form, as well as the dynamics of human settling in this area, across nearly three millennia.

Acknowledgements

This project is supported by the Commission for Foreign Excavations (French Ministry of Foreign Affairs), the National Centre of Scientific Research (CNRS, UMR 8215 *Trajectoires*) and the Panthéon-Sorbonne University. The present work is also supported by the project EthnosalRo managed by M. Alexianu (CNCS-UEFISCDI, PN-II-ID-PCE-2011-3-0825, 219/5.10.2011).

References

Alexianu, M., Dumitroaia, G. and Monah, D. 1992. Exploatarea surselor de apă sărată din Moldova: o abordare etnoarheologică. *Thraco-Dacica* 13/1-2, 317-327.

Alexianu, M., Weller, O., Brigand, R., Curcă, R.-G., Cotiugă, V. and Moga, I. 2011. Salt springs in today's rural world. An ethnoarchaeological approach in Moldavia (Romania). In: Alexianu, M., Weller O. and Curcă, R.-G. eds. *Archaeology and Anthropology of Salt: A Diachronic Approach.* Proceedings of the International Colloquium, 1-5 October 2008 Al. I. Cuza University (Iaşi, Romania). BAR International Series 2198. Oxford: Archaeopress, 7-23.

Alexianu, M., Weller, O. and Brigand, R. 2012. EthnosalRo: an ethnoarchaeological project on Romanian salt. *The European Archaeologist* 38, 17-22.

Boghian, D. 2004. *Comunităţile cucuteniene din bazinul Bahluiuluii.* Suceava: Ed Univ. Ştefan cel Mare.

Brigand, R., Asăndulesei, A. and Nicu, I.C. 2014. Autour de la station éponyme de Cucuteni: paysage et peuplement (Valea Oii, Iasi, Roumanie). *Tyragetia* 8/1, 89-106.

Brigand, R. and Weller, O. 2012. Natural resources and settlements dynamics during Later Prehistory in central Moldavia (Romania). An integrated GIS for spatial archaeological studies. In: Cotiugă, V. and Caliniuc, Ş. eds. *Interdisciplinarity research in archaeology.* Proceedings of the first Arheoinvest congress, 10-11 june 2011 (Iaşi, Romania). BAR International Series 2433. Oxford: Archaeopress, 1-18.

Brigand, R. and Weller, O. 2013. Neolithic and Chalcolithic settlement patterns in central Moldavia (Romania). *Documenta Praehistorica* XL, 194-207.

Conolly, J. and Lake M. 2006. *Geographical Information Systems in archaeology.* Cambridge Manuals in Archaeology. Cambridge: University Press.

Dumitroaia, G. 1987. La station archéologique de Lunca-Poiana Slatinei. In: Ursulescu, N., Monah, D. and Chirica, V. eds. *La civilisation de Cucuteni en contexte européen.* Biblioteca Archaeologica Iassiensis I. Iaşi, 253-258.

Ellis, L. 1984. *The Cucuteni-Tripolye Culture. A Study in Technology and the Origins of Complex Society.* BAR 217. Oxford: Archaeopress.

Harding, A. 2013. *Salt in Prehistoric Europe.* Leiden: Sidestone Press.

Lazarovici, G. and Lazarovici, C.M. 2003. The Neo-Eneolithic architecture in Banat, Transylvania and Moldavia. In: Grammenos, D.V. ed. *Recente Research in the Prehistory of the Balkans.* Publications of the Archaeological Institute of Northern Greece 3. Thessaloniki, 369-486.

Llobera, M. 2003. Extending GIS-based Visual Analysis: the Concept of Visualscapes. *International Journal of Geographical Information Science* 17/1, 25-48.

Lupaşcu, G. 1996. *Depresiunea Cracău-Bistriţa. Studiu pedogeografic.* Iaşi: Corson.

Mareş, I. 2002. *Metalurgia aramei în neo-eneoliticul României.* Suceava: Cetate de Scaun.

Mareş, I. 2012. *Metalurgia aramei* în *civilizaţiile Precucuteni şi Cucuteni.* Suceava: Ed Univ. Ştefan cel Mare.

Marinescu-Bîlcu, S. 1974. *Cultura Precucuteni pe teritoriul României.* Bucharest: Ed. Academiei Republicii Socialiste România.

Meruţiu, V. 1912. Sarea în pământul românesc. *Buletinul Societăţii Regale Române de Geografie* 33/1–2, 69-162.

Monah, D. and Cucoş, Ş. 1985. *Aşezările culturii Cucuteni din Romania.* Iaşi: Junimea.

Monah, D., Dumitroaia, G., Monah, F., Preoteasa, C., Munteanu, R. and Nicola, D. 2003. *Poduri-Dealul Ghindaru. O Troie în Subcarpaţii Moldovei.* Piatra Neamţ: Constantin Matasă.

Pétrequin, P. and Weller, O. 2008. L'exploitation préhistorique des sources salées dans le Jura français. Application et critiques d'un modèle prédictif. In: Weller, O., Dufraisse, A. and Pétrequin, P. eds. *Sel, eau et forêt. D'hier à aujourd'hui.* Cahiers de la MSHE 12. Besançon: Presses Universitaires de Franche-Comté, 255-279.

Pétrequin, P., Weller, O., Gauthier, E., Dufraisse, A. and Piningre J.-F. 2001. Salt springs exploitations without pottery during Prehistory. From new Guinea to the French Jura. In: Pétrequin, P. and Beyries, S. eds. *Ethno-archaeology and its transfert.* BAR International Series 983. Oxford: Archaeopress, 37-65.

Petrescu-Dîmboviţa, M. and Văleanu, M.C. 2004. *Cucuteni-Cetăţuie. Monografie arheologică.* Bibliotheca Memoriae Antiquitatis XIV. Piatra-Neamţ: Constantin Matasă.

Rodier, X. ed. 2011. *Information spatiale et archéologie.* Paris: Errance.

Şandru, I. 1952. Contribuţii geografico-economice asupra exploatării slatinelor în Bucovina de Sud. *Studii şi Cercetări Ştiinţifice* 1–4/III, 407-428.

Şandru, I. 1961. Contribuţii geografice economice asupra evoluţiei aşezărilor omeneşti în depresiunea subcarpatică Oneşti. *Analele Ştiinţifice ale Universităţii "Al. I. Cuza" din Iaşi*, VII, fasc. 1, 215-230.

Văleanu, M.-C. 2003. *Aşezări Neo-eneolitice din Moldova*. Iaşi: Helios.

Velcea, V. and Savu, A. 1982. *Geografia Carpaţilor şi a subcarpaţilor Românesti*. Bucharest: Ed. Didactică si pedagogică.

Ursulescu, N. 1977. Exploatarea sării din saramură în neoliticul timpuriu, în lumina descoperirilor de la Solca (jud. Suceava). *Studii şi Cercetări de Istorie Veche* 28/3, 307-317.

Ursulescu, N. 1995. L'utilisation des sources salées dans le néolithique de la Moldavie (Roumanie). In: Otte, M. ed. *Nature et culture*. ERAUL 68. Liège, 487-495.

Weller, O. 2002. Aux origines de la production du sel en Europe. Vestiges ; fonctions et enjeux archéologiques. In: Weller, O. ed. *Archéologie du sel: techniques et sociétés dans la Pré et Protohistoire européenne*. Internationale Archäologie, ASTK 3. Rahden: VML GmbH, 163-175.

Weller, O., Brigand, R. and Alexianu, M. 2007. Cercetări sistematice asupra izvoarelor de apă sărată din Moldova. Bilanţul explorărilor din anii 2004-2007 efectuate în special în judeţul Neamţ. *Memoria Antiquitatis* 24, 121-190.

Weller, O., Brigand, R. and Alexianu, M. 2010b. Recherches systématiques autour des sources salées de Moldavie. Bilan des prospections 2008-2010. *Memoria Antiquitatis* 25/26, 437-504.

Weller, O., Brigand, R., Nuninger, L. and Dumitroaia, G. 2011. Spatial analysis of Prehistoric salt exploitation in Eastern Carpathians (Romania). In: Alexianu, M., Weller O. and Curcă, R.-G. eds. *Archaeology and Anthropology of Salt: A Diachronic Approach*. Proceedings of the International Colloquium, 1-5 October 2008 Al. I. Cuza University (Iaşi, Romania). BAR International Series 2198. Oxford: Archaeopress, 69-80.

Weller, O., Brigand, R., Dumitroaia, G., Garvăn, D. and Munteanu, R. 2015 (in press). A pinch of salt in the Prehistoric Eastern Carpathians Mountains (Romania). In: Alexianu, M., Curcă, R.-G. and Cotiugă, V. eds. *Salt Effect*. 2nd international symposium ArheoInvest, Univ. Al.I. Cuza, april 2012, Iaşi (Romania). BAR International Series. Oxford: Archaeopress.

Weller, O. and Dumitroaia, G. 2005. The earliest salt production in the world. An early Neolithic exploitation in Poiana Slatinei-Lunca, Romania. *Antiquity* 79, 306.

Weller, O., Dumitroaia, G., Sordoillet, D., Dufraisse, A., Gauthier, E. and Munteanu, R. 2010a. Lunca-*Poiana Slatinei* (jud. Neamţ): Cel mai veche sit de exploatara a sării din preistoria europeană. Cercetări interdisciplinare. *Arheologia Moldovei* 32, 2009, 21-39.

Weller, O. and Nuninger, L. 2005. Les eaux salées de Moldavie roumaine: étude interdisciplinaire autour d'une ressource structurante du territoire. In: Berger, J.-F., Bertoncello, F., Braemer, F., Davtian, G. and Gazenbeek, M. eds. *Temps et espaces de l'homme en société. Analyses et modèles spatiaux en archéologie.* XXVe rencontres internationales d'archéologie et d'histoire d'Antibes. Antibes: APDCA, 511-516.

Wilson, J.P. and Gallant, J.C. ed. 2000. *Terrain analysis. Principles and applications.* New-York: Wiley.

Yokoama, R., Shirasawa, M. and Pike, R.J. 2002. Visualizing topography by openness: a new application of image processing to digital elevation models. *Photogrammetric Engineering and Remote Sensing* 68, 251-266.

Zaharia, N., Petrescu-Dîmbovița, M. and Zaharia, E. 1970. *Așezări din Moldova. De la Paleolitic și pînă în secolul al XVIII-lea.* Bucharest: Ed. Academiei Republicii Socialiste România.

Part Four

Historical themes

The salt of Rome. Remarks on the production, trade and consumption in the north-western provinces

Ulrich STOCKINGER

University of Cologne, Archaeological Institute, Albertus-Magnus-Platz, 50923 Cologne, Germany

Abstract. In spite of the 'white gold's' eminent importance for daily life in the *Roman Empire* and numerous pre- and protohistoric studies dedicated to this topic, this resource has not received intensified attention in the archaeological research on the Rhine and Danube provinces until the last few decades. Several research projects suggest a collapse of inland salt extraction and a shift of the production sites to the coastlines in connection with the integration of Central Europe into Rome's sphere of control. This study compiles some of the scattered evidence for salt extraction in this region from the imperial period and discusses the demand and the channels of trade, as well as the economic importance of this mineral resource. The site of Michlhallberg (Bad Aussee, Austria) and connected trade routes leading to *Ovilava* resp. *Virunum* illustrate that some rock salt deposits in the eastern Alpine area were extracted in Roman times.

Keywords. Antiquity, Central Europe, Roman Empire, trade, diet.

Résumé. Malgré l'importance éminente de « l'or blanc » pour la vie quotidienne dans l'Empire romain et de nombreuses études pré- et protohistoriques consacrées à ce sujet, cette ressource, jusque dans les décennies récentes, n'a pas attiré l'attention intensive des chercheurs sur les provinces rhéno-danubiennes. Plusieurs projets de recherche suggèrent un déclin de la saliculture intérieure et un déplacement des centres de production vers les zones maritimes, évolutions liées à l'intégration de l'Europe centrale dans le monde romain. Cette étude compile quelques-unes des traces éparses de la production saline dans cette région pendant la période impériale et discute la demande, les routes commerciales ainsi que l'importance économique de cette ressource minérale. Le site de Michlhallberg (Bad Aussee, Autriche) et les voies commerciales qui le reliaient avec *Ovilava* respectivement *Virunum* indiquent que certains gisements de sel gemme dans la région alpine orientale ont été exploités à l'époque romaine.

Mots-clés. Antiquité, Europe centrale, Empire romain, commerce, alimentation.

Salt played a vital role for the functioning of both economy and society until the modern age. Cassiodorus' remark that "*potest aurum aliquis minus quaerere, nemo est qui salem non desideret invenire*" (Cassiod. *var.* 12.24.6) pointedly illustrates the importance of this resource in Late Antiquity. Similarly to oil in the recent past, salt stimulated numerous military conflicts during the Roman Empire as well as in baroque Central Europe. After all, the use of salt was the most common method for the conservation of foods before the gradual electrification since the 1880s, thus being almost indispensable to any form of transport and storage of most perishables. Furthermore, salt served, *inter alia*, as a condiment for meals, as an important addition to livestock feed, as flux in metallurgy and for medical applications.

Rome's rise to power was closely connected to its control over the salterns on the Tiber estuary and the *via Salaria* leading to the Sabine territory (cf. Dion. Hal. *ant.* 2.55.5; Liv. 1.33.9; Plin. *nat.* 31.89; Strab. 5.3.1). Livy (Liv. 29.37.3) bears testimony to state supervisory measures as early as towards the end of the Second Punic War when censor M. Livius earned his cognomen *Salinator* by introducing a new tax on salt. In spite of the 'white gold's' eminent importance for daily life in the *Roman Empire* and numerous pre- and protohistoric studies dedicated to this topic (*e.g.* Nenquin 1961; Gouletquer 1971; Jodłowski 1977a; 1977b; Alexander 1985; Saile 2000; Fries-Knoblach 2001; Litchfield *et al.* 2001; Weller 2002; Jülich 2007; Monah *et al.* 2007; Fries-Knoblach 2010; Alexianu *et al.* 2011), this resource and merchandise has not received intensified attention in the archaeological research on the Rhine and Danube provinces until the last few decades. This study should contribute towards filling this chronological and geographical gap.

Methods and objectives

Based on a thorough compilation of different types of sources, it should be possible to roughly determine the places, routes and volumes of salt production, trade and consumption in the north-western provinces and beyond the frontiers. Thus, the predominant thesis claiming a shift of the extraction of salt in continental Europe from inland to coastlines in connection with the integration into the Roman Empire (Saile 2000, 172-175; 2013, 212-215) will be reassessed although it can only be exemplified in this article (cf. Stockinger forthcoming). In the following, the eastern Alpine area shall illustrate that salt could have acted as an important factor for the infrastructural, economic and cultural development of regions which were disadvantaged regarding the transport geography, the topography or the climate. This paper will also attempt to outline salt's economic development during the first centuries AD by comparing the isolated written documents which grant information on the organisation, administration and legal character of salt commerce.

Figure 1. Map of Central Europe with probable salt production sites from La Tène to the Early Middle Ages.

Geological situation

The area under investigation features numerous natural mineral deposits (Buschman 1909; Berg 1929, 112-118; Fulda 1938; Lotze 1938; Kollmann 1994; Walter 1995, 438-439; Hauber 1997), of which several had already been extracted before the Roman conquest of continental Europe north of the Alps in Caesarean and Augustan times (Hocquet 1994; Saile 2000; Stöllner 2012, 47-48, 65-67, 80-84). The most important salt deposits in Central Europe are situated in the area from the United Kingdom to Poland, from eastern France to south-western Germany and in the Alps (Walter 1995, 438-439). In the Alpine region, the salt formation of Upper Permian evaporate sediments had already been exploited for rock salt and natural brine in prehistory (Kern *et al.* 2008).

Production, trade and consumption of salt in the east Alps under Roman rule

The expansion of the Roman hegemony to the north of the Alps in Julio-Claudian times clearly had a significant impact on the administrative, social and economic structures in this region, not least stimulated by the extension of the road networks and the establishment of a single market with strong state control and taxation. However, this did not entail a complete collapse of the salt production in inland Europe and parallel replacement with marine salt from Mediterranean production sites. In spite of an extensive network for long-distance commerce in the Roman Empire, transport costs accounted for the greater part of most goods' prices, especially affecting merchandises which were low-priced and more difficult to transport. In unfavourable climate, the extraction of salt from marine sources could require up to ten times more combustible material than that from inland brine springs, due to the small proportion of salt (on average 3%) in sea water (Hocquet 1994, 15-18).

According to Pliny the Elder (Plin. *nat.* 31.73-83), the Roman salt producers used mainly three different raw material sources: marine water, brine springs and rock salt. Archaeological research proves that extraction included both natural (*e.g.* sun, wind, sedimentation) and anthropogenic (*e.g.* clarifying basins, artificial evaporation, mining) methods of purification, graduation and crystallisation to finally obtain sufficiently pure salt (cf. Shepherd 1980, 221-228; Bradley 1992; Woodiwiss and Bond 1992; Wollmann 1996; Grabherr 2001; Lane *et al.* 2001; Hurst 2006; Morris 2007; Lane *et al.* 2008; Williams and Reid 2008). However, the salt deposits in the eastern Alpine region are not explicitly emphasised in the Roman sources (Gostenčnik 2005; Moinier 2007).

The infrastructural development measures undertaken and the relative flourishing of topographically and agriculturally unfavourable settlements in the mountainous regions of the eastern Alps during the first centuries AD seem to document economic strength of some kind. The eponym site of the Hallstatt period drew its importance primarily from the solid rock salt deposits there, which were mined at least from the Bronze Age onwards (Kern *et al.* 2008). Numerous archaeological finds and structures document Roman presence in the high valley and in particular on the lakeside but no direct traces of montane activities have come to light so far (Igl 2008; Kern 2011, 419). This applies largely to other locations in the Salzkammergut such as Bad Dürrnberg/Hallein, Bad Ischl and Bad Reichenhall (Saile 2000, 173; Stöllner 2012, 101; Pollak 2013, 18) where salt production at least for the local demand seems probable because of the geological situation, previous production and archaeological discoveries but is not directly attested. Based on the name Ἀλαυνοί for a Noric tribe given by Ptolemy (Ptol. 2.13.2), the intensive extraction of some salt resources in the Alps during the Iron Age was not completely neglected by the Romans.

While the extent to which salt production and distribution were commercial factors for the archaeologically documented prosperity in the *vicus* of Hallstatt-Lahn and surroundings or in Bad Reichenhall is still speculative, substantial archaeological evidence for the continued extraction of Alpine rock salts in the Salzkammergut was discovered at the Michlhallberg site at the southern foot of the Sandling (Bad Aussee, Austria) (Grabherr 2001). This *vicus* was situated in the mountainous heart of *Noricum* at *c.* 1000 m above sea level but nevertheless well integrated in the provincial road network; recent surveys have shown that the Roman road made a detour climbing up the slopes of the Sandling right to Michlhallberg and connected this site with the alpine uplands of *Ovilava* in the north and *Virunum* in the south (Pollak 2003; Windholz-Konrad 2008; Pollak 2013, 15-19).

The geological situation, finds of miner's tools in the settlement, the toponym and salt extraction in the late Middle Ages and the early modern period at this site documented in literature make a Roman salt production in this area highly plausible. According to the datable finds from the excavations, the site was occupied from the later 2nd until the end of the 4th century AD; furthermore, the spectrum of fibulas might indicate the presence of soldiers or officials. Direct correlations between the establishment of this salt production site and the appointment of the *legio II Italica* to Albing resp. *Lauriacum*/Lorch after the Marcomannic Wars cannot be verified but seem worth considering since this would have caused a considerable increase in the demand for salt provisions.

Excursus on the economic value of salt in Roman times

While the importance of salt, the 'white gold', for the daily life of Roman soldiers and citizens is well documented in the literary sources (cf. Carusi 2008a, 15-30; 2008b; Tsigarida 2012) and has been widely appreciated in modern research, our knowledge of salt's economic value in antiquity still remains limited (Drexhage 1991, 39-41; Carusi 2008a, 162-165). This is particularly due to the alleged absence of explicit direct sources and to fundamental incalculabilities regarding the supply and demand of salt in Roman times. In addition to the possibilities and problems of reconstructing prices in antiquity pointed out by Szaivert and Wolters (2005, 10-17), it has to be emphasised that there are still considerable difficulties in the determination of some measures used in the Roman Empire, for example the *castrensis modius* or the Egyptian *artaba*, the latter not following a global standard but might having been equivalent to *c.* 38.78 l in most cases and regions (Pommerening 2005, 166-173). Recent studies (*e.g.* Polfer 2000; Herz 2005; Carusi 2007; Morère Molinero 2011; Ruffing 2012; Rothenhöfer 2013) have shed more light on the Roman economic and fiscal policy, which provided the framework for the development of salt prices in the Roman Empire.

Several papyri from Egypt list salt and concrete figures without specifying the exact amount that was purchased or provided (cf. Carusi 2008a, 164, n. 31). Nevertheless, it can be stated that the sums given are generally very modest and rarely exceed a few obols. Taking the special natural conditions in Egypt into account, this might not be astonishing: salt was quite easily available in most parts of the country (Alavedra i Regàs 2007) and the Nile acted as a north-south transversal which connected the most important settlements lined up along it.

More detailed information on the prices is documented in the report on a meeting of the salt merchants' association at *Tebtunis*/Umm al-Buraiǧāt (Faiyum, Egypt) in Claudian times (*P.Mich.* V 245; cf. Drexhage *et al.* 2002, 254-255 M46). The sale of salt was publicly licensed and firmly organised, and minimum prices were fixed at two and a half resp. two obols resp. one and one-half obol per metron. The three different denominations corresponding with a difference of more than 33 or 66% compared to the low-budget ἅλς λεπτότερος have been tentatively related with three sorts of salt in respect of the production technique: marine salt, rock salt and rock salt powder (Cadell 1966, 282-283; Drexhage 1991, 39).

Figure 2. Map of Egypt with find spots of the discussed papyri and schematic areas of salt extraction.

However, the interpretation as stepped levels of quality and refinement mooted more recently (Drexhage *et al.* 2002, 254; Carusi 2008a, 163) seems to be supported more by both the Greek termini and the geological and topographic situation. The determinatives might even correspond to different classes of bulk density and thence weight, λεπτός indicating a thin and light salt, which could have been due to different extraction sources or methods as well as to different degrees of impureness or contamination[1]. Thanks to a contemporary papyrus from the same site (*P.Mich.* II 127) the prices for salt can be compared to those of other basic resources such as wheat (*c.* 1:2.4) and lentils (*c.* 1.1:1)[2].

A customs account from AD 114 (*P.Wisc* II 80) records the import of one artab of ἅλς λεπτός, which accounts for a tax of three obols. The same sum was paid several times for two artabs of black beans according to this document; since the

---

1   The latter would offer an explanation for the use of καλός to describe the highest quality, although this denomination could be due to various other reasons, for instance its usefulness for certain purposes.

2   Ratio in comparison to the medium salt price.

DATE	DOCUMENT	PLACE	COMMODITY	AMOUNT stated	litres	PRICE stated	asses	ASSES/L	ANNOTATION
47 AD	P.Mich. V 245	Tebtunis	ἅλς καλός	1 metron	c. 3.9	2 obols 4 chalci	1 2/3	c. 0.43	minimum price (salt merchants)
47 AD	P.Mich. V 245	Tebtunis	ἅλς λεπτός	1 metron	c. 3.9	2 obols	1 1/3	c. 0.34	minimum price (salt merchants)
47 AD	P.Mich. V 245	Tebtunis	ἅλς λεπτότερος	1 metron	c. 3.9	1 obol 4 chalci	1	c. 0.26	minimum price (salt merchants)
111 AD	Tab.Vind. 186	Vindolanda	sal	≥85 pondera	c. 23.2*	≥2 asses	≥2	c. 0.52**	purchase by soldier through Audax (merchant?)
150–199 AD	SB XIV 11960 col. 1	Oxyrhynchites	ἅλς	2 metra	c. 7.8	2 drachmas 2 chalci	4 1/6	c. 0.53	estate's account
258–259 AD	P.Lond. III 1170 verso col. 3	Theadelphia	ἅλς	1 metron	c. 3.9	1 drachma	2	c. 0.51	estate's account
301 AD	Edict. Diocl. 3.8	Roman Empire	sal	1 castrensis modius	c. 11.6	100 denarii communes	-	-	maximum price
301 AD	Edict. Diocl. 3.9	Roman Empire	sal conditum	1 sextarius	c. 0.5	8 denarii communes	-	-	maximum price

*based on a bulk density of 1.2 kg/l
**based on a price of 12 asses and a bulk density of 1.2 kg/l

Table 1. Prices of salt attested to in written sources from the Roman imperial period.

bulk density of salt is approximately twice that of beans, the customs for these resources per kilo were similar. The converted weight of *c.* 47 kg of salt suggests – regardless of the exact tare – that Onnos's donkey was only half loaded and carried also goods which were exempt from duty or his owner. The average carrying capacity of these pack animals can be estimated at approximately 93 kg based on to the other goods' amounts mentioned in this papyrus (cf. Mayerson 1999; Drexhage *et al.* 2002, 138), although the loads differed much (standard deviation *c.* ± 24.6 kg). In comparison to the sums documented in other papyri from Egypt, the customs would have contributed roughly 10% to this salt's retail price.

According to the admittedly scant information given in the papyri, the mean inflation rate for salt was moderate in the Faiyum region from the mid-first century AD to Gallienic times, about 0.33% per annum. Furthermore, salt was a basic and low-priced good with no exceptional fiscal position (cf. Moinier 2007, 235). While no direct evidence attests to a public monopoly on the salt production, the commerce was subject to public supervision and taxation. Costs for all commodities might have varied significantly not only chronologically but also according to distance from deposits or production sites, type of purchaser and specific circumstances (*e.g.* disturbances of trade routes caused by political or military conflicts, climatic changes).

Several tablets from Vindolanda (*Tab.Vind.* 176[?], 182[?], 185, 186, 191, 202[?]) record purchases of salt and highlight the importance of salt in the military diet, which is also attested to in literary sources (cf. Davies 1989, 188-189, 204-205). Of particular interest is the Trajanic tablet 186 containing an account of miscellaneous commodities such as beer or hobnails with concrete quantities and cash equivalents. The anonymous soldier had purchased not less than 85 pondera (*c.* 27.83 kg) of salt through Audax. Transferred to a measure of capacity, as commonly used for quantifying salt, this equals approximately 23.19 l or a little less than three Italic modii[3]. Unfortunately, the section with the paid expenses is fragmentary but a minimum of 12 *asses* has been suggested (Bowman and Thomas 1994, 147). Based on this reading, one litre of salt would have roughly cost one semis, doubling the quadrans paid for the same amount of salt of poor quality in Egypt some 60 years earlier; compared to the beer also purchased by the auxiliary soldier stationed at Vindolanda, the salt could not be considered a bargain (*c.* 2.5:1). This does not correspond to the ratio between these two commodities documented in Diocletian's Edict (*c.* 1.18:1), which could be due to various hardly calculable factors (*e.g.* difference in price trends, in logistics or in supply as well as price rigging) or to an incorrect completion of the account[4].

Diocletian's Edict on Maximum Prices from AD 301 (Lauffer 1971) provides insights on the economic value of salt during the tetrarchy, in a period after the galloping inflation which accompanied the beginning of the last third of the 3rd century. Edict. Diocl. 3.8-9 specifies the upper limit for a castrensis modius of standard salt at 100 and for an italic sextarius of *sal conditus* at 8 denarii communes.

---

3   Based on a bulk density of salt of *c.* 1.2 g/cm³ (cf. Schulze 2006, 20-21; Carusi 2008a, 23).
4   In order to be in the most similar ratio, the sum in *Tab.Vind.* 186 would have to be read as *VII asses*, a surprisingly low but still possible price for salt in Trajanic Britain.

The value of standard salt corresponds to that attributed to grain (Edict. Diocl. 1.1). According to the prevalent conversion of the involved units of measurement (cf. Bagnall 2009, 187), the spiced salt was at the most little more than one and a half times more expensive than the basic commodity. Pliny the Elder (Plin. *nat.* 31.87) praises the taste of odoriferous salts, and Apicius 1.27 gives us a recipe for *sales conditi*, which he describes as a medicine *ad multa* (*e.g.* indigestion, epidemics). This panacea consisted of common and ammoniac salt and several condiments like thyme, oregano, anise or pepper and required – admittedly manageable – preparation; the considerable price difference resulting of this is comparable to the ratio between the costs of the best and second grade honey (Edict. Diocl. 3.10-11).

Results

Although direct evidence for salt extraction during the imperial period is scarce, saline production seems probable for several sites in Noricum when the geological and topographic situation is taken into account. Practical reasons, scattered archaeological remains, several epigraphic pieces of evidence and the documented knowledge of production techniques and the continuity of former infrastructure might indicate a greater importance of salt production, trade and consumption in Roman inland Europe than directly reflected in the archaeological record. Salt extraction in this region in the subsequent Early Middle Ages is better certified in written sources but there are hardly any archaeological finds which can be convincingly connected to it; hence, the supposed 'absence of salt' in the north-western provinces of the Roman Empire might partially be due to a bias induced by the available sources.

The dynamic developments in the eastern Alpine salt production centres were presumably not directly correlated with the Roman occupation of the former *Regnum Noricum*. At some sites (Hallstatt, Dürrnberg/Hallein), the decline of the salt extraction commences already in the La Tène period (LT A resp. D). This could be explained with the gradual integration into the Roman trading networks preceding the conquest of Central Europe but might as well be due to regional reasons, *e.g.* ecological factors or transforming commercial structures and market areas. Furthermore, the exploitation of some salt deposits (Hallstatt, Bad Reichenhall, Michlhallberg) may have experienced a new upswing or even started in the first centuries AD.

Local salt production has to be taken into consideration as well for the Gallo-Roman region since the production of cured meat products, which required great amounts of salt, is sufficiently documented in both literary (cf. Moinier 2007, 241) and archaeological sources (Peters 1998; Amrein *et al.* 2012, 142-152). At the moment, it remains unsettled if and to which extent the accumulation of workshops specialised in meat processing for instance in *Augusta Raurica*/Augst was possible because of a supposed local (*e.g.* Kaiseraugst, Schweizerhalle, Liestal, Rheinfelden, Allschwill) or regional (*e.g.* Franche-Comté, Saunlnois) salt production or if it even made an intensified extraction necessary.

Prospects

During the last decades, several research projects focussed on the role of salt in the Roman Empire, and detailed studies on the Gallo-Roman, Romano-British and Dacian salt industry (general: Chevallier 1991; Ørsted 1998; Moinier 2011; Morère Molinero 2011; Moinier 2012. Roman Gaul and Britain: Brisay *et al.* 1975; Hocquet 1994; Daire 2003; Morris 2007; Tsigarida (in this volume). Roman Dacia: Medeleţ 1995; Wollmann 1996; Dordea *et al.* 1999; Balla 2000) provide the framework for a survey undertaken by the author (Stockinger forthcoming). Its research area comprises the provinces *Germania Inferior* and *Superior*, *Raetia* and *Noricum* and the barbaric *Germania* beyond the frontiers of the Roman Empire. Neither geographical nor chronological limitations will be considered as absolute in order to reconstruct developments from the late La Tène period to the Early Middle Ages and to view them in the broader context of the so-called archaically globalised Europe. Besides, the interactions between the Roman provinces and the barbaric tribes shall be brought into sharper focus.

The analysis of the archaeological material will provide an insight into technical possibilities and developments, and this shall be complemented by literary sources, ethnographic studies and experimental archaeologists' findings. This study will combine archaeological finds and features, epigraphic evidence, literary sources and iconographic attestations, as well as results of geological and medical research projects. Taking economic, topographic, social, political and historico-cultural aspects into account, this interdisciplinary approach will contribute to a more vivid picture of the food supply, diet and daily routine in Roman antiquity.

Acknowledgements

I would like to thank Th. Fischer (Cologne) for giving the impetus and helpful suggestions during my studies on this topic. This research project could be conducted thanks to a generous sponsorship by Verband der Kali- und Salzindustrie e.V. I am much obliged to H. Behnsen and D. Krüger (both Berlin) for their interest and enthusiasm. I am also deeply indebted to P. Allsobrook (Cologne) and H. Stockinger (Salzburg) for their assistance with the English and French translations as well as to J. Szczepanski (Cologne) for her support and encouragement. All maps and illustrations were produced by the author and are licenced under the Creative Commons licence CC BY-NC-SA 4.0.

References

Alavedra i Regàs, J. 2007. Economia de la sal i el natró a l'antic Egipte. In: Fíguls i Alonso, A. and Weller, O. eds. *La Trobada internacional d'arqueologia envers l'explotació de la sal a la prehistòria i protohistòria.* Cardona, 6-8 de desembre del 2003. Archaeologia Cardonensis 1. Cardona: Institut de recerques envers la Cultura (IREC), 241-255.

Alexander, J. 1985. The Production of Salt and Salt Trading Networks of Central and Western Europe in 1st Millenium BC. In: Liverani, M., Palmieri, A. and Peroni, R. eds. *Studi di paletnologia in onore di Salvatore M. Puglisi.* Rome: Università di Roma "La Sapienza", 563-569.

Alexianu, M., Weller, O. and Curcă, R.-G. eds. 2011. *Archaeology and Anthropology of Salt: A Diachronic Approach.* Proceedings of the International Colloquium, 1-5 October 2008 Al. I. Cuza University (Iaşi, Romania). BAR International Series 2198. Oxford: Archaeopress.

Amrein, H., Carlevaro, E., Deschler-Erb, E., Deschler-Erb, S., Duchauvelle, A. and Pernet, L. 2012. *Das römerzeitliche Handwerk in der Schweiz. Bestandsaufnahme und erste Synthesen.* Monographies instrumentum 40. Montagnac: Monique Mergoil.

Bagnall, R.S. 2009. Practical Help: Chronology, Geography, Measures, Currency, Names, Prosopography, and Technical Vocabulary. In: Bagnall, R.S. ed. *The Oxford Handbook of Papyrology.* Oxford: Oxford University Press, 179-196.

Balla, L. 2000. Contribution à l'histoire de l'extraction du sel et de fer dans les mines de la Dacie romaine. In: Szabó, E. ed. *Studia Dacica. Collected Papers.* Hungarian Polis Studies 5. Debrecen: University of Debrecen, 135-143.

Berg, G. 1929. *Vorkommen und Geochemie der mineralischen Rohstoffe. Einführung in die Geochemie und Lagerstättenlehre.* Leipzig: Akademische Verlagsgesellschaft.

Bowman, A.K. and Thomas, J.D. eds. 1994. *The Vindolanda Writing-Tablets.* Tabulae Vindolandenses II. London: British Museum Press.

Bradley, R. 1992. Roman Salt Production in Chichester Harbour. Rescue Excavations at Chidham, West Sussex. *Britannia* 23, 27-44.

Brisay, K.W.de and Evans, K.A. eds. 1975. *Salt. The Study of an Ancient Industry.* Report on the Salt Weekend. Essex 20-22 September 1974. Colchester: Colchester Archaeological Group.

Buschman, J.O.F.v. 1909. *Das Salz. Dessen Vorkommen und Verwertung in sämtlichen Staaten der Erde. I. Europa.* Leipzig: Wilhelm Engelmann.

Cadell, H. 1966. Problèmes relatifs au sel dans la documentation papyrologique. In: *Atti dell'XI congresso internazionale di papirologia.* Milano 2-8 Settembre 1965. Milan: Istituto Lombardo di Science e Lettre, 272-285.

Carusi, C. 2007. Régimes d'exploitation et fiscalité du sel dans le monde grec et romain. In: N. Morère Molinero ed. *Las salinas y la sal del interior en la historia: economía, medio ambiente y sociedad.* Madrid: Dykinson, 257-279.

Carusi, C. 2008a. *Il sale nel mondo greco (VI a.C.-III d.C.). Luoghi di produzione, circolazione commerciale, regimi di sfruttamento nel contesto del Mediterraneo antico.* Pragmateiai 15. Bari: Edipuglia.

Carusi, C. 2008b. Le sel dans les auteurs grecs et latins. In: Weller, O., Dufraisse, A. and Pétrequin, P. eds. *Sel, eau et forêt. D'hier à aujourd'hui*. Les Cahiers de la MSHE Ledoux 12. Besançon: Presses Universitaires de Franche-Comté, 353-364.

Chevallier, R. 1991. Réflexions sur le sel dans l'histoire romaine: un produit de première nécessité insaisissable. In: Blásquez, J.M. and Montero S. eds. *Alimenta. Festschrift Dr. Michel Ponsich*. Gerion Anejos 3. Madrid: Complutense, 53-60.

Daire, M.-Y. 2003. *Le sel des Gaulois*. Collection des Hespérides. Paris: Errance.

Davies, R.W. 1989. *Service in the Roman Army*. Edinburgh: Edinburgh University Press.

Dordea, I., Slotta, R. and Wollmann, V. eds. 1999. *Silber und Salz in Siebenbürgen*. Katalog zur Ausstellung im Deutschen Bergbau-Museum vom 27. August bis zum 31. Dezember 2000. Veröffentlichungen aus dem Deutschen Bergbau-Museum Bochum 85. Bochum: Deutsches Bergbau Museum.

Drexhage, H.-J. 1991. *Preise, Mieten/Pachten, Kosten und Löhne im römischen Ägypten bis zum Regierungsantritt Diokletians*. St. Katharinen: Scripta Mercaturae.

Drexhage, H.-J., Konen, H. and Ruffing, K. 2002. *Die Wirtschaft des Römischen Reiches (1-3 Jahrhundert). Eine Einführung*. Studienbücher Geschichte und Kultur der Alten Welt. Berlin: Akademie Verlag.

Fries-Knoblach, J. 2001. *Gerätschaften, Verfahren und Bedeutung der eisenzeitlichen Salzsiederei in Mittel- und Nordwesteuropa*. Leipziger Forschungen zur ur- und frühgeschichtlichen Archäologie 2. Leipzig: Professur für Ur- und Frühgeschichte der Universität.

Fries-Knoblach, J. 2010. The Impact of Salt Production on Iron Age Central Europe. In: Shuicheng, L. and von Falkenhausen, L. eds. *Salt Archaeology in China 2. Global Comparative Perspectives*. Beijing: Ke xue chu ban she, 261-283.

Fulda, E. 1938. *Die Salzlagerstätten Deutschlands*. Deutscher Boden 6. Berlin: Borntraeger.

Gostenčnik, K. 2005. Schriftquellen zu Rohstoffgewinnung und handwerklicher Produktion in Noricum. In: Polfer, M. ed. *Artisanat et économie romaine: Italie et provinces occidentales de l'Empire*. Actes du 3e colloque international d'Erpeldange (Luxembourg) sur l'artisanat romain, 14-16 octobre 2004. Monographies instrumentum 32. Montagnac: Monique Mergoil, 97-109.

Gouletquer, P.L. 1971. Le sel en Europe avant l'histoire. *Archéologia* 42, 56-63.

Grabherr, G. 2001. *Michlhallberg. Die Ausgrabungen in der römischen Siedlung 1997-1999 und die Untersuchungen an der zugehörigen Straßentrasse*. Schriftenreihe des Kammerhofmuseums Bad Aussee 22. Bad Aussee: Verein der Freunde des Kammerhofmuseums.

Hauber, L. 1997. Salzlagerstätten. In: Schweizerische Geotechnische Kommission ed., *Die mineralischen Rohstoffe der Schweiz*. Zurich: Schweizerische Geotechnische Kommission, 357-370.

Herz, P. 2005. Der römische Staat und die Wirtschaft. Staatliche Eingriffe in das Wirtschaftsleben (Kontrolle von Ressourcen). In: Polfer, M. ed. *Artisanat et économie romaine: Italie et provinces occidentales de l'Empire*. Actes du 3e colloque international d'Erpeldange (Luxembourg) sur l'artisanat romain, 14-16 octobre 2004. Monographies instrumentum 32. Montagnac: Monique Mergoil, 17-30.

Hocquet, J.-C. 1994. Production et commerce du sel à l'Âge du Fer et à l'époque romaine dans l'Europe du Nord-Ouest. *Revue du Nord – Archéologie* 76, 9-20.

Hurst, D. ed. 2006. *Roman Droitwich: Dodderhill Fort, Bays Meadow Villa, and Roadside Settlement*. Council for British Archaeology Research report 146. York: Council for British Archaeology.

Igl, R. 2008. Römische Spuren in Hallstatt. In: Kern, A., Kowarik, K., Rausch, A.W. and Reschreiter, H. eds. *Salz-Reich. 7000 Jahre Hallstatt*. Veröffentlichungen der Prähistorischen Abteilung 2. Vienna: Verlag des Naturhistorischen Museums Wien, 176-179.

Jodłowski, A. 1977a. Die Salzgewinnung auf polnischem Boden in vorgeschichtlicher Zeit und im frühen Mittelalter. *Jahresschrift für mitteldeutsche Vorgeschichte* 66, 85-103.

Jodłowski, A. 1977b. Saliny i kopalnie soli w państwach starożytnych strefy Śródziemnomorskiej. *Meander. Miesięcznik poświęcony kulturze świata starożytnego* 32, 40-53.

Jülich, S. 2007. *Die frühmittelalterliche Saline von Soest im europäischen Kontext*. Bodenaltertümer Westfalens 44. Mainz: Zabern.

Kern, A. 2011. Ergebnisse und der Stand der Forschung in Hallstatt. In: Chytráček, M., Gruber, H., Michálek, J., Rind, M.M., Schmotz, K., Sandner, R. and Zápotocká, M. eds. *Archäologische Arbeitsgemeinschaft Ostbayern/West- und Südböhmen/Oberösterreich*. Fines Transire 20. Rahden/Westf.: Leidorf, 411-421.

Kern, A., Kowarik, K., Rausch, A.W. and Reschreiter, H. eds.2008. *Salz-Reich. 7000 Jahre Hallstatt*. Veröffentlichungen der Prähistorischen Abteilung 2. Vienna: Verlag des Naturhistorischen Museums Wien.

Kollmann, H.A. 1994. Alpine Salzlagerstätten. In: Dopsch, H., Heuberger B. and Zeller, K.W. eds. *Salz. Ausstellungskat. Salzburger Landesausstellung Hallein Pernerinsel Keltenmuseum 1994*. Salzburg: Salzburger Landesausstellungen, 50-56.

Lane, T. and Morris, E.L. 2001. *A Millenium of Saltmaking. Prehistoric and Romano-British Salt Production in the Fenland*. Lincolnshire Archaeological and Heritage Reports 4. Sleaford: The Heritage Trust of Lincolnshire.

Lane, T., Peachey, M. and Morris, E.L. 2008. Excavations on a Roman Saltmaking Site at Cedar Close, March, Cambridgeshire. *Proceedings of the Cambridge Antiquarian Society* 97, 89-109.

Lauffer, S. 1971. *Diokletians Preisedikt*. Texte und Kommentare 5. Berlin: de Gruyter.

Litchfield, C.D., Palme, R. and Piasecki, P. eds. 2001. *Le Monde du Sel. Festschrift Jean-Claude Hocquet*. Journal of Salt-history 8/9. Hall: Berenkamp.

Lotze, F. 1938. *Steinsalz und Kalisalze. Geologie.* Die wichtigsten Lagerstätten der Nicht-Erze 3/1. Berlin: Borntraeger.

Mayerson, P. 1999. Measures (μετρηταί) and Donkeyloads of Oil in *P.Wisc.* II.80. *Zeitschrift für Papyrologie und Epigraphik* 127, 189-192.

Medeleţ, F. 1995. Über das Salz in Dakien. *Archäologie Österreichs* 6/2, 53-57.

Moinier, B. 2007. Éléments pour une géographie du sel dans l'antiquité. In: Monah, D., Dumitroaia G., Weller, O. and Chapman, J. eds. *L'exploitation du sel à travers le temps.* Bibliotheca Memoriae Antiquitatis 18. Piatra Neamţ: Constantin Matasă, 235-257.

Moinier, B. 2011. Salt in the Antiquity: a Quantification Essay. In: Alexianu, M., Weller, O. and Curcă, R.-G. eds. *Archaeology and Anthropology of Salt: A Diachronic Approach.* Proceedings of the International Colloquium, 1-5 October 2008 Al. I. Cuza University (Iaşi, Romania). BAR International Series 2198. Oxford: Archaeopress, 137-148.

Moinier, B. 2012. *Le sel dans la culture antique.* Archaeologica et Anthropologica I. Kaiserslautern/Mehlingen: Parthenon Verlag.

Monah, D., Dumitroaia, G., Weller, O. and Chapman, J. eds. 2007. *L'exploitation du sel à travers le temps.* Bibliotheca Memoriae Antiquitatis 18. Piatra Neamţ: Constantin Matasă.

Morère Molinero, N. 2011. Historical Development of the 'salinae' in Ancient Rome: from Technical Aspects to Political and Socio-Economic Interpretations. In: Alexianu, M., Weller, O. and Curcă, R.-G. eds. *Archaeology and Anthropology of Salt: A Diachronic Approach.* Proceedings of the International Colloquium, 1-5 October 2008 Al. I. Cuza University (Iaşi, Romania). BAR International Series 2198. Oxford: Archaeopress, 155-161.

Morris, E.L. 2007. Making Magic. Later Prehistoric and Early Roman Salt Production in the Lincolnshire Fenland. In: Moore, T. and Haselgrove, C. eds. *The Later Iron Age in Britain and beyond.* Oxford: Oxbow Books, 430-443.

Nenquin, J.A.E. 1961. *Salt. A Study in Economic Prehistory.* Dissertationes archaeologicae Gandenses 6. Bruges: De Tempel.

Ørsted, P. 1998. Salt, Fish and the Sea in the Roman Empire. In: Nielsen, I. and Nielsen, H.S. eds. *Meals in a Social Context. Aspects of the Communal Meal in the Hellenistic and Roman World.* Aarhus Studies in Mediterranean Antiquity 1. Aarhus: Aarhus Univ. Press, 13-35.

Peters, J. 1998. *Römische Tierhaltung und Tierzucht. Eine Synthese aus archäozoologischer Untersuchung und schriftlich-bildlicher Überlieferung.* Passauer Universitätsschriften zur Archäologie 5. Rahden/Westf.: Leidorf.

Polfer, M. 2000. CRAFTS – Projet de recherche international. Structures, implantation et rôle économique de l'artisanat antique en Italie et dans les provinces occidentales de l'Empire romain. *Instrumentum* 12, 31.

Pollak, M. 2003. Funde entlang der Oberen Traun zwischen Hallstätter See und Traunsee. Kombinierter römischer Land-Wasser-Verkehr im Salzkammergut, Oberösterreich. *Fundberichte aus Österreich* 42, 331-385.

Pollak, M. 2013. Wege zum Wohlstand. Technologie und Infrastruktur in den Zentralalpen. In: Fischer, T. and Horn, H.G. eds. *Straßen von der Frühgeschichte bis in die Moderne. Verkehrswege – Kulturträger – Lebensraum*. Akten des Interdisziplinären Kolloquiums Köln Februar 2011. Schriften des Lehr- und Forschungszentrums für die antiken Kulturen des Mittelmeerraumes – Centre for Mediterranean Cultures (ZAKMIRA) 10. Wiesbaden: Reichert, 11-41.

Pommerening, T. 2005. *Die altägyptischen Hohlmaße*. Studien zur altägyptischen Kultur. Beihefte 10. Hamburg: Buske.

Rothenhöfer, P. 2013. Die Wirtschaft der Römer: Produktionszentren und Handelswege in römischer Zeit. In: Fischer, T. and Horn, H.G. eds. *Straßen von der Frühgeschichte bis in die Moderne. Verkehrswege – Kulturträger – Lebensraum*. Akten des Interdisziplinären Kolloquiums Köln Februar 2011. Schriften des Lehr- und Forschungszentrums für die antiken Kulturen des Mittelmeerraumes – Centre for Mediterranean Cultures (ZAKMIRA) 10. Wiesbaden: Reichert, 109-121.

Ruffing, K. 2012. *Wirtschaft in der griechisch-römischen Antike*. Darmstadt: WBG.

Saile, T. 2000. Salz im ur- und frühgeschichtlichen Mitteleuropa – Eine Bestandsaufnahme. *Berichte der Römisch-Germanischen Kommission* 81, 129-234.

Saile, T. 2013. Ungleicher Wettbewerb – Salzwerke um die Zeitenwende. In: Edelmann-Singer B. ed. Salutationes – *Beiträge zur Alten Geschichte und ihrer Diskussion*. Berlin: Frank & Timme, 207-218.

Schulze, D. 2006. *Pulver und Schuttgüter. Fließeigenschaften und Handhabung*. Berlin: Springer.

Shepherd, R. 1980. *Prehistoric Mining and Allied Industries*. London: Academic Press.

Stockinger, U. forthcoming. *Rom und das Salz. Studien zu Produktion, Handel und Konsum von Salz in den Nordwestprovinzen und im angrenzenden Barbaricum*. Master's thesis, University of Cologne.

Stöllner, T. 2012. Der vor- und frühgeschichtliche Bergbau in Mitteleuropa bis zur Zeit der Merowinger. In: Bartels, C. and Slotta, R. eds. *Geschichte des deutschen Bergbaues. Band 1: Der alteuropäische Bergbau. Von den Anfängen bis zur Mitte des 18. Jahrhunderts*. Münster: Aschendorff, 25-110

Szaivert, W. and Wolters, R. 2005. *Löhne, Preise, Werte. Quellen zur römischen Geldwirtschaft*. Darmstadt: WBG.

Tsigarida, I. 2012. Zur Bedeutung der Ressource Salz in der griechisch-römischen Antike. Eine Einführung. In: Olshausen, E. and Sauer, V. eds. *Die Schätze der Erde – Natürliche Ressourcen in der antiken Welt*. Stuttgarter Kolloquium zur Historischen Geographie des Altertums 10. Geographica Historica 28. Stuttgart, 377-396.

Tsigarida, I. (in this volume). Salt in Roman Britain. Leiden: Sidestone Press.

Walter, R. 1995. *Geologie von Mitteleuropa*. 6th ed. Stuttgart: E. Schweizerbart.

Weller, O. ed. 2002. *Archéologie du sel: techniques et sociétés dans la Pré- et Protohistoire européenne*. Actes du Colloque 12.2 du XIVe Congrès de UISPP, 4 septembre 2001, Liège, et de la Table Ronde du Comité des Salines de France, 18 mai 1998, Paris. Rahden/Westf.: Leidorf.

Williams, M. and Reid, M. 2008. *Salt: Life and Industry. Excavations at King Street, Middlewich, Cheshire, 2001-2002*. BAR British Series 456. Oxford: Archaeopress.

Windholz-Konrad, M. 2008. Archäologische Altwegforschung im Salzkammergut. In: Hofer, N. ed. *Schätze.gräber.opferplätze. traunkirchen.08. Archäologie im Salzkammergut. Ausstellungskat. 2008*. Fundberichte aus Österreich. Materialhefte A 6. Vienna: Bundesdenkmalamt, 44-47.

Wollmann, V. 1996. *Mineritul metalifer, extragerea sării și carierele de piatră în Dacia romană. Der Erzbergbau, die Salzgewinnung und die Steinbrüche im römischen Dakien*. Bibliotheca Musei Napocensis 13 [=Veröffentlichungen aus dem Deutschen Bergbau-Museum Bochum 63]. Cluj-Napoca: Muzeul de Istorie.

Woodiwiss, S. and Bond, J. 1992. *Iron Age and Roman Salt Production and the Medieval Town of Droitwich: Excavations at the Old Bowling Green and Friar Street*. Council for British Archaeology research report 81. London: Council for British Archaeology.

Competing on unequal terms: saltworks at the turn of the Christian era

Thomas SAILE

Chair of Prehistory and Early History, Institute of History, University of Regensburg, 93040 Regensburg, Germany

Abstract. In the Late Pre-Roman Iron Age, salt production in Central Europe reached its highest point. At the same time, in the Mediterranean region salt was being produced under significantly more favourable conditions and was evidently also being consumed in great quantities. The estimated demand for salt in Central Europe, even if calculated as relatively modest, could not have been met by the production of the major saltworks of this region. The existence of a considerable number of smaller, seasonally operated production sites of local importance must also be taken into account; the salt produced here would have been of low quality. The gradual introduction of Mediterranean salt could have offset this shortfall. However, since the salt trade was a Roman state monopoly, this process could only come into full effect after the expansion of Rome into the region north of the Alps. The gradually squeezing out of local-scale salt production took place at the same time as various Central European saltworks ceased to operate. Only in the north-west did large-scale salt extraction continue under Roman rule.

Keywords. Salt production and trade, Mediterranean region, Central Europe, Iron Age, Roman Empire.

Résumé. La production du sel en Europe Centrale atteint son plus haut niveau à la fin de l'Age du Fer. Au même moment, dans les régions méditerranéennes, le sel est produit dans des conditions plus favorables et naturellement consommé en grande quantité. L'estimation de la demande en sel pour l'Europe Centrale, relativement modeste, ne peut pas prendre en compte la seule production des majeures salines de cette région. L'existence d'un nombre considérable de sites de production modestes et saisonniers, d'importance locale, doit aussi être considérée; le sel alors produit devait être de qualité réduite. L'introduction progressive du sel méditerranéen aurait pu contrebalancer ce déficit. Cependant, puisque le commerce du sel est sous monopole de l'Etat romain, ce processus aurait été effectif seulement après l'expansion de Rome au nord des Alpes. La diminution progressive des productions locales s'effectue alors que diverses salines centre-européennes cessent de fonctionner. C'est seulement dans le nord-ouest qu'une production de sel à large échelle se poursuit dans le cadre des règles posées par Rome.

Mots-clés. Production et commerce du sel, région méditerranéenne, Europe Centrale, Age du Fer, Empire romain.

Many climatically and morphologically suitable areas along the coastal belt of the Mediterranean are taken up by salt pans. For example, in western Sicily extensive ponds for salt production from seawater stretch along the beach between Trapani and Marsala. On Sardinia large lagoons with sea salt production facilities extend west and east of Cagliari. Likewise, ancient Ostia, the first colony of Rome, initially rose to importance due to the production of salt from the coastal marshes (Liv. 1.33.9); in 204 BC, for example, this produced an income totalling a remarkable four tonnes of silver. There were salt pans at the mouth of the Arno, not far from Pisa, and likewise in the delta of the Po at Comacchio and Cervia; the same is true of the estuary of the Rhone and the Camargue. At the beginning of the last century Sicilian salt was still being sent primarily to Scandinavia. In the 19th century the salt pans of the Po delta, with an annual production of more than 25,000 t, supplied the northern part of the Papal State, in addition to which a proportion of the salt extracted here was exported. We may compare this against the total European salt production for 1870, estimated by Matthias Jakob Schleiden (1875, 184) at 3,800,000 t. This article discusses various facts and ideas relating to the quantity, quality and distribution of salt in the Mediterranean and the zone north of the Alps during the centuries around the time of Christ.

For salt production by solar evaporation, seawater was channelled into pools in early summer, so that it was exposed to the process of evaporation under the effect of sun and wind during summer. In the salt pans, seawater flows through several large, shallow evaporation ponds, where the concentration of the brine increases each time. Because seawater includes a range of dissolved compounds and salts, the production of table salt demands a degree of technical expertise. This is because, in the course of the evaporation process, sodium chloride will be deposited after gypsum and clay, but before magnesium salts – impurities in cooking salt that give a bitter taste. The wet salt, generally recovered in late autumn, is dried in tent-shaped piles, and is subsequently ground in salt mills in order to obtain a consistent grain size. During the production phase, in the summer half of the year, the salt ponds must be protected from intruders.

In antiquity salt was used, among other purposes, as a condiment, a preservative, a technical raw material and health remedy (Tsigarida 2012a). The demand for salt was enormous and salt production correspondingly high. The economic value of salt was limited, because of the range of different opportunities for producing it (Hantos 1996); even so, it could be used as an economic weapon, as shown by the example of the Salassi (App. Ill. 17). The use of salt served as a mark of higher

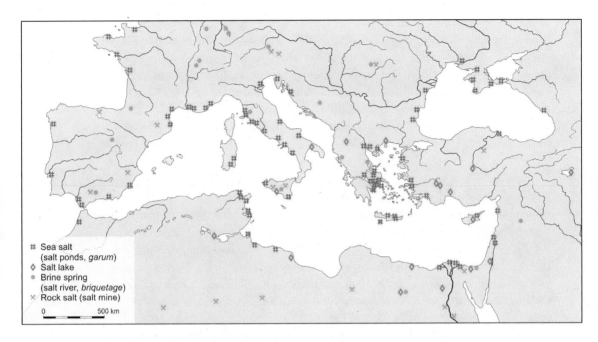

Figure 1. Saltworks in antiquity (after Carusi 2008, supplemented and modified).

civilisation (Hiob 6.6). This important substance, held in high esteem and playing a role in cult and ritual, also earned an abiding place in literature (Strässle 2009).

There were numerous salt production sites in the Mediterranean region: some are specifically mentioned in the ancient sources, while the existence of others can be inferred (Carusi 2008; Hoffmann-Salz 2011, 90 ff., 407 ff.). Sea salt production was extensive (fig. 1). In the east, salt lakes were extensively exploited. In the southern regions, rock salt deposits and brine springs played a relatively minor role; the salt mines and *briquetage* finds in the north indicate that these sources were of greater importance there.

The beginnings of sea-salt extraction and the fluctuations in the volume of production can hardly be traced with any degree of certainty by archaeological means, since salt is a hydrophilic substance, and the simple facilities used to obtain it required continual maintenance and rebuilding[1]. Only at Vigo in Galicia are the remains of a sea-salt production sites preserved from Roman times (Castro Carrera 2008). Salt pans were more economic to operate than inland salt production. Mining for rock salt, in particular, required considerable investment, and not only in the initial phase. The only exception in this regard was the exploitation of surface outcrops, for example at Cardona in Catalonia. Admittedly, rock salt was mined in Roman times, too, as Pliny (nat. hist. 31. 77-80. 85-86) has recorded *inter alia* with respect to Sicily, the Iberian Peninsula and Cappadocia. In Dacia

---

1   The presence of salt production sites has been variously identified on the basis of spatial concentrations of archaeological sites, rich find assemblages or the distribution of prestige goods. In many cases such observations have led researchers to infer the existence of economic activities on a corresponding scale, in some cases even going back to the Neolithic. See: Chapman and Gaydarska 2003; Ivanova 2010; Saile 2012.

in the 2nd/3rd century salt mines and saltworks, owned by the state, were leased to private operators (*conductores*) (Tsigarida 2012b). Utilisation of the comparatively rarer brine springs – for example those at Volterra – which required considerable quantities of fuel in the cooler, more northerly regions (Saile 2007), could have been economically viable if we consider the distance-related increase in the cost of transporting sea salt to regions remote from the coast.

Apart from *fleur de sel*, which forms on hot, windless days, the salt crystals in salt pans contain suspended particles and sediment, which may give the salt a grey colour. Rock salt also contains impurities, which lend it a variety of colours. In order to obtain salt of the finest quality, Cato the Elder (agr. 88) advises that extracted salt should be washed and purified through re-crystallisation. In order to meet quality requirements, processing of unrefined salt, which would generally have been rather unsightly, undoubtedly became necessary in the zone north of the Alps, too. However, we can only guess at the quality of the salt produced in the north. In the east Alpine region of rock salt deposits, the Dürrnberg salt was of considerably lower purity than that produced at Hallstatt. The quality of the prehistoric salt was probably more similar to that of the salt produced at the present day for industry or feeding to livestock than to modern-day cooking salt.

A product that had such diverse uses and was required in such quantities became the cause of conflict when there were shortages in supply or distribution. At least from the time of the Middle Republic, the wholesale trade in salt was taken out of the hands of private merchants and placed under state supervision. On the other hand, the production of salt from the sea was essentially free from state monopoly. Certainly, a private individual could only sell that part of the yield which exceeded his own needs with the participation of a *publicanus*. This may also explain the disadvantageous situation of many salterns. It was not the production of salt, only the trade in it that was under state control (Ørsted 1998, 21 ff.; Bekker-Nielsen 2012, 11 f.).

In prehistoric Central Europe salt production reached a high point in the Iron Age (Saile 2000; Weller 2002; Fries-Knoblach 2010; Hees 2010; Harding 2013). In qualitative terms this is reflected in the range of different production methods that came into use. These varied from salt mining to inland production by evaporation to sea salt production, which would in part have taken the form of leaching salt-enriched sands. In quantitative terms it is indicated by the growing number of major production centres. It will suffice here to refer to the saltworks of Lorraine (*briquetage de la Seille*) and the Free County of Burgundy as well as Schwäbisch Hall, Bad Reichenhall, Bad Nauheim, Werl, Halle an der Saale and Lesser Poland (Laumann 2000; Kull 2003; Vogt 2003; Olivier and Kovacik 2006), along with the east Alpine salt mines of Hallstatt and Dürrnberg (Stöllner 2007; Kern *et al.* 2008; Tiefengraber and Wiltschke-Schrotta 2013). To these we may add the sea-salt production regions along the south coast of the North Sea and the English Channel (Daire 2003; van den Broeke 2005 – on Britain see: Kinory 2012) and the salt-producing areas of the Carpathian region and Transylvania (Harding and Kavruk 2013). Over the course of time the salt production activities in these areas would, presumably, have been subject to fluctuations in yield and quality, which

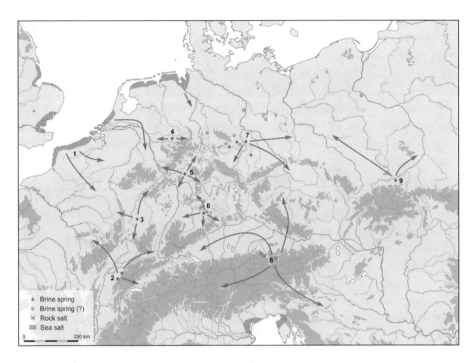

Figure 2. Iron Age salt production areas and probable main directions of the salt trade in Central Europe (after Saile 2000 and Stöllner 2002, supplemented and modified). 1: North Sea coast, 2: Jura, 3: Lorraine, 4: Westphalia, 5: Wetterau, 6: North Württemberg, 7: Saale region, 8: Eastern Alps, 9: Lesser Poland.

are difficult to assess. From this point of view the picture presented by Marie-Yvane Daire (2003, 130 ff.) of a progression from dominant rock salt production in the Early Iron Age through the prevalence of *briquetage* in the Late Iron Age to the dominance of salt pans starting from the first centuries after Christ, although attractive, appears rather too schematic.

The inland salt trade was integrated into extensive exchange networks with large areas being supplied by the major production sites (fig. 2) (Saile 2000, 161, fig. 9; Stöllner 2002, 61, fig. 7). However, the salt trade cannot be characterised adequately, a problem due, first and foremost, to the non-preservation of the trade item itself. Finds of imported goods do offer points of reference for conclusions based on analogy. Certainly, in the case of the specialised major production centres, we can assume there were broad and stable exchange patterns.

In the time of the Roman Empire we can observe a significant decrease in salt production in Central Europe as a whole, which affected both mining and evaporation. In the east Alpine mining area, salt extraction was probably disrupted already at the close of the oppida period (Stöllner 2007, 345). Such statement may appear surprising at the first instance, since the demand for this desirable product can hardly have decreased. Thus, for example, it is reported that the Gauls living in the hinterland of coasts and rivers consumed salted fish (Athen. 4.152a), while the Sequani exported cured pork as far as Rome (Strab. 4.3.2). Only at Schwäbisch Hall does the saltworks seem to have remained in operation during the Roman period (Smettan 1996). At the same time armed conflicts developed between the German tribes over salt sites. It is significant that two written sources, among the small number that we have on events within Germania, refer to conflicts over salt. Tacitus (ann. 13.57) mentions a battle in the summer of AD 58 in which the Hermunduri triumphed over the Chatti, fighting over a boundary river that produced plenty of salt, probably the Werra. Ammianus Marcellinus (rer. gest. 28.5.11) records disputes over salt sources and boundaries between the Burgundians and the Alemanni in the year AD 369. These salt deposits are thought to have been located mainly in north Württemberg, probably at Schwäbisch Hall.

In contrast to the conditions in the Central European interior, along the Continental North Sea and Channel coast in the Roman period a noticeable extension of sea salt extraction can be documented. In Britain, too, coastal salt extraction developed under Roman rule. Two inscriptions found in the 19th century at Rimini, dating from the time of Emperor Vespasian (CIL XI 390–391 [= AE 1964, Nr. 202]) and dedicated to a Roman centurion (*L. Lepidius Proculus*), who was engaged in salt provision for the legionary camp of *Novaesium*, underscore the importance of coastal salt extraction and the salt trade directed towards the interior; these had been left by the salters of the Menapii (*salinatores civitatis Menapiorum*) and the Morini (*salinatores civitatis Morinorum*). A trade in fish sauces, salted foods and salt from the Rhineland to Britain is reflected in four votive altars in the sanctuary of the native deity *Dea Nehalennia* at Collijnsplaat in the ancient Scheldt and Rhine delta; these were erected in the late 2nd and first half of the 3rd century by *negotiatores salarii* from Cologne and Trier to ensure a safe crossing (AE 1973, Nr. 362, 364 and 378; AE 2001, Nr. 1464 [= AE 2003, Nr. 1228]). The imperial salt trade is also reflected epigraphically in Dacia (Tsigarida 2012b). Various opinions have been expressed regarding the existence and volume of salt trade between *Germania magna* and the Roman Empire. Certainly, the prohibition against the export of Roman salt in the 3rd century can be seen as evidence that previously it had indeed been exported to the barbarian lands.

We may use a description by Cato (agr. 58) to estimate the annual requirement of salt in the Roman Empire: *Salis unicuique in anno modium satis est*. He estimated about 8.75 l or 7 kg of salt per year as sufficient for one slave. Taking into account the salt requirements for livestock and food preservation, the average annual per capita requirement has been calculated as up to 30 kg (Carusi 2011, 149). The population of the Roman Empire (covering more than 5 million km^2) is generally regarded as having exceeded 50 million. Using as a starting point the statement by Cato and taking into consideration various other factors, the annual demand for salt has been estimated at 350,000 t (Moinier 2011, 143 f.). Difficult to evaluate is the need for salt in fish processing, especially in the production of *garum* (Carusi 2011, 152 ff.).

As regards Iron Age Central Europe, with a mean population density of 5 inhabitants per km^2 (Zimmermann 1996) and an area of about 1 million km^2, it could have required about 35,000 t; in the first centuries AD about 17,500 t would have been needed in the areas beyond the Roman frontier. On the other hand Walter Dörfer (2012, 100) gives the minimum annual requirement for cooking salt as only 312 g per head! According to Albrecht Jockenhövel (2012, 240), a Bronze Age settlement of about 75 people, excluding their livestock, required 150-300 kg of salt per annum. Proceeding from an estimated consumption of 7.5 g of salt per person per day, Heinz Grünert (1985, 263) calculated that the 75 inhabitants of a Germanic settlement would have had an annual requirement of about 200 kg, not considering the preservation of foods and raw materials, or the provision of salt for ruminants. For Bohemia in the La Tène Period Vladimír Salač (2013, 109 ff.) established on the basis of a calculated 200,000 inhabitants and an annual per capita requirement of about 1 kg a total need of about 200 t of salt. Recalculated on the Central European scale, this comes to about 5000 t.

How much salt was being produced in Central Europe? According to a rough estimate subject to various imponderables, the Dürrnberg had an annual production of about 2 t (Pauli 1995, 206); a figure of 16 t has been given for Bad Nauheim (Deffner and Dresely 2002, 51). Individual salt production sites along the French Atlantic coast may have produced some 10 t of salt per year (Daire 2003, 127). Assuming that the rock salt production of Hallstatt and salt production by evaporation at the major prehistoric saltworks in the north zone of the Alps had a yield on the same order of magnitude, we might estimate an annual volume of production of perhaps 100 t. The amount could have been slightly greater if we add coastal salt production. It seems likely that the proto-industrial saltworks of Central Europe were in reality somewhat more productive. Nevertheless, the output of the major saltworks could hardly have met the calculated demand, even if we take into account that the estimate is subject to various imponderables. For supply to have kept up with demand, disregarding quality considerations, we have to envisage local production on a substantial scale, practiced on a seasonal basis (Vogt 2003, 472). There is a considerable amount of archaeological evidence for this in the form of minor salt production sites, some of them at locations that might initially seem inappropriate (Hoppe 2002; Taieb 2004; Pfeifer 2007). We must also take into account that part of salt production which leaves no archaeological traces (Künzler 2001; Alexianu et al. 2012). However, the import of Mediterranean sea salt could also have made up for the calculated deficit in supply within the north zone of the Alps. The salt trade in the Roman Empire was strictly regulated. On the other hand, the purchase of Roman salt became progressively easier along with the expansion of the empire[2].

This cursory description permits us to make the following inference and formulate a working hypothesis: in the Late Pre-Roman Iron Age salt production in Central Europe reached a high point. At the same time in the Mediterranean region salt was being produced under significantly more favourable conditions and was evidently also being consumed in large amounts. The Central European

2   Only in the Late Middle Ages and the beginning of the Early Modern Era does a sufficient supply of salt appear to have been ensured. At the beginning of the 13th century Lüneburg may have produced about 5000 t of salt, increasing to over 20,000 t by the end of the 16th century (Witthöft 2010). The estimated total annual production at Bochnia and Wieliczka could have reached about 7300 t in 1499. At Timbuktu, which owed its importance largely to the salt trade, in 1900 about 50,000 bars of salt from Taudeni, with a total weight of 1800 t, were traded.

demand, although calculated as comparatively modest, could not have been met by the yield of the region's major saltworks. We must take into account the presence of a much greater number of small, seasonally operated production sites that were of local importance. The quality of the salt produced here would have been low. Mediterranean salt slowly could gradually offset this shortfall in supply. Since the trade in salt was, however, a Roman state monopoly, this process could only have come into full effect after the expansion of Rome into the zone north of the Alps. At the same time as local salt production was being gradually squeezed out, various Central European saltworks also ceased operating. Only in the northwest did salt production continue on a large scale under Roman rule. At the same time, brine springs began to be used as therapeutic baths, for example at *Aquae Mattiacorum* or Fontaines-Salées.

References

Alexianu, M., Weller, O., Brigand, R. and Curcă, R.-G. 2012. Ethnoarchäologische Forschungen zu den Salzwasserquellen der moldauischen Vorkarpaten, Rumänien. In: Nikolov, V. and Bacvarov, K. eds. *Salz und Gold: die Rolle des Salzes im prähistorischen Europa*. Akten der internationalen Fachtagung (Humboldt-Kolleg) in Provadia, Bulgarien, 30. September-4. Oktober 2010. Provadia-Veliko Tarnovo: Faber, 155-172.

Bekker-Nielsen, T. 2012. Die Schätze des Meeres. In: Olshausen, E. and Sauer, V. eds. *Die Schätze der Erde – Natürliche Ressourcen in der antiken Welt*. Stuttgarter Kolloquium zur Historischen Geographie des Altertums 10, 2008. Geographica Historica 28. Stuttgart, 9-17.

van den Broeke, P.W. 2005. Salt makers along the North Sea coast: the production of salt for the hinterland. In: Louwe Kooijmans, L.P., van den Broeke, P.W., Fokkens, H. and van Gijn, A. L. eds. *The Prehistory of the Netherlands 2*. Amsterdam 2005, 513-518.

Carusi, C. 2008. *Il sale nel mondo greco (VI a.C. – III d.C.). Luoghi di produzione, circolazione commerciale, regimi di sfruttamento nel contesto del Mediterraneo antico*. Pragmateiai 15. Bari.

Carusi, C. 2011. Hypotheses, Considerations – and unknown Factors – regarding the Demand for Salt in Ancient Greece. In: Alexianu, M., Weller, O. and Curcă, R.-G. eds. *Archaeology and Anthropology of Salt: A Diachronic Approach*. Proceedings of the International Colloquium, 1-5 October 2008, Al. I. Cuza University (Iaşi, Romania). BAR International Series 2198. Oxford: Archaeopress, 149-154.

Castro Carrera, J.C. 2008. La saline romaine de « O Areal », Vigo (Galice): architecture d'une installation industrielle de production de sel. In: Weller, O., Dufraisse, A. and Pétrequin, P. eds. *Sel, eau et forêt. D'hier à aujourd'hui*. Les Cahiers de la MSHE Ledoux 12. Besançon: Presses Universitaires de Franche-Comté, 381-399.

Chapman, J. and Gaydarska, B. 2003. The provision of salt to Tripolye mega-sites. In: Korvin-Piotrovskiy, O.G. eds. *Tripil'ski poselennya-giganti. Materiali mizhnarodnoy konferentsiy. Tripolian settlements-giants*. The international symposium materials. Kiiv, 203-211.

Daire, M.-Y. 2003. *Le sel des Gaulois*. Paris.

Deffner, A. and Dresely, V. 2002. Gesalzene Überraschung. *Archäologie in Deutschland* 18/6, 51.

Dörfler, W. 2012. Salz als ein bestimmender Faktor für das Bevölkerungswachstum und die Agrarökonomie vorgeschichtlicher Bauern. In: Stobbe, A. and Tegtmeier U. eds. *Verzweigungen. Eine Würdigung für A. J. Kalis und J. Meurers-Balke*. Bonn, 91-103.

Fries-Knoblach, J. 2010. The Impact of Salt Production on Iron Age Central Europe. In: Shuicheng, L. and Falkenhausen, L.v. eds. *Salt Archaeology in China 2. Global Comparative Perspectives*. Beijing, 261-283.

Grünert, H. 1985. Zur germanischen Salzversorgung in den Jahrhunderten um die Wende unserer Zeitrechnung. In: Horst, F. and Krüger, B. eds. *Produktivkräfte und Produktionsverhältnisse in ur- und frühgeschichtlicher Zeit. XI.* Tagung der Fachgruppe Ur- und Frühgeschichte vom 14. bis 16. Dezember 1981 in Berlin. Berlin, 263-269.

Hantos, T. 1996. Cum grano salis… In: Elkar, R.S., Neutsch, C., Roth, K.J. and Schawacht, J.H. eds. *"Vom rechten Maß der Dinge". Beiträge zur Wirtschafts- und Sozialgeschichte. Festschrift für Harald Witthöft zum 65.* Geburtstag, St. Katharinen, 211-225 (Siegener Abhandlungen zur Entwicklung der materiellen Kultur 17).

Harding, A. 2013. *Salt in Prehistoric Europe*. Leiden: Sidestone Press.

Harding, A. and Kavruk, V. 2013. *Explorations in Salt Archaeology in the Carpathian Zone*. Archaeolingua Main Series 28. Budapest.

Hees, M. 2010. Prehistoric Salt Production in Southwest Germany. In: Shuicheng, L. and Falkenhausen, L.v. eds. *Salt Archaeology in China 2. Global Comparative Perspectives*. Beijing 2010, 219-237.

Hoffmann-Salz, J. 2011. *Die wirtschaftlichen Auswirkungen der römischen Eroberung. Vergleichende Untersuchungen der Provinzen Hispania Tarraconensis, Africa Proconsularis und Syria*. Historia Einzelschriften 218. Stuttgart.

Hoppe, M. 2002. *Keltische Salzsieder in Würzburg?* Das archäologische Jahr in Bayern 2001 (2002), 64-65.

Ivanova, S.V. 2010. Prirodnye resursy i èkonomika drevnih obŝestv. Natural Resources and Economics of Ancient Societies. *Stratum plus* 2010 (2), 49-97.

Jockenhövel, A. 2012. Bronzezeitliche Sole in Mitteldeutschland: Gewinnung – Distribution – Symbolik. In: Nikolov, V. and Bacvarov, K. (eds.). *Salz und Gold: die Rolle des Salzes im prähistorischen Europa*. Akten der internationalen Fachtagung (Humboldt-Kolleg) in Provadia, Bulgarien, 30. September-4. Oktober 2010. Provadia-Veliko Tarnovo: Faber, 239-257.

Kern, A., Kowarik, K., Rausch, A.W. and Reschreiter, H. eds. 2008. *Salz-Reich. 7000 Jahre Hallstatt*. Veröffentlichungen der Prähistorischen Abteilung (VPA) 2. Wien.

Kinory, J. 2012. *Salt Production, Distribution and Use in the British Iron Age*. BAR British Series 559. Oxford: Archaeopress.

Künzler, N. 2001. Gedanken zum Nachweis prähistorischer Salzgewinnung aus Sole. In: *Experimentelle Archäologie. Bilanz 2000*. Archäologische Mitteilungen aus Nordwestdeutschland Beiheft 37. Oldenburg, 41-47.

Kull, B. ed. 2003. *Sole und Salz schreiben Geschichte. 50 Jahre Landesarchäologie, 150 Jahre Archäologische Forschung in Bad Nauheim.* Mainz am Rhein.

Laumann, H. 2000. Hallstattzeitliche Salzsiederei in Werl. In: Horn, H.G., Hellenkemper, H., Isenberg, G. and Koschik H. eds. *Fundort Nordrhein-Westfalen. Millionen Jahre Geschichte.* Schriften zur Bodendenkmalpflege in Nordrhein-Westfalen 5. Mainz, 250-251.

Moinier, B. 2011. Salt in the Antiquity: a Quantification Essay. In: Alexianu, M., Weller, O. and Curcă, R.-G. eds. *Archaeology and Anthropology of Salt: A Diachronic Approach.* Proceedings of the International Colloquium, 1-5 October 2008, Al. I. Cuza University (Iaşi, Romania). BAR International Series 2198. Oxford: Archaeopress, 137-148.

Olivier, L. and Kovacik, K. 2006. The 'Briquetage de la Seille' (Lorraine, France): proto-industrial salt production in the European Iron Age. *Antiquity* 80, 558-566.

Ørsted, P. 1998. Salt, Fish and the Sea in the Roman Empire. In: Nielsen, I. and Sigismund Nielsen, H. eds. *Meals in a Social Context. Aspects of the Communal Meal in the Hellenistic and Roman World.* Aarhus Studies in Mediterranean Antiquity 1. Aarhus, 21-35.

Pauli, L. 1995. Salzgewinnung und Salzhandel in vor- und frühgeschichtlicher Zeit zwischen Alpen und Mittelgebirge. In: Treml, M., Jahn, W. and Brockhoff, E. eds. *Salz Macht Geschichte.* Veröffentlichungen zur Bayerischen Geschichte und Kultur 29. Regensburg: Aufsätze, 204-211.

Pfeifer, S. 2007. Ein hallstattzeitlicher Salzsiedeofen bei Löbnitz-Bennewitz, Lkr. Leipziger Land. *Arbeits- und Forschungsberichte zur sächsischen Bodendenkmalpflege* 47 (2005(2007)), 21-49.

Saile, T. 2000. Salz im ur- und frühgeschichtlichen Mitteleuropa – Eine Bestandsaufnahme. *Bericht der Römisch-Germanischen Kommission* 81, 130-234.

Saile, T. 2007. Salz und Holz: Salinen als Großverbraucher von Brennholz. Anmerkungen zur Lüneburger Saline. *Archäologie in Niedersachsen* 10, 54-57.

Saile, T. 2012. Salt in the Neolithic of Central Europa: production and distribution. In: Nikolov, V. and Bacvarov, K. eds. *Salz und Gold: die Rolle des Salzes im prähistorischen Europa.* Akten der internationalen Fachtagung (Humboldt-Kolleg) in Provadia, Bulgarien, 30. September-4. Oktober 2010. Provadia-Veliko Tarnovo: Faber, 225-238.

Salač, V. 2013. O rychlosti dopravy v době laténské a jejích hospodářských, politických a kulturních dopadech na společnost. *Archeologické rozhledy* 65, 89-132.

Schleiden, M.J. 1875. *Das Salz. Seine Geschichte, seine Symbolik und seine Bedeutung im Menschenleben. Eine monographische Skizze.* Leipzig.

Smettan, H. 1996. Vorgeschichtliche Salzgewinnung und Eisenverhüttung im Spiegel württembergischer Pollendiagramme. In: Jockenhövel, A. ed. *Bergbau, Verhüttung und Waldnutzung im Mittelalter. Auswirkungen auf Mensch und Umwelt.* Ergebnisse eines internationalen Workshops (Dillenburg, 11-15 Mai 1994. Wirtschaftshistorisches Museum „Villa Grün"). Vierteljahrschrift für Sozial- und Wirtschaftsgeschichte Beiheft 121. Stuttgart, 84-92.

Stöllner, T. 2002. Salz als Fernhandelsgut in Mitteleuropa während der Hallstatt- und Latènezeit. In: Lang, A. and Salač, V. eds. *Fernkontakte in der Eisenzeit.* Konferenz Liblice 2000. Praha, 47-71.

Stöllner, T. 2007. Siedlungsdynamik und Salzgewinnung im östlichen Oberbayern und in Westösterreich während der Eisenzeit. In: Prammer, J., Sandner, R. and Tappert, C. eds. *Siedlungsdynamik und Gesellschaft*. Beiträge des internationalen Kolloquiums zur keltischen Besiedlungsgeschichte im bayerischen Donauraum, Österreich und der Tschechischen Republik, 2.-4. März 2006 im Gäubodenmuseum Straubing. Jahresbericht des Historischen Vereins für Straubing und Umgebung, Sonderband 3. Straubing, 313-362.

Strässle, T. 2009. *Salz. Eine Literaturgeschichte*. München.

Taieb, P. 2004. *Salz, Sieder, Siedlungen am Salzigen und Süßen See im Mansfelder Land des Mitteldeutschen Trockengebietes*. Antiquitates 28. Hamburg.

Tiefengraber, G. and Wiltschke-Schrotta, K. 2013. *Der Dürrnberg bei Hallein. Die Gräbergruppe Moserfeld-Osthang*. Dürrnberg-Forschungen 6. Rahden/Westf.

Tsigarida, I. 2012a. Zur Bedeutung der Ressource Salz in der griechisch-römischen Geschichte. Eine Einführung. In: Olshausen, E. and Sauer V. eds. *Die Schätze der Erde – Natürliche Ressourcen in der antiken Welt*. Stuttgarter Kolloquium zur Historischen Geographie des Altertums 10, 2008. Geographica Historica 28. Stuttgart, 377-396.

Tsigarida, I. 2012b. Bereiche der zentralen Einflussnahme auf Salz im Römischen Reich am Beispiel der Provinz Dakien. In: Nikolov, V. and Bacvarov, K. eds. *Salz und Gold: die Rolle des Salzes im prähistorischen Europa*. Akten der internationalen Fachtagung (Humboldt-Kolleg) in Provadia, Bulgarien, 30. September-4. Oktober 2010. Provadia-Veliko Tarnovo: Faber, 313-322.

Vogt, U. 2003. Bemerkungen zur Technologie vorgeschichtlicher Salinen im Mittelgebirgsraum. In: Stöllner, T., Körlin, G., Steffens, G. and Cierny, J. eds. *Man and Mining – Mensch und Bergbau. Studies in honour of Gerd Weisgerber on occasion of his 65th birthday*. Der Anschnitt Beiheft 16 = Veröffentlichungen aus dem Deutschen Bergbau-Museum Bochum 114. Bochum, 465-473.

Weller, O. ed. 2002. *Archéologie du sel. Techniques et sociétés dans la pré- et protohistoire européenne*. Actes du Colloque 12.2 du XIVᵉ congrès de l'UISPP, 4 septembre 2001, Liège, et de la table ronde du Comité des Salines de France, 18 mai 1998, Paris. Internationale Archäologie. Arbeitsgemeinschaft, Symposium, Tagung, Kongress 3. Rahden/Westf.

Witthöft, H. 2010. *Die Lüneburger Saline. Salz in Nordeuropa und der Hanse vom 12-19 Jahrhundert. Eine Wirtschafts-und Kulturgeschichte langer Dauer*. De Sulte 22. Rahden/Westf.

Zimmermann, A. 1996. Zur Bevölkerungsdichte in der Urgeschichte Mitteleuropas, in: Campen, I., Hahn, J. and Uerpmann, M. eds. *Spuren der Jagd – Die Jagd nach Spuren. Festschrift für Hansjürgen* Müller-Beck. Tübinger Monographien zur Urgeschichte 11. Tübingen, 49-61.

Salt in Roman Britain

Isabella TSIGARIDA

University of Zurich, Faculty of Arts, Department of History, Karl Schmid-Str. 4, CH-8006 Zurich, Switzerland

Abstract. Following the Roman expansion into Britain where large parts of Roman military forces were based, this paper discusses how the growing demand for salt – one of the most vital resource in ancient times – was ensured long term and whether any increase in salt production could be ascertained. It will also look at salt production methods and related infrastructural measures during the Roman settlement in Britain, as supported by archaeological evidence.

Keywords. Production techniques, Britain, briquetage, wooden tank, lead pan, Romans, military.

Résumé. Suite à l'expansion romaine en Grande-Bretagne où une grande partie des forces militaires romaines était basée, ce document explique comment la demande croissante en sel – l'une des ressources les plus vitales dans les temps anciens – a été assurée à long terme et si une augmentation de la production de sel pouvait être assurée. Ce document se penchera également sur les méthodes et les infrastructures liées à l'exploitation du sel durant la colonisation romaine en Grande-Bretagne, basé sur des preuves archéologiques.

Mots-clés. Techniques de production, Britannia, briquetage, bassin de bois, poêle de fer, Romains, militaire.

Roman expansion in the north meant that from the 1st century AD onwards, a large part of Rome's military forces were concentrated in the Empire's northern regions. The maintenance of the military was ensured not only through the necessary infrastructure, which was created by building roads and suitable means of transport; long-distance trade was also essential in providing troops with supplies. Delivering a constant supply of goods to deployed troops posed a strategic challenge and was key to the success of large-scale military operations. For reasons of cost alone, it was not left up to chance. Accordingly, logistic preparations for building camps, expanding the local maintenance of troops and a functioning replenishment system for imports from the Mediterranean were vital if military operations were to succeed (cf. Thomas 2008; Erdkamp 2006, 287 f.).

Regarding army supplies, the state was responsible for providing and financing the goods essential for maintaining the troops, and organised their delivery using the *annona* system[1]. At the same time, garrisons' supplies were also regulated predominantly through contracts with private businessmen, such as *navicularii*, who delivered a great variety of goods, usually in large quantities, to certain places on behalf of the Roman state; at the same time they also had scope for private deals. There were also countless other private dealers who profited from the transport routes supplying the troops and who could conduct their trade under relatively secure conditions (cf. Tsigarida 2014; Morris 2010, 92; cf. also Monfort 2002 and Scardigli 2007).

This is the background against which the following study intends to use the resource of salt as an example to outline both the need and, accordingly, the demand for this commodity in Roman Britain and by the Roman troops stationed there. Salt is well-suited for this kind of study, as not only can it be used in many different ways, but is also vital for both human and animals in terms of nutrition physiology. As a preservative, salt made it possible to render vegetables and foods containing protein such as cheese, fish and meat non-perishable and transportable, so that they kept over the winter and could be traded across great distances (on the different uses of salt, cf. Tsigarida 2012). Furthermore, the mineral was also used in animal husbandry, as a medicine and as an auxiliary agent in tanning, ancient metallurgy and glass production.

Generally, it can be assumed that the greater part of salt trade activity took place on a local or regional level, that is, that local salt trade was the most common form of salt exchange. Long-distance trade was presumably linked to particular circumstances, for example if the value of salt was enhanced due to its status as a luxury item, if it was a scarce commodity as it was not produced locally, or if there was increased demand for it.

In his Geographika, Strabo gives an account of this kind of long-distance salt trade by Phoenician traders, who imported salt and other products to the Cassiterides, a group of islands off the British coast, exchanging them for tin, lead and other commodities (Strab. 3.5.11).

This reference to long-distance trade activity suggests that not only did corresponding supply and demand exist, but also that established communication and trade relationships were in place that guaranteed a constant supply of scarce or desirable commodities. Although removing the resource from the place of production caused its cost to increase due to the expense of transportation, this kind of trade seems to have been financially worthwhile for various reasons – whether the products were used as barter goods, scarce commodities, and presents or as cargo for outward or return journeys.

---

[1] Before Diocletian's reign, not only taxes but also rents and rent in kind (mainly cereals) were collected in order to provide for the population of the city of Rome and the Roman army. Under Diocletian, these extraordinary payments in kind (*annona*) were instituted as regular rents in kind throughout the Empire as a new main tax, also called *annona*. On *annona* in general, cf. Höbenreich (1997) and Mitthof (2001), as well as Kolb (2000, 228) and Demandt (2007, 67 f.).

The extent to which both the demand for salt and the trade structure were altered by Roman expansion into Britain will now be examined using the example of local British salt production. Roman interest in Britain is already evident in the two campaigns led by Caesar. The province of Britannia was finally created in AD 43 when parts of Britain were conquered by Claudius (Wesch-Klein 2008, 240).

The arrival of the Romans opened up new ways of utilising conquered areas; however, most of these primarily served military purposes. In order to do this, the Romans established an impressive infrastructure of land and water routes as well as ports. The water routes were the most important of these for the transportation of goods. One example that can be mentioned in this context is the Car Dyke, a navigable canal eighty-five miles long in the fenlands of eastern England[2].

Besides drainage works and the construction of canals and dams, agriculture was also used more intensely in order to ensure adequate provisions for the army stationed in the region. In the following it will be examined what interesting innovations were made to the production of salt, which was counted as part of agriculture in ancient times.

In general, there were different ways in which salt production on the British coast could take place (Rippon 2000, 42; Saile 2000, 136-138): either by boiling salt water, by filtering or leaching salt from peat (Plin. nat. 16.4) or sand (Hocquet 1993, 39 f.) permeated with salt, or by collecting salt water in shallow basins, where the water evaporated in sunlight. Although the latter method was the most common in the Mediterranean, it was less suited to the northern coastal regions due their less clement climate. Nonetheless, there is evidence from south-eastern England (the red hills in Essex) that suggest a modified form of solar salt production. Here, sea water was collected in clarifying basins and after most of it had evaporated, the rest of the brine was heated in briquetage containers until the salt formed crystals (cf. Saile 2000, 144; De Brisay 1975, 5). On the coast, peat served as the main fuel besides wood.

The salt production process ended with drying the salt, which often took place in briquetage vessels. As a so-called "salt block", the salt was impervious to moisture and could be transported either with or without a briquetage vessel (Fries-Knoblach 2001, 5). In order to get at the salt, the vessel could be broken or shattered. Use of the briquetage technique was widespread in coastal salt production and in areas rich in brine, particularly in Central Europe. The briquetage vessels, usually reddish-coloured pottery, vary in form depending on their region and epoch; thus there were cup-, chalice- and vase-shaped containers and both rod- and plate-shaped supporting elements (*ibid.*, 5-18).

---

2   The construction of the Car Dyke may be linked to salt production. It seems that the construction of the canal made it possible to halt the decline in Iron Age salt production caused by the sinking sea levels in this particular location by changing and stabilising the inflow of water. This shifted the facilities about 1 to 3 miles to the east. Besides reactivating the production of salt, these measures combined with drainage works also made it possible to reclaim and utilise new land. Cf. Simmons 1979, 196. Tacitus mentions other impressive canals in the Rhine-Meuse delta, cf. Tac. ann. 2.8.1 on the *fossa Drusiana* (12 BC); Tac. ann. 11.20.2 on the *fossa Corbulonis* (AD 47).

There is already evidence of salt production by boiling salt water in early Bronze Age Britain (*ibid.*, 10). Besides coastal salt production, there was also widespread inland salt production in Britain that used the briquetage salt production method, as evidenced by briquetage vessels, oven structures and fuel. Here it can be noted that Iron Age and Roman production facilities were often not located in the same places, which may be due to changes in the coastline in coastal areas (cf. Saile 2000, 171 f., 174; Thoen 1975, 58-60; 1981, 250 f.; 1991, 41-43; Fries-Knoblach 2001, 22; Rothenhöfer 2005, 214).

During the Iron Age, it was mainly the south and east coast of Britain that were used for the production of salt; further inland, it was predominantly the inland salt water springs in the west of England.

The sites of production stretch from Hampshire as far as Cornwall on the south coast, with a strong concentration around Dorset. In Hampshire and Sussex, the decline in salt production can be dated to around AD 100 (Bradley 1975, 20-25).

Along the east coast, there is evidence of production sites from Kent up as far as Durham, with north Kent, Essex and south Lincolnshire with its "red hills" as the most notable of these (Fries-Knoblach 2001, 11). The so-called "red hills" developed over centuries as the result of salt production processes in which salt water was conducted into clay basins in the marshes. After evaporation of the sea water (in the summer), the salt crust and salt-permeated clay could be extracted. The latter was burnt and rinsed with salt water, and the brine was then crystallised in briquetage vessels. Many of the briquetage vessels discovered in the red hills were located in the ash and wood coal layers used for firing[3].

In western England, besides findings on the north Somerset coast it is mainly the inland salt water springs in Cheshire and Worcestershire that are of importance, as evidenced for the Iron Age in archaeological findings from Droitwich and Worcestershire along the river Salwarpe (Fries-Knoblach 2001, 12). The advantage of salt water springs lay in the fact that they already had a very high saline content; in Droitwich, this lay at around 25%, close to saturation point.

When the Romans came to Britain, salt production using the briquetage technique common during the Iron Age was already widespread; as mentioned above, salt was harvested from sea water and salt water springs. During Roman times, too, salt production took place both along the coast, particularly the Fenlands of east England, as well as inland. The central area of inland salt production was north-western England, particularly Cheshire and the towns of Northwich, Nantwich and Middlewich (Arrowsmith and Power 2012, 2).

In Northwich (Condate), the Romans even erected an auxiliary fort, probably as its strategic position near the river Weaver and the rich salt water springs provided good conditions; in Middlewich (Salinae), there is likewise evidence of a fort near Harbutts Field.

---

3   For the east coast two different types of briquetage can be identified, the "East Coast group" and the "Thames-mouth group".

Besides the two abovementioned important salt production locations in Cheshire, it is worth to take a closer look at Nantwich, the third significant inland place of salt production in this area during Roman times. It is here that two well-preserved wooden tanks for salt water dating from Roman times were dug up in Kingsley Fields (for the following account, cf. part. *ibid.*, 174-182). Most of the findings date from the 2nd century AD, whilst some are from the 3rd century AD. The 2nd-century findings are of particular interest here, as they provide information both on how the salt water was stored and on the actual salt production itself.

In the excavation area, two wooden constructions (tank 1182 and 1207) were found, which were apparently built to store salt water. Close to the wooden salt water tanks, further wooden constructs were found that were possibly used for storage purposes, conceivably for salt besides other resources. In the northern part of the excavation area, a small group of ovens were identified; these were probably used to heat the salt water. It is assumed that a larger number of ovens are located between the two tanks and the road, outside the excavation area itself. The clay fragments discovered suggest that evaporation was used as a production method. Thus it seems likely that the wooden salt water tanks set into the ground were connected to the salt water springs by natural or artificially constructed trenches and river branches. The water collected in the wooden tanks was partially evaporated by the sunlight and probably also by the wind, and the sediment settled at the bottom of the tank. Following this, the salt water was filled into the briquetage vessels and probably heated in the ovens until the salt crystallised.

The briquetage findings and the dendrological analysis of the wooden tanks suggests this production site was probably used around AD 130-137 (tank 1182). The examination of salt water tank 1207 and its dendrological analysis, which dates it to AD 114-142, provide evidence of increased usage of the production site during the Antonine period. Samian wares found in the tank date another period of usage to around AD 150. Further briquetage and coin findings reveal that the production site declined around AD 180 (*ibid.*, 176).

Interestingly, another discovery was made in the north of Kingsley Fields and in Shavington to the east of the settlement; here, shallow pans made of lead were found. Inscriptions on the pans reveal that salt production was still active in the area during the 4th and 5th century AD and suggest that it was managed by the church (*ibid.*, 181; Penney and Shotter 1996). These pans could also be seen as first evidence for the use of lead evaporation pans instead of briquetage vessels in the salt production process in Roman Britain[4].

That shallow pans made of lead were indeed used to boil salt water instead of briquetage vessels is proved by the total of 18 lead pans (some of them complete) that have survived from Roman times, all of which come from the county of Cheshire (Hocquet 1993, 38; Jülich 2003, 39; 2005, 29; 2007, 128-130; Lane 2005, 19-26).

---

4 The specimen preserved from Shavington is 0.9 × 1 m in size, the pans from Nantwich are
   c. 1 × 1 × 0.12-0.18 m. Cf. Fries-Knoblach 2001, 21.

Prior to this discovery, the use of pans made of lead, bronze or iron instead of ceramic vessels to boil salt water was only evidenced for the Early Middle Ages, particularly in Central Europe. While they may only represent exceptions, these Roman salt boiling pans – the oldest discovered so far – may also show that the salt-boiling techniques and methods used during Roman times were more advanced than previously assumed.

In summary, the archaeological evidence in Nantwich leads to the conclusion that the salt water springs there were not used prior to the arrival of the Romans in the area (Arrowsmith and Power 2012, 181 f.).

In contrast to Northwich and Middlewich, in Nantwich there was no Roman fort, only a small settlement possibly connected with some kind of "industrial production". This assumption may be supported by the fact that the settlement was fairly remote, that is, away from the road network, and a road had to be newly built to access it. The increased activity in the salt production process identified for the Hadrianic period may suggest an increased demand for salt and an intensified salt production during this period. This may be linked to supplies for the Roman army in this area and the increased number of troops identified during the 2nd century AD in Chester. One conceivable reason for this might be the expansion of Hadrian's Wall. The decline in salt production activity around AD 180 may be linked to unrest in Britannia at this time. The resumption of salt production at the beginning of the 3rd century is possibly connected to Severus's activities in Scotland.

Even though much remains uncertain, the following can be stated: Roman presence in Britain leads to an identifiable change in the salt production process both for inland and coastal salt production. It seems that the solar production method common in the Mediterranean was combined here with the briquetage technique that was predominantly widespread in Central Europe during the Iron Age. This can be seen in the aforementioned example of salt production in south-eastern England (the red hills in Essex) and in the example of Nantwich. Findings from Belgium also point in this direction (Thoen 1991, 40). Besides natural bays that served as salt pans, salt production also used wooden constructions in the tidal marshlands as well as in inland salt production. As already mentioned above, these tanks were set into the ground and connected to the salt water springs by natural or artificially constructed trenches and river branches. The water collected in the wooden tanks evaporated partially in sunlight and wind, and the sediment settled at the bottom of the tank. The salt water was then filled into briquetage vessels and heated (probably in an oven) until the salt crystallised.

There are many examples of the construction of this kind of Roman saltworks along the continental North Sea coast, in Brittany and in England (Saile 2000, 173, im. 11 and 174), suggesting intensified salt production and an increase in production volume.

The saltworks mentioned fulfill certain criteria that suggest their expansion was planned strategically. Besides access to sea water and/or salt springs, these criteria include the availability of peat for firing, clay as a material for the construction of salt boiling ovens and briquetage vessels, and a location with good transport connections for trade and distribution. Given the archaeological findings on the construction and expansion of the saltworks, the assumption that they were of interest to Roman decision makers for strategic reasons does not seem unreasonable. This makes sense against the background of Roman expansion in the northern provinces. Thus the province Britannia of interest here became a central area of military concern due to the higher numbers of troops stationed there. In order to pursue the aims of foreign policy and support military operations, it was necessary to constantly supply the stationed troops with goods. Logistic preparations for the construction of forts, a reliable supply of imports from the Mediterranean and the expansion of local supply routes proved indispensable (Thomas 2008; Erdkamp 2006, 287 f.), which is why infrastructural conditions were created that ensured the troops were adequately supplied. The increased demand for and provision of salt can be mentioned in this context. In Roman Britain for example, during the 1st century AD, around 15,000 soldiers besides the local population and additional auxiliary troops, consisting of a further 15,000 men, needed to be supplied with salt. The same number of troops can be assumed for the 2nd century[5].

For this reason it can be assumed that salt production during the 1st century AD mainly took place in the Mediterranean saltworks, even though this incurred the additional costs for transport and distribution that went hand in hand with long-distance trade. As the increased demand could not be met initially through local production in the northern provinces, it was necessary to import large quantities of salt to ensure the need for salt was catered to.

The archaeological findings in the Roman saltworks show that the increased demand for salt created by Roman expansion was accounted for both in that the constant supply of salt to the troops was ensured through Mediterranean imports, and in that salt production was gradually adapted to the rise in demand. This means that the trade in Mediterranean salt was gradually replaced by the expansion of local salt production facilities. Both the facilities in the northern provinces and the production methods were adapted to natural and local conditions, so that the best possible local salt harvest could be achieved. Technological innovation in the salt production process consisted of expanding the technical know-how of Mediterranean salt production by including and blending it with the briquetage technique common in the northern coastal regions with that of the Mediterranean.

The effectiveness of the Roman frontier guard depended not only on its military bases but also on supplying the troops stationed there with agricultural products. Impressive infrastructural measures were taken to ensure this, particularly in regard to the road and water networks. This not only ensured that the army was supplied with goods and resources, but also created optimal conditions for trade within the

---

5   Cf. Verboven 2007, 303 f. It is also to consider that every year a certain number of veterans settled in the areas near the military camps, then there are a further *c.* 10,800 veterans for Britannia during the 1st century AD Furthermore, there were also the relatives, slaves and freedmen and the traders, contractors and so on following the army, so that maintaining all of these people besides the local population became a task of considerable proportions.

province and with other provinces, including the trade in salt. It was possible to meet the increased demand for salt not least due to the creation of new lines of supply, structures of trade and reliable lines of distribution.

Accordingly, the long-term deployment of an army had a significant influence on structures of production and distribution (Jacobsen 1995, 183). With the movement of Roman troops into the northern provinces, the former periphery of the Empire developed into a central military area. The presence of the army resulted both in comprehensive infrastructural measures and in technical innovations and economic developments, all of which restructured the Central European region in both economic and cultural terms.

The given conditions of the landscape, its shape and resources were optimised for agricultural usage by the Romans by adapting technical methods. This reveals their political significance, and against this background the expansion of saltworks to increase salt production makes sense. It should be pointed to the Romans' neat transfer in joining two existing salt production methods to create a new one, by combining the familiar Mediterranean technique of salt production in shallow basins and using sunlight with the technique practised in the Iron Age on the North Sea coast and inland of evaporation in briquetage vessels (sometimes also in salt boiling ovens). To do this, the Romans constructed artificial (wooden) basins where the deposition of sediment from the sea water could take place and the brine could then be filled into briquetage vessels or metal shallow pans and crystallised by heating it. This new method of salt production made it possible to meet increased demand locally and dispense with imports from the south. Roman presence in Britain thus resulted – as has been shown for the field of salt production – in a change in land use methods and a simultaneous intensification of salt production.

References

Arrowsmith, P. and Power, D. 2012. *Roman Nantwich: A Salt-Making Settlement. Excavations at Kingsley Fields 2002*. BAR British Series 557. Oxford: Archaeopress.

Bradley, R. 1975. Salt and Settlement in the Hampshire Sussex Borderland. In: De Brisay, K.W. and Evans, K.A. eds. *Salt. The Study of an Ancient Industry*. Report on the Salt Weekend Held at the University of Essex, September 1974. Colchester: Colchester Archaeological Group, 20-25.

De Brisay, K.W. 1975. The Red Hills of Essex. In: De Brisay, K.W. and Evans, K.A. eds. *Salt. The Study of an Ancient Industry*. Report on the Salt Weekend Held at the University of Essex, September 1974. Colchester: Colchester Archaeological Group, 5-11.

Demandt, A. 2007. *Die Spätantike. Römische Geschichte von Diocletian bis Justinian 284-565 n. Chr.* München: C.H. Beck Verlag.

Erdkamp, P. 2006. Army and society. In: Rosenstein, N. and Morstein-Marx, R. eds. *A companion to the Roman Republic*. Malden: Blackwell, 278-296.

Fries-Knoblach, J. 2001. *Gerätschaften, Verfahren und Bedeutung der eisenzeitlichen Salzsiederei in Mittel- und Nordwesteuropa*. Leipziger Forschungen zur ur- und frühgeschichtlichen Archäologie. Leipzig: Professur für Ur- und Frühgeschichte der Universität Leipzig.

Hocquet, J.-C. 1993. *Weißes Gold. Das Salz und die Macht in Europa von 800 bis 1800*. Stuttgart: Klett-Cotta.

Höbenreich, E. 1997. *Annona. Juristische Aspekte der stadtrömischen Lebensmittelversorgung im Prinzipat*. Graz: Leykam.

Jacobsen, G. 1995. *Primitiver Austausch oder freier Markt? Untersuchungen zum Handel in den gallisch-germanischen Provinzen während der römischen Kaiserzeit*. St. Katharinen: Scripta Mercaturae Verlag.

Jülich, S. 2003. Blei und Salz, Gott erhalt's, *Archäologie in Deutschland* 1, 38f.

Jülich, S. 2005. An Overview of Early Salt Making in Germany. In: Fielding, A.M. and Fielding, A.P. eds. *Salt works and Salinas. The Archeology, Conservation and Recovery of Salt Making Sites and their Processes*. Lion Salt Works Trust Monograph Series, Research Report n°2. Northwich: Lion Salt Works Trust, 27-32.

Jülich, S. 2007. Römische Tradition in mittelalterlicher Siedetechnik? In: Melzer, W. and Capelle, T. eds. *Bleibergbau und Bleiverarbeitung während der römischen Kaiserzeit im rechtsrheinischen Barbaricum*. Soester Beiträge zur Archäologie 8. Soest: Westfälische Verlagsbuchhandlung Mocker & Jahn, 125-133.

Kolb, A. 2000. *Transport und Nachrichtentransfer im Römischen Reich*. Klio Beihefte Neue Folge Band 2. Berlin: Akademie Verlag.

Lane, T. 2005. Roman and Pre-Roman Salt Making in the Fenland of England. In: Fielding, A.M. and Fielding, A.P. eds. *Salt works and Salinas. The Archeology, Conservation and Recovery of Salt Making Sites and their Processes*. Lion Salt Works Trust Monograph Series, Research Report n°2. Northwich: Lion Salt Works Trust, 19-26.

Mitthof, F. 2001: *Annona militaris. Die Heeresversorgung im spätantiken Ägypten. Ein Beitrag zur Verwaltungs- und Heeresgeschichte des Römischen Reiches im 3. bis 6. Jh. n. Chr.* Florenz: Gonnelli.

Monfort, C.C. 2002. The Roman military supply during the principate. Transportation and staples. In: Erdkamp, P. ed. *The Roman Army and the Economy*. Amsterdam: Brill Academic Pub, 70-89.

Morris, F.M. 2010. *North Sea and Channel Connectivity during the Late Iron Age and Roman Period (175/150 BC-AD 409)*. BAR International Series 2157. Oxford: Archaeopress.

Penney, S. and Shotter, D.C.A. 1996. An Inscribed Roman Salt-Pan from Shavington, Cheshire. *Britannia* 27, 360-365.

Rippon, S. 2000. *The Transformation of Coastal Wetlands. Exploitation and Management of Marshland Landscapes in Northwest Europe during the Roman and Medieval Periods*. Oxford: Oxford University Press.

Rothenhöfer, P. 2005. *Die Wirtschaftsstrukturen im südlichen Niedergermanien. Untersuchungen zur Entwicklung eines Wirtschaftsraumes an der Peripherie des Imperium Romanum*. Kölner Studien zur Archäologie der römischen Provinzen 7. Leidorf: VML Verlag Marie Leidorf.

Saile, T. 2000. Salz im ur- und frühgeschichtlichen Mitteleuropa – Eine Bestandsaufnahme. *Bericht der Römisch-Germanischen Kommission* 81, 130-234.

Scardigli, B. 2007. I rifornimenti per l'esercito in età repubblicana: una rassegna. In: Papi, E. ed. *Supplying Rome and the Empire*. The Proceedings of an International seminar held at Siena-Certosa di Pontignano on May 2-4, 2004 on Rome, the Provinces, Production and Distribution. Journal of Roman Archaeology, Supplementary Series 69. Portsmouth, 179-192.

Simmons, B.B. 1979. The Lincolnshire Car Dyke: Navigation or Drainage? *Britannia* 10, 183-196.

Thoen, H. 1975. Iron Age and Roman Salt-Making Sites on the Belgian Coast. In: De Brisay, K.W. and Evans, K.A. eds. *Salt. The Study of an Ancient Industry*. Report on the Salt Weekend Held at the University of Essex, September 1974. Colchester: Colchester Archaeological Group, 56-60.

Thoen, H. 1981. The Third Century Roman Occupation in Belgium. The Evidence of the Coastal Plain. In: King, A. and Henig, M. eds. *The Roman West in the Third Century. Contributions from Archaeology and History*. BAR International Series 109. Oxford: Archaeopress, 245-257.

Thoen, H. 1991. Neue Ergebnisse über antike Salzgewinnung und –handel an den nordatlantischen Küsten (Nord-Frankreich, Belgien und Holland). *Mitteilungen Österreichischer Arbeitsgemeinschaft für Ur- und Frühgeschichte* 37, 1987 [1991], 39-49.

Thomas, R. 2008. For starters. Producing and supplying food to the army in the Roman north-west provinces. In: Stallibras, S. and Thomas, R. eds. *Feeding the Roman Army. The Archaeology of Production and Supply in NW Europe*. Oxford: Oxbow Books, 1-17.

Tsigarida, I. 2012. Zur Bedeutung der Ressource Salz in der griechisch-römischen Antike. Eine Einführung. In: Olshausen, E. and Sauer, V. eds. *Die Schätze der Erde – Natürliche Ressourcen in der antiken Welt*. Stuttgarter Kolloquium zur Historischen Geographie des Altertums 10, 2008. Stuttgart: Franz Steiner, 377-396.

Tsigarida, I. 2014. Auf den Spuren der Salzhändler. In: Olshausen, E. and Sauer, V. eds. *Mobilität in den Kulturen der antiken Mittelmeerwelt*. Stuttgarter Kolloquium zur Historischen Geographie des Altertums 11, 2011. Stuttgart: Franz Steiner, 505-516.

Verboven, K.S. 2007. Good for business. The Roman Army and the Emergence of a 'Business Class' in the Northwestern Provinces of the Roman Empire (1st century BC–3rd century CE). In: De Blois, L. and Lo Cascio, E. eds. *The Impact of the Roman Army (200 BC-AD 476). Economic, Social, Political, Religious and Cultural Aspects*. Proceedings of the Sixth Workshop of the International Network Impact of Empire (Roman Empire, 200 BC-AD 476), Capri, March 29 - April 2, 2005. Leiden, Boston: Brill Academic Pub, 295-314.

Wesch-Klein, G. 2008. *Provincia. Okkupation und Verwaltung der Provinzen des Imperium Romanum von der Inbesitznahme Siziliens bis auf Diokletian. Ein Abriss*. Antike Kultur und Geschichte 10. Berlin: LIT.

Authors info

Marius-Tiberiu ALEXIANU, Ph.D., is Associate Professor and head of the Ethnoarchaeology section of the Arheoinvest Research and Training Platform from the "Alexandru Ioan Cuza" University of Iasi, Romania. He is the main author of the first ethnoarchaeological study in Romania (published in 1992) and of the first book on the ethnoarchaeology of the salt springs from Eastern Romania (2007). After the entry of Romania into the EU, he has won two national research projects with international French cooperation regarding the ethnoarchaeology of the salt springs and salt mountains from extra-Carpathian areas of Romania (2007-2010 and 2011-2015). He is the first editor of the collective volume *Archaeology and Anthropology of Salt* (Archaeopress, 2011). Recently, he applied for the first time the saturated model in the field of ethnoarchaeology, a study published by Springer in 2013. E-mail: alexianumarius@yahoo.com.

Andrei ASĂNDULESEI is currently a Researcher in the Department for Interdisciplinary Research – Field Science within the "Alexandru Ioan Cuza" University of Iași, Romania. His main research interest is prehistoric archaeology, with special focus on interdisciplinary investigations of prehistoric sites. In 2012 he successfully defended his Ph.D. thesis in the field of Prehistoric Archaeology entitled *Applications of geographical and geophysical methods in the interdisciplinary investigation of Cucutenian settlements from Moldavia. Case studies.* Both during the Ph.D. studies and after their completion, he has been involved as member in several ethnoarchaeological or interdisciplinary-archaeological research projects, having as main tasks GIS spatial analyses and non-destructive prospecting. Since 2014 he has coordinated a research project aimed at elaborating and applying a model of non-intrusive research in prehistoric sites from the region of Moldavia. He is member of the editorial board of a specialised journal, has participated to multiple national and international scientific gatherings, and has published several papers in ranked journals. E-mail: andrei.asandulesei@yahoo.com.

Mihaela ASĂNDULESEI is a Ph.D. student at "Alexandru Ioan Cuza" University of Iași (Romania), Faculty of History, her main research line being cultural anthropology of salt in rural world of the Eastern-Carpathian Romania. She has been involved, as a Research Assistant, in two research projects: *The ethnoarchaeology of the salt springs and salt mountains from the extra-Carpathians areas of Romania*, coordinated by Associated Professor Ph.D. Marius Alexianu and *Non-destructive approaches to complex archaeological sites. An integrated applied research model for cultural heritage*, coordinated by Ph.D. Researcher Andrei Asăndulesei. She participated, alone or in collaboration with other authors, in several international conferences. E-mail: mihaela.asandulesei@yahoo.com.

Antonia ARNOLDUS-HUYZENDVELD graduated in Amsterdam in physical geography, has worked as a consultant and independent researcher mainly in Italy (Latium, Tuscany), first in soil science and mapping and then, from the 1980s on, in the field of geoarchaeology. Over the last two decades she has been a contract professor at the University of Siena and "La Sapienza" University of Rome. Website: www.digiter.it. E-mail: digiter@libero.it.

Józef BEDNARCZYK is Assistant Professor at the Institute of Prehistory of the Adam Mickiewicz University (Poznań, Poland). His main research lines are, firstly, the pre-Roman and Roman periods in the European *Barbaricum*, with special emphasis on the study and analysis of the settlement structures in the region of Kujavia; second, the development of the sources, methods and techniques of the archaeological fieldwork. His research has been also related to the systematic and rescue excavations in the regions of Great Poland and Kujavia related to the transit of several infrastructures (roads and gas pipelines). He has been involved in several research projects in Poland and abroad and has participated in more than 60 conferences and congresses, at a regional, national and international level. He is editor and author of articles in the series *Via Archaeologica Posnaniensis* 1-4 (2010-2011) and a collective volume, *Od długiego domu najstarszych rolników do dworu staropolskiego* (2004). He has also been involved in several initiatives related to the dissemination of his work, in particular several exhibitions, such as "Pipeline of Archaeological Treasures" (1998) in the Palais de l'Europe (Strasbourg). E-mail: jotbe@amu.edu.pl.

Robin BRIGAND received a Ph.D. in Archaeology from the Universities of Franche-Comté (Besançon, France) and Padua (Italia). He is currently a post-doctorate researcher at UMR 8215 *Trajectoires* and UMR 7218 *LAVUE* (Paris, France). His studies on the spatial impact of former societies focus – using various scales – on site systems and their environments, settlement patterns, raw material acquisition and distribution, landscape dynamics, *etc*. Within this framework, he is involved in an ethnoarchaeological study on territorial practices surrounding salt uses and circulation in Romanian Moldavia. Besides these research developments, he is particularly interested in understanding ways in which human societies create, use and transform cultural heritage from a planimetric point of view. E-mail: robin.brigand@cnrs.fr.

Ștefan CALINIUC is an M.A. graduate at the Department of History and Archaeology within the "Alexandru Ioan Cuza" University of Iași, Romania. His research interests include archaeology, archaeological heritage, digital research in archaeology, and data visualization. He has been involved in several research projects including the project of the National Romanian Research Council on *The ethno-archaeology of the salt springs and salt mountains from the extra-Carpathians areas of Romania* coordinated by Assoc. Prof. Dr Marius Alexianu (ethnosalro.uaic. ro). E-mail: stefan.caliniuc@uaic.ro.

Marianne CARDALE SCHRIMPFF is an Independent Researcher (M.A. Edinburgh University, D.Phil. Oxford University, resident in Colombia), a member of Pro Calima since 1979. Research interests include pre-Columbian salt winning, technology (particularly textiles and metal), road systems and agriculture. She is currently part of a team investigating the origins of the Formative period in southwestern Colombia with a focus on the alluvial valley of the upper river Cauca. E-mail: marianne@procalima.org.

Roxana-Gabriela CURCĂ is Assistant Professor at the Faculty of History and member of the *Arheoinvest* Research Platform – Ethnoarchaeology section ('Al. I. Cuza' University (Iaşi, Romania). She has organized and participated as key-speaker in numerous international conferences, and published different papers on the anthropology of salt, particularly on the study of halotherapy. She is also co-editor of the proceedings volume *Archaeology and Anthropology of Salt. A Diachronic Approach* and Visiting Professor at the University at Buffalo (USA), University of Adelaide (Australia), Universidad de Valparaíso (Chile), and Universidad Nacional de La Plata (Argentina). E-mail: roxanigabriela@yahoo.com.

Alessandra FACCIOLO is graduated in Prehistoric and Protohistoric Archaeology at the University of Rome 'La Sapienza'(prof. A. Manfredini) and postgraduate in Prehistoric Ecology. She works from 1995 among Soprintendenza al Museo Nazionale Preistorico Etnografico L. Pigorini, department of Paleontologia del Quaternario e Zoologia (Rome). From 2001 she works with Soprintendenza Speciale ai Beni Archeologici of Rome, offices of Ostia. E-mail: alessandra. facciolo@gmail.com.

Pierre GOULETQUER is retired, formerly researcher at the CNRS (Centre de Recherche Bretonne et Celtique, Brest, France). His researches concerned the salt production on the Atlantic coast of France during Iron Age, the general question of the briquetages and the Mesolithic period in Brittany. He was interested by the ethnoarchaeological and technological approaches of salt productions in West Africa.

Maria Cristina GROSSI is graduated in Classical Archaeology at the University of Rome 'La Sapienza' (prof. A. Carandini), postgraduate in Museologia and Museografia. She works from 1998 among Soprintendenza Speciale dei Beni Archeologici of Rome according preventive archaeology programs; she worked on Roman necropolis (publications 1998-2003) and on drainage systems in Roman settlements (publications 2003 until today). E-mail: mcristigrossi@hotmail.com.

Joanna JAWORSKA works as Assistant Professor at the Institute of Geology of the Adam Mickiewicz University (Poznań, Poland). Her main research areas are Permian evaporites (including salt tectonics). She has been specialized in the mineralogy and digenesis of salt rocks, deformation of crystals and also in the phenomena related to gypsum-anhydrite dissolution and recrystallisation. She has participated in several international and national symposia, and published various contributions on the geology of evaporites. E-mail: veronika@amu.edu.pl.

Takamune KAWASHIMA is Assistant Professor at the Archaeological Museum of the Yamaguchi University, which conducts archaeological excavation in the university campuses as well as exhibitions. He received his Ph.D. in archaeology from the University of Tsukuba in 2009. In his research he investigates the social structure of the Jōmon from the viewpoints of production and feasting in comparison with archaeological and ethnographic examples outside Japan. He regards salt production as one of the important clues to consider the social organization of the Jōmon society. He was awarded the title of Docent in Slovenia, while he was teaching Japanese history, culture, and language at the Department of Asian and African Studies at the Faculty of Arts, University of Ljubljana, from 2009 to 2012. This experience benefited him when he was involved in the international education program at the University of Tsukuba from 2012 to 2013. E-mail: takamune@yamaguchi-u.ac.jp.

Cornelia-Magda LAZAROVICI. Her research focuses on Neolithic and Copper Age. She investigated some Starčevo-Criş sites, as well as other sites of the Cucuteni culture and recently Cheile Turzii-Peştera Ungurească cave (Bodrogkeresztúr culture). She is also involved in application of interdisciplinary methods in archaeology, contributing to the establishment of an absolute chronology through radiocarbon dating (for Neolithic and Copper Age, including transition period to the Bronze Age). She is also involved in application of other interdisciplinary methods (archaeomagnetism, magnetic prospecting, databases for Cucuteni culture, databases for gold and salt). In the last years has organized several expeditions for identification of areas with flint deposits used by prehistoric communities. She published alone or in collaboration with other authors several books and articles related with Cucuteni culture, but also regarding cultures of Transylvanian area. She has co-organized ethnoreligion symposia meant to better understand the use and meaning of signs and symbols in prehistory and later periods. Her interests and concerns in the Neolithic and Copper Age are also illustrated by the two volumes regarding the architecture of the Neolithic and Copper Age cultures on Romanian territory. E-mail: magdamantu@yahoo.com.

Gheorghe LAZAROVICI. His activity is mainly focused on the investigation of the Neolithic and Copper Age of Transylvania and Banat. He conducts excavations in several sites from these areas. He has established periodization systems and chronologies for different archaeological cultures, such as Starčevo-Criş, Banat, Vinča, Zau and Tiszapolgár. He has been involved in various interdisciplinary researches such as archaeometry, ethnoarchaeology and ethnoreligion (studies and organizing symposia). Together with specialists in other fields he makes and publishes analyses for pottery, copper, gold, salt, flint and obsidian. He organized together with J. Nandris (London Institute of Archaeology and University), ethnoarchaeological expeditions in the mountain areas of Transylvania, Banat and Maramureş. He is involved in application of mathematics in Romanian archaeology, creating data bases and information database, guiding his Ph.D. for using and supplementing these databases. Together with mathematicians and computer scientists he develops programs for database management, for their classification and ordering. He wrote studies and monographs for computer use in research and in the application of modern methods. He is the author and co-author of several archaeological monographs. E-mail: ghlazarovici@yahoo.com.

Arkadiusz MARCINIAK is Associate Professor at the Institute of Prehistory of the Adam Mickiewicz University (Poznań, Poland). His research interests are related to the theory and methodology of archaeology, the Neolithic Anatolia and Central Europe and the social theory and its archaeological applications. He has directed several research projects, and currently is the director of the research team excavating the Late Neolithic at Çatalhöyük (central Turkey). He is a member of various national and international institutions and scientific organizations, such as the European Association of Archaeologists, several commissions in the Polish Academy of Sciences, the World Archaeological Congress or the International Council for Archaeozoology. Among his several publications are many books such as (with P.F. Biehl and A. Gramsch eds.) *Archaeologies of Europe. History, Methods and Theories* (2002); *Placing animals in the Neolithic. Social zooarchaeology of prehistoric farming communities* (2005); (with M. Kok and H. van Londen eds.) *E-learning Archaeology: The Heritage Handbook* (2012). E-mail: arekmar@amu.edu.pl.

Cinzia MORELLI, managing director of Interporto excavations and project, is Soprintendenza Speciale ai Beni Archeologici di Roma's functionary. She has coordinate for years the archaeological activities in the regions of *Fiumicino* and *Portuense*. E-mail: cinzia.morelli@beniculturali.it.

Maria Lucrezia RINALDI is graduated in Prehistoric and Protohistoric Archaeology at the University of Rome 'La Sapienza' (prof. A. Manfredini). She works from 1998 among Soprintendenza Speciale dei Beni Archeologici of Rome according preventive archaeology programs. From 2001 she works especially in Fiumicino's area. E-mail: ma.lucrezia @gmail.com.

Gheorghe ROMANESCU is a Ph.D. Professor at the Geography and Geology Faculty from the "Alexandru Ioan Cuza" University of Iaşi, Romania. Main activities and responsibilities are as follow: scientific research, educational activities, Director of the Laboratory of Geoarchaeology. Between 2003 and 2010 he was Head of the Department of Physical Geography from the aforementioned institution. His areas of expertise are: fluvial hydrology, hydrogeology, geomorphology, wetlands. He has been a member of the Ethnosal and EthnosalRo projects on the ethno-archaeology of the salt springs and salt mountains from the extra-Carpathians areas of Romania. He has organized and participated in several international and national symposia, and published several contributions on the hydrogeology of salt. E-mail: romanescugheorghe@gmail.com.

Daria RUGGERI has a Ph.D. in Prehistory from the University of Rome, La Sapienza. Since more than 15 years she works in preventive archaeological excavations in Rome, mainly in the Fiumicino area, and in different sities from Central and South Italy. She studies lithic industries from the Upper Palaeolithic and works in projects of Cultural Heritage. E-mail: daria.ruggeri@gmail.com.

Maria RUIZ DEL ARBOL MORO is Científica Titular (Tenured Scholar) at the Department of Archaeology at the Institute of History of the Spanish National Research Council (Madrid, Spain). The fundamental axis of her research is the archaeological study of the formation and transformation processes of ancient landscapes in the provinces of the Roman Empire. The concrete ambits of her research are: the analysis of Roman occupation in provincial territories, in mining areas such as Las Médulas (León, Spain) and Las Cavenes (Salamanca, Spain), the study of integration processes of the peninsular communities in the Roman Empire; the development of a specific methodology for the study of ancient agrarian landscapes and the formation of the archaeological record; and the integration of archaeological heritage into territorial planning and management. E-mail: maria. ruizdelarbol@cchs.csic.es.

Thomas SAILE has studied prehistory and early history, medieval and modern history as well as soil science at the Universities of Frankfurt am Main, Marburg, Kiel and Dublin (UCD). He concluded his studies with a doctoral thesis at the Goethe University in Frankfurt in 1995. The thesis, awarded the Friedrich Sperl Prize, was devoted to the ancient and early historical settlement of the Wetterau in Hesse. He has been employed as Research Assistant at the Seminar for Prehistory and Early History, Göttingen University, focussing, among other subjects, on the Slavic settlement in the lower middle Elbe region. In 2006 the Faculty of Philosophy of the Georg August University in Göttingen granted him the *venia legendi* for the subject *Prehistory and Early History*. In 2008/2009 he was interim Professor of Prehistoric and Early Historical Archaeology at the Otto-Friedrich University in Bamberg, and in 2009 was acting Chair of Prehistory and Early History at the Friedrich Schiller University in Jena. In the winter semester of 2010/2011 Thomas Saile was appointed to a Chair of Prehistory and Early History at the Institute of History of the University of Regensburg. His research interests focus mainly on Neolithic settlement and landscape archaeology in Central Europe. Thomas Saile is a corresponding member of the German Archaeological Institute. E-mail: thomas.saile@ur.de.

Ion SANDU is a Ph.D. Professor of Cultural Heritage Goods Preservation and Director of the Scientific Laboratory of Artefact Expertise from the "Alexandru Ioan Cuza" University of Iaşi, Romania. His areas of expertise are scientific investigation, preservation and restoration of the cultural heritage, environmental science and engineering, forensic science and inventics. His main research lines are, foremost, the development of new methods and techniques of investigation in order to evaluate the conservation state and the archaeometric characteristics of old artefacts, with special emphasis on the study and analysis of the chemical and physical structure of the surface and interior of archaeological objects; second, new procedures for the preservation and restoration of object discovered during archaeological fieldwork. His expertise in physical-chemical sciences was applied in two research projects on the salt springs and salt outcrops from the Romanian extra-Carpathian areas (Ethnosal and EthnosalRo). In this sense, he has investigated the impact of the saline aerosols (solions) on the human and animal